DATE DUE

racial
oppression
in
america

racial oppression in america

ROBERT BLAUNER
University of California, Berkeley

Harper & Row, Publishers
New York   Evanston   San Francisco   London

To the memory of two writers
  My father, Samuel Blauner, who encouraged me to write in the essay form; and George Jackson, who was to be the subject of an essay that I could not write—may his death be avenged.

Cover photo: Michel Cosson

Racial Oppression in America

Copyright © 1972 by Robert Blauner
Printed in the United States of America. All rights reserved. No part of this book may be used or reproduced in any manner whatsoever without written permission except in the case of brief quotations embodied in critical articles and reviews. For information address Harper & Row, Publishers, Inc., 10 East 53rd Street, New York, N.Y. 10022.

Standard Book Number: 06-040771-9

Library of Congress Catalog Card Number: 72-77484

contents

preface

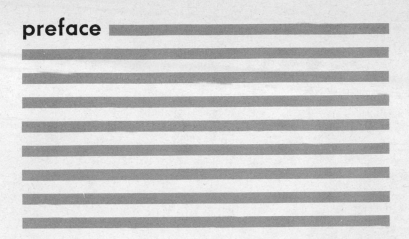

Because life tends to race ahead of our understanding of it, the likelihood that one's work will be outdated soon after it appears is an occupational hazard that all writers face. How much more true this is for the sociologist who analyzes contemporary American society—and for one who was brazen enough to try to make sense out of the shifting currents and conflicts that surrounded racial politics in the decade of the 1960s.

If the analyses in this book have any enduring value in the face of such volatility, it will be because I have succeeded in interpreting the specific crises of the late 1960s and early 1970s in terms of persisting patterns in American social structure. Fundamental to my perspective is the notion that racial groups and racial oppression are central features of the American social dynamic. The thesis that racial minorities are internal colonies of American capitalism is not original; however, I have tried to develop this idea systematically and, at the same time, critically. The strategic role of racism within American culture is another theme that recurs in these essays, along with the profound yet paradoxical impact of oppression on the culture of colonized minorities. Finally, the studies may be read as critical rejoinders to dominant liberal outlooks on race in the United States—forms of liberalism expressed in popular viewpoints, in governmental policies, in professional and institutional ideologies, and in the theories of academic sociology.

As I look back on the period in which this book was written, I wonder now at the temerity that impelled me through a sea of tensions and dilemmas. In the late 1960s, the white scholar who persisted in the sociology of race had his back up against the wall. Or, to shift metaphors, he was at least caught between the priorities and perspectives of subordinated groups—including his or her own students—and those of the academic community. My own developing framework probably owes more to the social movements of the oppressed than to standard sociology. At times, I have played the ambiguous role of interpreting the perspectives of the colonized to the more liberal colonizers. At other times, I felt as though I were balancing on a tightrope between sociological analysis that deals with the complexity of social reality and a radical commitment that speaks to the necessity of changing those realities.

Because these essays were written over a long period, it is difficult to acknowledge everyone who contributed to the book's present form. Besides those writers and scholars whose work I cite within, the most important influence has been the students with whom I have tested and exchanged ideas on race relations and American society, in settings that have ranged from classes of four hundred or more undergraduates to intimate seminars and small working groups of graduates. Earlier versions of some chapters have been published previously. They have all, however, been rewritten, and with the addition of new material more than half of the contents of this volume is new.

The point of view in this book was worked out in close collaboration with David Wellman. Presently teaching at the University of Oregon, Dave was a student in the first graduate course on racial and ethnic relations that I taught at Berkeley in 1965. Shortly afterward, we began to develop research plans which later materialized into a study supported by a grant from the National Institute of Mental Health. Although the report of this three-year project is not yet completed, the staff discussions and student seminars that Dave and I organized created a context in which the racial conflicts of the day were analyzed in terms of their theoretical, political, and social research implications by an unusually enthusiastic and sophisticated group of students. Within this circle, Hardy Frye stands out for the unique energy of his participation and his ever-questioning critical mind. Other valuable members who contributed both to these seminars and to the research project included Barbara Ballis,

Douglas Davidson, William Dorsey, Sheila Gibson, Bruce Johnson, Ricardo Muratorio-Posse, Alex Papillon, Jeffrey Prager, Lillian Rubin, John Spier, and Nick Vaca. I remain in debt to David Wellman for his role in creating the climate of these seminars, as well as for his dedication to the project, general friendship, and many careful and critical readings of virtually every draft of the chapters that are included in the present book.

On the Berkeley campus, three research institutes provided facilities and other help: the Institute of Industrial Relations, the Institute of Race and Community Relations, and the Center for the Study of Law and Society. For off-campus research opportunities, I am grateful to Miriam Johnson and the Adult Opportunity Center in the Fillmore district of San Francisco, and to Harry Specht, to the late Anatole Shaffer, and particularly to the new careerists in the Richmond Community Development Project.

Lloyd Street made an especially valuable contribution to Chapter 6, and his critical comments on several other essays are also appreciated. Sheldon Messinger and David Matza could always be counted on for comments that proved to be sensible and helpful in my rewriting. Some of the most useful criticisms came from Nathan Glazer. I appreciate the running dialogue we were able to maintain despite the considerable differences in theoretical and political outlook.

The list of individuals whose critical responses to specific drafts or chapters made a difference to me and the book is a long one. It includes Bennett Berger, Gerald Berreman, Leon Bramson, Jan Dizard, Erving Goffman, Nathan Hare, Bruce Johnson, Dale Johnson, Ira Katznelson, Charles Keil, William Kornhauser, Gilbert Kushner, Lawrence Levine, Gary Marx, Huey Newton, Lee Rainwater, Lisa Rubens, Philip Selznick, Bill Sommerville, Art Stinchcombe, Immanuel Wallerstein, Carol Walton, Ortiz Walton, James Wood, and Robert Wood.

Lincoln Bergman, Kris Dymond, E. Homer Price, and Lisa Rubens undertook various research tasks along the way. Lynn Turner typed many of the early drafts, and Christine Egan typed the bulk of the final manuscript. Carol Hatch and Kris Dymond also typed several chapters. I appreciate all of this.

Finally I would like to thank my wife Rena, who suffered the

inconveniences that protracted writing brought about with as much
graciousness as could be expected, and who instructed our children
Marya and Jonathan to respect the privacy of their father's work.

I am indebted to the Society for the Study of Social
Problems for "Internal Colonialism and Ghetto Revolt,"
Social Problems, vol. 16, no. 4 (Spring 1969), 393-408; to
the Free Press, Division of Macmillan Company, for "Black Culture:
Myth or Reality," in Norman Whitten and John Szwed, *Afro-
American Anthropology*, 1970; to *Trans*-action, Inc., New Brunswick,
N.J., for "The Chicano Sensibility," (*Trans*-action, Copyright,
February 1971) and "Whitewash over Watts," (*Trans*-action,
Copyright, March–April, 1966); to the National Lawyer's Guild and
Ann Ginger for "Sociology in the Courtroom," from *Minimizing
Racism in Jury Trials*, Ed. Ann Ginger, 1969.

                                                     Robert Blauner

part I
theoretical
perspectives

The present crisis in American life has led to the questioning of long-accepted frameworks. The pressure of events has forced intellectuals and social scientists to reexamine old definitions of the character of our society, the role of racism, and the workings of basic institutions. The depth and volatility of contemporary racial conflict challenge sociologists in particular to assess the adequacy of the theoretical models by which we have explained American race relations in the past.

The essays in this book owe their origin to my dissatisfaction with the state of theory in the study of contemporary race relations. In my view social theory should identify the significant social forces and trends of an historical period and in the least illuminate the relations among them. As a sociologist who was attempting to analyze the big news of the 1960s,[1] I found that general sociological theory, as well as the more specific "theories" in the race relations field, was pointing in the wrong direction. These theories not only failed to predict and illuminate new developments—the shift from civil rights to group power strategies, the outbreak of rebellions in the urban ghettos, the growth of militant nationalism and ethnic consciousness— in short, the deepening of racial awareness and conflict in America. The "theories" actually obscured the meaning of these issues, making them more difficult to comprehend. In 1965 I began searching for alternative ways of conceptualizing American racial realities. The essays in this volume are the results of that effort.

The Sociology of Race: An Alternative Framework Needed

The present work parts company with the leading ideas and implicit assumptions that until recently, at least, have guided most American social scientists in their study of (or reluctance to consider) our racial order: First, the view that racial and ethnic groups are neither central nor persistent elements of modern societies. Second, the idea that racism and racial oppression are not independent dynamic forces but are ultimately reducible to other causal determinants, usually economic or psychological. Third, the position that the most important aspects of racism are the attitudes and prejudices of white Americans. And, finally, the so-called *immigrant analogy*, the assumption, critical in contemporary thought, that there are no essential long-term differences—in relation to the larger society— between the *third world* or racial minorities and the European ethnic groups.

In his *Crisis of the Negro Intellectual* Harold Cruse describes
how Marxist interpretations of race and nationality came to dominate
the perspectives of leading Afro-American theorists and political
figures, even though this framework of analysis arose out of specific
European conditions, which varied considerably from American
realities.[2] In my view, sociology in the United States experienced
a somewhat similar distortion which had profound consequences for
its outlook on race—although in this case it was not only Marxism
but the larger structure of European social thought that steered
American scholars off course. Despite the fact that the young
discipline of sociology was not theory conscious before World War
II, the limited and pragmatic concepts it utilized were predominantly
home-grown. Therefore the leading figures of its developing years—
such men as Albion Small, William Graham Sumner, W. I. Thomas,
Charles Cooley, and Robert Park—gave major attention to race
relations in their writings.[3] The life conditions and problems of
immigrant groups and racial minorities were perhaps the predominant
research emphasis. After the war the prestige of European social
theory overpowered the contributions of the indigenous American
sociologists and provided the basis for the conceptual schemes that
today inform social science analysis of modern societies, including the
United States.

For my purpose the most important assumption in this body of
social theory is the idea that as industrial societies develop and
mature, race and ethnicity become increasingly irrelevant as
principles of group formation, collective identity, and political action.
This assumption, so strikingly at odds with contemporary realities
in the modern world as a whole as well as in the United States, can
be traced directly to the impact of European social analysis.[4]

Karl Marx, Max Weber, Emile Durkheim, Ferdinand Toennies,
and Georg Simmel stand as the great pioneers of sociology. Diverse
as were their theories, a concern with interpreting the new bourgeois
industrial order which had replaced a more traditional feudal society
was a central intellectual priority for each of these scholars. In
analyzing the modern world and the social forces that gave rise to
it, they devoted relatively scant attention to ethnic and racial division
and conflict. They saw such social bonds as essentially parochial
survivals from preindustrial societies, and fundamentally opposed to
the logic of modernity. Marx assumed that national differences would

dissolve as the world proletariat developed a vision and practice based on class consciousness; he saw the more complex social differentiation of the past giving way to a dynamic of simplification and polarization that was leading to the predominance of only two classes as significant social forces. Durkheim and Toennies developed ideal types of traditional and modern social structures: *mechanical solidarity* versus *organic solidarity*, and the *gemeinschaft-gesellschaft* dichotomy, respectively. Ethnic solidarity belonged to the earlier social forms. Their conceptions of modern social arrangements precluded sentimental attachments based on race or ethnicity, or at least the likelihood that men would act on them consistently and frequently. Simmel saw the city as a metropolitan way of life in which such primordial bonds (to use Edward Shils's term) must lose their power and persistence.[5] And for Max Weber, perhaps the least disposed among them to an evolutionary perspective and incidentally the theorist whose constructs are potentially the most fruitful for analyzing race and ethnicity, the basic historical dynamic—the movement from tradition to rationality—also appeared to indicate a weakening of these ties.[6] Thus the general conceptual frame of European theory implicitly assumed the decline and disappearance of ethnicity in the modern world; it offered no hints in the other direction. Without significant alteration, American sociology synthesized this framework into its models of social structure and change.

Rather than race, ethnicity, and nationality,* the characteristic features of modern industrial societies were the centrality of classes and social stratification (Marx, Weber), the growth and ubiquity of large-scale bureaucratic organizations (Weber, Robert Michels), the trend toward occupational and professional specialization (Durkheim), and the dominance of the metropolis and its distinctive patterns and problems over less urban areas and concerns (Simmel, Toennies, and Durkheim). After World War II the subfields of

* Religion also was seen as a social phenomenon somehow more appropriate to traditional societies. However, the great interest Weber and Durkheim devoted to its study is one reason why the sociology of religion has prospered in the United States. The fact that none of the European "giants" gave major attention to race or ethnicity has been consequential, since American sociology has used their aura and prestige to legitimate its own choice of research problems and theoretical development.

sociology devoted to these phenomena were favored by the overall logic of social theory; specialties such as stratification, organizations, politics, urban studies, and so on, were thereby linked to the major theoretical paradigms and fertilized with the seminal ideas and conceptual schemes that were the European legacy to the American discipline. These fields also attracted the most talented scholars because their concerns penetrated the heart of modern society and its dynamics. After a promising start in the early period, the study of race and ethnic relations suffered correspondingly. With little room for ethnic and racial phenomena in the macroscopic models of social structure and process, the field was isolated from general sociological theory and particularly from those leading conceptual themes that might have provided coherence and useful lines of inquiry: stratification, culture, community.[7] The study of race relations developed in a kind of vacuum; no overall theoretical framework guided its research and development. Not surprisingly it has failed to attract leading social scientists, particularly during the past 25 to 30 years. While the fields of organization and bureaucracy, industry and occupation, interaction and deviance, have grown in depth and sophistication during the past generation, the same has not been true of the study of race relations, especially in terms of theoretical advancement.*[8]

Without support from a general social theory, the study of race relations in sociology became organized around a variety of disparate approaches or foci of analysis. The leading approaches developed in *ad hoc* fashion. They were not well integrated with one

* In the subsequent period, American sociology has not produced an analysis of race comparable in significance to Gunnar Myrdal's *An American Dilemma* published in 1944.[9] Virtually all the new insights about racism and the experience of the oppressed have been provided by writers whose lives and minds were uncluttered by sociological theory. Probably the best have come from outside the academic establishment entirely— for example, *The Autobiography of Malcolm X* and Harold Cruse's *The Crisis of the Negro Intellectual*.[10] The most important new theoretical work by university and professional scholars is from other academic fields, notably history, where the contributions of Eugene Genovese and Winthrop Jordan are especially significant, and psychiatry.[11] The most valuable products of the sociological method have been case studies rather than theoretical understanding—for example, E. Franklin Frazier's *Black Bourgeoisie* and Elliot Liebow's *Tally's Corner*.[12]

another;[13] of particular significance, none of them was able to articulate racial and ethnic phenomena to the structure and dynamics of the larger society satisfactorily.[14] These approaches—with perhaps one exception that I discuss below—shared the key assumption of general sociology that racial groups and racial conflict were epiphenomenal and ephemeral. Thus the dominant perspectives within the subfield of race—among which the most representative have been Robert Park's theory of the race relations cycle and its present-day expression in the study of assimilation and ethnic groups, the caste-class model, the analysis of prejudice and discrimination, and the immigrant analogy—made it inevitable that sociological experts would miss the thrust of social change and movement during the past decades. A closer look at some of their key assumptions might help us understand why sociologists (not unlike other Americans) were caught napping by the intensity and scale of civil rights protest, the furor of ghetto revolt, and the rapidity with which black power, cultural nationalism, and other militant third world perspectives emerged and spread.

The Assimilationist Bias
The most influential theory within the sociology of American racial studies has been that of the *race relations cycle* advanced by Robert Park. According to Park, when dominant and minority groups come into contact, they enter a series of relationships that he characterizes in terms of successive stages of competition, accommodation, and assimilation. Though Park and his students never clarified the dynamics that would inevitably lead from one stage to the next, the assumption that assimilation and integration were the likely end-products of ethnic and racial diversity has dominated American sociology. On the question of black people, Park was ambivalent and ambiguous. At times he saw them as a group in the process of being assimilated, at other times as an exception to the cyclical scheme.[15]

In addition to supporting the idea that American society is based on a dynamic of integration, the "assimilationist bias" distorted the analysis of the attitudes and movements of minority groups. Louis Wirth, a student and colleague of Park, granted the possibility that minorities could have other goals—separation, cultural pluralism, militant dominance. However, his view that in America the assimilationist goal was the only viable one became standard.[16]

Afro-Americans were considered even more assimilation oriented than the European immigrants because it was believed that they had no ethnic culture of their own. In recent years third world nationalists have pointed out the ideological repressiveness implicit in the assumption that the cultural traditions of people of color are either nonexistent or less valuable than those of the dominant society. They have noted how social scientists have tended to ignore or distort the experiences and values of such groups as Indians and Mexicans, who have long histories of resistance to assimilation. Although some sociologists have developed the concept of assimilation in less dogmatic directions and qualified the rigid assumption of a *melting pot* solution (Milton Gordon and Nathan Glazer, especially),[17] most scholars did not seriously consider the possibility that racial minorities might prefer to build their own cultures and community institutions rather than choose absorption into the mainstream.

Caste and Class

The idea that assimilation and integration are the most probable outcomes of racial as well as ethnic heterogeneity rests on the assumption that racial oppression is an aberration rather than a fundamental principle of American society. The only major challenge to this premise within academic sociology has come from a group led by W. Lloyd Warner known as the *caste-class school*. Warner suggested that Negroes might be an exception to the general tendency toward ethnic assimilation because of the special power of color prejudice among white Americans.[18] In a series of studies of Southern towns undertaken by his associates, John Dollard, Allison Davis, and Burleigh and Mary Gardner, the researchers were impressed by the similarity between the racial order they discovered and the historic caste system of India. They oriented their investigations around the castelike nature of the color line separating white and black, the class structure of each racial group, and the relations between these two principles of stratification.[19] This theoretical approach was useful for analyzing small communities over a limited period, and the idea of color caste had the special virtue of treating race and racial oppression as independent realities. But lacking the capacity to account for changes in racial patterns generated from within the system, it was a static conception.[20] The only possibilities the caste-class school envisioned for obliterating the color line were Southern industrialization and black migration to Northern cities, processes that would thrust blacks and Southern whites alike into the overall class system. Furthermore, this approach, like all the others, assumed, first, that a rigid racial order was a peculiarly rural phenomenon; second, that there was a fundamental disparity between Northern and Southern social structure; and third, that the North would be the spearhead of democratic racial change.

The Focus on Prejudice

Each of these three assumptions has been shattered by recent history. Although the emergence of the civil rights movement, and particularly its Southern provenience, took sociology by surprise, the movement of the 1950s did not at first call into question the assimilationist premise. The predominant goal of Southern blacks was integration and equality in institutional treatment. In a few years, however, massive white resistance and a growing realization of the limits of the movement's very success began to shake up prevailing thought about race in America. Most critically, the civil rights period exposed the depth and pervasiveness of racism in a society that appeared, on the surface, to be moving toward equality.[21]

Social science experts assumed that this movement toward equality depended primarily on the reduction of prejudice in the white majority, rather than upon the collective actions of the oppressed groups themselves or upon basic transformations in the society. Here sociologists were reflecting the general ethos of American culture, which minimizes a consciousness of, and concern with, group power—with the structure of institutions and their constraints—emphasizing in their stead the ideas and attitudes of individuals. Myrdal had written in 1944 that all major transformations in American race relations would stem from determinants on the white side of the color line.[22] Sociologists and psychologists began to focus their research on racial attitudes (a development that was also furthered by a fascination with the unparalleled power of anti-Semitism in Nazi Germany), and public opinion surveys noted that from the thirties through the fifties and sixties there was a consistent decline in racial prejudice and stereotypic thinking.[23] The 1954 decision by the Supreme Court appeared to confirm the idea that powerful white institutions would respond in time to these changes in attitudes. Yet very soon afterwards, with the Montgomery bus boycott and subsequent civil rights actions, the initiative toward change in race relations passed out of white hands. The continuing deepening of racial crisis and conflict made it more and more apparent that white attitudes were peripheral rather than primary determinants of racial arrangements. There were still sociologists celebrating the impressive decline in racial prejudice at the very moment that Watts burst into flames.*

I would not deny that ideas of white superiority are powerful in their impact, and that stereotypes of racial minorities have a tenacious hold on the conscious and unconscious mind. But prejudiced attitudes are not the essence of racism. Racism is unfortunately too often equated with intense prejudice and hatred of the racially different—thus with men of evil intent. This kind of racial extremism—while all too prevalent and very likely on the upswing among some segments of the American people today—is not necessary for the maintenance of a racist social structure. Virulent prejudice tends to be reduced, and crude stereotypes changed, by education and by exposure to more sophisticated environments. The men of goodwill and tolerance who identify racism with prejudice can there-fore exempt themselves from responsibility and involvement in our system of racial injustice and inequality by taking comfort in their own "favorable" attitudes toward minority groups.

The error in this point of view is revealed by the fact that such men of goodwill help maintain the racism of American society and in some cases even profit from it. This takes place because racism is institutionalized. The processes that maintain domination—control of

* For a number of intellectual and political reasons, including the rejection of Marxist perspectives, sociologists were caught short without a systematic theory of social oppression, one that could stipulate the conditions under which oppressed groups would challenge their long-standing subjugation. Two related concepts have been used by social scientists to explain "The Negro Revolution" of the past two decades. The two ideas, "relative deprivation" and "rising expectations," imply that group protest may arise from the improvement of social and economic status when that improvement places the group in a position to compare itself with more favored social strata, and when changes in objective situation lag behind expanding subjective goals and aspirations. Though not without merit, these concepts are inadequate as social theory because they are not connected to a holistic model of American society that stresses the systematic oppression of social groups, especially racial minorities.

whites over nonwhites—are built into the major social institutions. These institutions either exclude or restrict the participation of racial groups by procedures that have become conventional, part of the bureaucratic system of rules and regulations. Thus there is little need for prejudice as a motivating force. Because this is true, the distinction between racism as an objective phenomenon, located in the actual existence of domination and hierarchy, and racism's subjective concomitants of prejudice and other motivations and feelings is a basic one.

The Immigrant Analogy and Economic Reductionism

The perspective that has become most widely accepted recently is the immigrant analogy. It is based on an alleged similarity between the historical experience of European ethnic groups and the contemporary situation of racial minorities, who have become predominantly urban as a result of migrations from more rural areas of the South and Southwest. The analogy posits a common dynamic in the American experience through which lower-class and ethnically diverse outsiders become incorporated into the national consensus. Thus it may be viewed as an updated and perhaps sophisticated version of the assimilationist position. Although the immigrant analogy need not deny the special impact of racism, in practice its advocates tend to discount or minimize the pervasiveness of racial oppression, especially as a reality of the present period. In their view racism tends to be located in our *past* heritage of slavery, segregation, and discrimination. These historical forces and their present-day effects on the racially oppressed have slowed the assimilation and social mobility of people of color, maintaining minority groups in lower-class status for a longer period than was the case for the European ethnics. But for the common man who subscribes to this folk sociology, as well as for its academic exponents, racism is now largely a thing of the past. Therefore, those who hold this perspective are not pessimistic, despite the massive economic imbalances and social problems correlated with race. They assume that black, Chicano, and even Native Americans will eventually follow the path of acculturation and "Americanization" marked out by the white immigrants. Thus the immigrant analogy serves to bolster a desperate need of many Americans to believe that our society can solve its internal problems; it is a contemporary version of the myth of progress and opportunity.

A variant of this perspective is the common view that the social position, life styles, and social problems of urban racial minorities in the North are predominantly reflections of poverty and economic class status, since a racial hierarchy has not been officially sanctioned. If "racial" problems are essentially problems of a recent arrival into urban lower-class position, then acclimation to city life and economic mobility will in time reduce the salience of race itself. This tendency to reduce race to class has been practiced by radical theorists as well as liberal policy-makers. Marxists have expected that a developing class consciousness cutting across ethnic and racial lines would eliminate national and racial considerations and lead to the collective solidarity of oppressed groups. Liberal sociologists expected race and ethnic concerns to recede as large numbers of individuals from the minority groups began to move into the middle class. Curiously enough, in the recent period it has more often been the mobile and middle-class elements from third world groups who have asserted their racial identities most aggressively.

The most important contemporary spokesman for economic class reductionism has been Daniel Patrick Moynihan. As Nixon's chief advisor on urban social problems, Moynihan suggested that the nation stop thinking and acting in terms of race and focus instead on the common problems associated with poverty and class. Moynihan and the Nixon administration assumed that racial groups and racial oppression would disappear as social forces if third world people and "liberal-radical" whites (to use Spiro Agnew's fine expression) ceased talking about them. Thus the economic class reductionism inherent in the conservative doctrine of *benign neglect* merges with the *color-blind approach* to social reality that many white liberals have long favored. These approaches are of course ostrichlike. Race and racism are not figments of demented imaginations, but are central to the economics, politics, and culture of this nation.

Colonialism and Racial Oppression

Perhaps the most important theme uniting the essays in this study is an insistence on the central and independent role of racial oppression in American life. Unfortunately social science lacks a model of American society and its social structure in which racial division and conflict are basic elements rather than phenomena to be explained (or explained away) in terms of other forces and determinants. To close this theoretical gap, in part, I rely on the framework of colonialism in the present study.

The connections between the American racial experience and the imperialism of Western societies have been blurred by the standard usage of the term "colonial America" in general parlance and in the field of history. In emphasizing the relations between the emerging nation of white settlers and the English mother country rather than the consolidation of white European control, the conventional usage separates the American experience from the matrix of Western European expansion. When we Americans think about European colonialism, it is the domination of Asia and Africa, which reached its peak in the late nineteenth century, that comes to mind. Yet American society has always been a part of this Western colonial dynamic, however isolated we were from the European center. Our own development proceeded on the basis of Indian conquests and land seizures, on the enslavement of African peoples, and in terms of a westward expansion that involved war with Mexico and the incorporation of half that nation's territory. In the present period our economic and political power penetrates the entire non-Communist world, a new American empire, basing its control on neocolonial methods, having supplanted the hegemony of the European nations. The democratic and liberal self-image of our national ethos has deeply repressed these realities of our heritage. But revolutions in the third world and the stirrings of colonized populations in our own society have brought into the foreground a new consciousness of both domestic colonialism and empire abroad.

A focus on colonialism is essential for a theory that can integrate race and racial oppression into a larger view of American social structure. The colonial order in the modern world has been based on the dominance of white Westerners over non-Western people of color; racial oppression and the racial conflict to which it gives rise are endemic to it, much as class exploitation and conflict are fundamental to capitalist societies. Western colonialism brought into existence the present-day patterns of racial stratification; in the United States, as elsewhere, it was a colonial experience that generated the lineup of ethnic and racial division. Just as developing capitalism in Europe produced social classes out of a medley of rural and urban strata and status groups, the colonial system brought into being races, from an array of distinct tribes and ethnic peoples. It was European conquest and colonial wardship that created "the Indian," an identity irrelevant to men who lived their lives as Crow, Sioux, or Iroquois. And as a result of slavery the "Negro race" emerged from the heterogeneity of African ethnicity.[24]

Yet the colonial perspective cannot by itself provide the theoretical framework necessary to grasp the complexities of race relations and social change in America. When the colonial model is transferred from the overseas situation to the United States without substantial alteration, it tends to miss the total structure, the context of advanced industrial capitalism in which our racial arrangements are embedded—a context that produces group politics and social movements that differ markedly from the traditional colonial society. I discuss these issues briefly in the book, but not enough work has gone into elaborating the main dimensions of the overall context and pursuing their implications for the social transformations of the future.

This suggests a major defect of my study. It lacks a conception of American society as a total structure beyond the central significance that I attribute to racism. Thus my perspective tends to suffer from the fragmented character of the approaches to American race relations that I have just criticized. Conceived to a great extent within the confines of the middle ranges of theory, there is no systematic exposition of capitalist structure and dynamics; racial oppression and racial conflict are not satisfactorily linked to the dominant economic relations nor to the overall distribution of political power in America. The failure of Marxism to appreciate the significance of racial groups and racial conflict is in part responsible for this vacuum, since no other existing framework is able to relate race to a comprehensive theory of capitalist development.

The new theoretical model needed to analyze and interpret American society might be based on the combined existence, historical interaction, and mutual interpenetration of the colonial–racial and the capitalist class realities. For America is clearly a mixed society that might be termed colonial capitalist or racial capitalist. Neither the explanatory framework of colonial theory nor conventional Marxist models of capitalism can adequately capture the complexity and paradoxes of racial oppression in relation to other compelling social forces. But it will be no simple mechanical task to merge these

two frameworks into a theory that is integrated and convincing.
Although I am currently working on such a theoretical conception,
I publish these essays now in the belief that their overall perspective
is valuable and the specific analyses relevant to contemporary
problems.

Outline of the Book

In Part I of this volume I advance a set of theoretical perspectives
that run counter to the dominant approaches discussed. Chapter 1
treats racial oppression as a guiding principle of American society
and analyzes some of its major components and themes—white
privilege; exploitation and control; the mechanisms of cultural domination, restricted mobility, and dehumanization. Chapters 2 and 3
introduce the colonial paradigm and attempt to rebut the immigrant
analogy. In Chapter 2 I argue that people of color in the United
States have been colonized minorities whose original entry into the
society, early labor status and subsequent economic history, and
relation to the dominant culture have all differed qualitatively from
the experiences of the European ethnic groups. In Chapter 3 I apply
the concept of *internal colonialism* to the relation between the black
ghetto and the larger society, focusing on the structural parallels
between our system of racial control and systems that undergirded
overseas colonial regimes.

The essays in Part II are responsive to the assimilationist bias
in the study of American race relations. This powerful assumption
contributed to the sociologist's denial of the ethnicity of Afro-
Americans and to his distortion of black cultural realities, the subject
of Chapter 4. In the discussion of Anglo-Chicano relations, as
illuminated by selected Mexican-American literature in Chapter 5,
some of the historical and contemporary conditions of the strong
antiassimilationist posture of the nation's second largest ethnic
minority are suggested. Part III is made up of a number of case
studies of institutional racism. Analyzing the ways in which racial
inequality is built into the operation of, and interaction among, specific
institutions, these essays approach racism as an objective, structured
system and question those alternative frameworks that emphasize
individual acts and prejudices.

NOTES

1. Robert Park, a pioneer in the sociology of ethnic and racial relations, was fond of the idea that sociologists were "superjournalists," who interpreted the "big news" of an era. I find this conception of the field still worthwhile, especially when so much research in the social sciences has become formalized to the point where human concerns and experience have disappeared from view. Park was originally a journalist, and today the best sociological journalism comes from the men of the press and not the academy.

2. Harold Cruse, *The Crisis of the Negro Intellectual* (New York: Morrow, 1967).

3. Peter I. Rose, *The Subject Is Race* (New York: Oxford University Press, 1968), pp. 27–66.

4. The publication of Talcott Parsons' *The Structure of Social Action* (New York: McGraw-Hill, 1937), was the most important prewar precursor of this development. More than any other individual, Parsons brought European theory to the forefront of American sociology. In an unreadable, yet somehow influential article of 53 pages on the theory of social stratification, Parsons gave less than two pages to "the ethnic factor": "a secondary basis of modification of the stratification pattern but . . . by no means unimportant." "A Revised Analytical Approach to the Theory of Social Stratification," in T. Parsons, *Essays in Sociological Theory*, rev. ed. (New York: The Free Press, 1954), pp. 424–425.

   In his recent book *Why Can't They Be Like Us?* (New York: Dutton, 1971), Andrew Greeley presents a similar critique of sociological theory, pointing out its failure to appreciate the importance of ethnic groups in American society.

5. Simmel also stressed social conflict in his work, and his essay on "the stranger" inspired the notion of "the marginal man" which Park and his students applied to minority relations in the United States.

6. Weber gave some attention to race and ethnicity in his writings; however, these insights were not incorporated into the summaries

of his work which had the most impact on American theory. See Ernst M. Manasse, "Max Weber on Race," *Social Research, 14* (June 1947), 191–221.

7. Rose makes the point that the study of race was part of the mainstream of sociology in Park's day, but is no longer. Rose, *op. cit.*, p. 153.

8. Rose speculates that "the slow pace of theoretical development in regard to racial and ethnic relations between the late 1930's and the early 1960's might be related to the prominence of structural-functional analysis and the neglect of conflict theory." *Ibid.*, p. 57.

9. Gunnar Myrdal, *An American Dilemma* (New York: Harper & Row, 1944).

10. *The Autobiography of Malcolm X* (New York: Grove, 1964), and Cruse, *op. cit.*

11. Eugene Genovese, *The Political Economy of Slavery* (New York: Random House, 1956) and *The World the Slaveholders Made* (New York: Pantheon, 1969); Winthrop Jordan, *White Over Black* (Chapel Hill: University of North Carolina Press, 1968). The most original psychiatric study is Joel Kovel's *White Racism: A Psychohistory* (New York: Pantheon, 1970).

12. E. Franklin Frazier, *Black Bourgeoisie* (New York: The Free Press, 1957) and Elliot Liebow, *Tally's Corner* (Boston: Little, Brown, 1967).

13. The point is stressed in T. Shibutani and K. Kwan, *Ethnic Stratification* (New York: Macmillan, 1956), pp. 14–15.

14. The dead-end consequences of this situation are suggested by Pierre Van Den Berghe who notes that "race is only a special case of more general social facts" and therefore "there can be no general theory of race and . . . race relations must be placed within the total institutional and cultural context of the society studied." *Race and Racism* (New York: Wiley, 1967), p. 7. Although I submit there is something special about racial phenomena, even as a type-case of the more general category of social oppression, Van Den Berghe's point is well taken, and suggests one reason for the abysmal failure of "race relations theory."

15. Robert Park, *Race and Culture* (New York: The Free Press, 1950).

16. Louis Wirth, "The Problem of Minority Groups" in Ralph Linton, ed., *The Science of Man in the World Crisis* (New York: Colum-

bia University Press, 1945), pp. 354–364, and Wirth, *The Ghetto* (Chicago: University of Chicago Press, 1928).

17. Milton Gordon, *Assimilation in American Life* (New York: Oxford University Press, 1964); Nathan Glazer and Daniel Patrick Moynihan, *Beyond the Melting Pot* (Cambridge: M.I.T. and Harvard University Press, 1963).

18. William Lloyd Warner, Introduction to Allison Davis, Burleigh Gardner, and Mary Gardner, *Deep South* (Chicago: University of Chicago Press, 1941), and Warner and Leo Srole, *The Social Systems of American Ethnic Groups* (New Haven: Yale University Press, 1945), pp. 284, 295. "Our class system functions for a large proportion of ethnics to destroy the ethnic subsystems and to increase assimilation. . . . The future of American ethnic groups seems to be limited; it is likely that they will be quickly absorbed. When this happens, one of the great epochs of American history will have ended, and another, that of race, will begin."

19. John Dollard, *Caste and Class in a Southern Town* (Garden City, N.Y.: Doubleday, 1957); Davis, Gardner, and Gardner, *Deep South, op. cit.*

20. This also has been a problem for caste theory in India. For an attempt to justify the comparison between India and the United States in a nonstatic framework, see Gerald Berreman, "Caste in India and the United States," *American Journal of Sociology, 66* (September 1960), 120–127.

21. Charles Silberman was one of the first white experts to make this point when he wrote in 1964 that "what we are discovering . . . is that the United States—all of it, North as well as South, West as well as East, is a racist society in a sense and to a degree that we have refused so far to admit, much less face." *Crisis in Black and White* (New York: Random House, 1964), pp. 9–10.

22. Myrdal, *op. cit.*, p. li: "All our attempts to reach scientific explanations of why the Negroes are what they are and why they live as they do have regularly led to determinants on the white side of the race line. In the practical and political struggles of effecting changes, the views and attitudes of the white Americans are likewise strategic. The Negro's entire life, and, consequently, also his opinions on the Negro problem are, in the main, to be considered as secondary reactions to more primary pressures from the side of the dominant white majority."

23. H. Hyman and P. Sheatsley, "Attitudes Toward Desegregation,"
    Scientific American (July 1964), 16–23.
24. Cf. Murray Wax, *Indian Americans* (Englewood Cliffs, N.J.:
    Prentice-Hall, 1971), p. 3.

chapter 1
on racial oppression
in america

The analysis of race by social scientists has been shaped by an under-lying assumption that the concern with color in human society is ultimately irrational or nonrational. The intellectuals and scientists who have labored to expose the falsity of popular racial conceptions have contributed immensely to the modern outlook—with its progres-sive and skeptical principles that remain essential to humanistic and egalitarian thought. Yet at the same time, in permeating the atmo-sphere in which racial realities have been investigated, this irrational or nonrational bias may have blocked a deeper, more complex under-standing of racial oppression and its causes and functions for modern societies.

Race Consciousness as a Rational Project

In a sense the study of race relations and racial groups remains in the same backward state as was the study of religion a century and more ago. Religion also was approached in terms of how its systems of belief and dogma deviated from what was construed as scientific reality. Today most scholars recognize that an institution so enduring cannot be the simple product of fear and ignorance. Religion obviously speaks to basic human needs; it is increasingly viewed as another path to apprehending the complex reality of the world, a mode of knowing as legitimate for its purposes as the scientific. Can there be something parallel in the phenomenology of race that similarly explains its re-markable persistence through the ages?*

* In a provocative paper, Edward Shils puzzles over the remarkable

Put differently, is there a rational substratum underlying the awareness and concern with color in the human family? In the form of racism, color consciousness becomes profoundly irrational, but man's interest in race also speaks to something deeply rational: the search to know himself and the human species. The shock of systematic color variation brought a form of order to man's early understanding of his kind. It dramatized the diversity of humankind in all its physical and cultural manifestations. The knowledge of racial difference (distorted as this "knowledge" was and often remains) served to help classify the bewildering variety of tribes, nations, and languages. Thus racial awareness must be distinguished from racism; the former must have emerged first in human evolution.[2]

Intertwined in the structure of racial thought is a dual reality, made up of rational as well as irrational elements. Race consciousness emerges out·of the need to classify and the search for group identity, but like all knowledge and principles of division, it contains the potential of human alienation. The wedge of racism separates men from others of their own species and blocks possibilities of common identification and mutual cooperation. Racism alienates men psychologically because it is also a flight from reality, distorting the human project of knowing the social world and covering up the facts of domination, exploitation, and injustice with ready-made but ever changing formulas about the relation between man's nature and his lot in life.

Where then did the impulse to know the other (and ultimately oneself too) in terms of color become perverted into the closed, rigid views of the relation between race and behavior, race and character, race and virtue, that we recognize today as genuine racism? The transition from color consciousness or racial awareness to racism may be too re-

---

salience of color in human identity despite its inherent "meaninglessness." He argues that "self-identification by color has its origins in the sense of primordial connection with which human beings find it difficult to dispense." Shils sees race and ethnicity replacing kinship and locality as the crucial primordial identifications, and he links such attachments to "man's need to be in contact with the point and moment of his origin and to experience a sense of affinity with those who share that origin."[1] Shils is unusual among modern scholars: he sees race and color as symbols that have a positive function for human group life. But in linking color with such values as kinship, nationality, and religion, the "primordial" approach continues to view racial identification in a nonrational, if not an irrational, framework.

mote or inaccessible in terms of available evidence to provide a definitive answer. However, in broad terms we can suggest an answer. The association of race consciousness with social relations based on the oppression of one group by another is the logical prerequisite for the emergence of racism. The conquest of people of color by white Westerners, the establishment of slavery as an institution along color lines, and the consolidation of the racial principle of economic exploitation in colonial societies led to the elaboration and solidification of the racist potential of earlier modes of thought.[3] Of course, cruel oppression and naked exploitation have long been a human affliction, without regard to race or national origin. What is distinctive about the modern period is the emergence of a racial order dominated by whites in which much of this exploitation and brutality has been channeled along the dimension of color. Fantastic structures of belief and ideology developed as justification; with the institutionalization of racial oppression, the irrational elements in racial thinking have flowered. Nevertheless, the rational core remains, both in the atavistic project of consciousness and in the form of social and economic interests that are associated with racial privilege and the relative position of different racial and ethnic groups.

The Problem of Racial Privilege

Oppression is usually studied for what it does to the oppressed; even in dictionary definitions the role of the oppressor is a shadowy one.* Yet all forms of social oppression, whatever their motivation, confer certain privileges on the individuals and groups that oppress or are able to benefit from the resultant inequalities. It is the creation and defense of group privileges that underlie the domination of one sex over the other, as well as the emergence of slavery, caste, and economic classes.[5] Privilege is the heart of racial oppression also—for Albert Memmi the colonizer's privilege was the essence of the colonial

---

* The new Random House dictionary lists these meanings for the verb "to oppress": "To lie heavily upon," "to burden with cruel or unjust impositions or restraints," to "subject to a burdensome or harsh exercise of authority or power," and "to weigh down, as sleep or weariness does." This source notes further that while the literal meaning of the term is to press down upon, its chief usage today is the figurative application to social and political situations: "To oppress is usually to subject (a people) to burdens, to undue exercise of authority, and the like."[4]

relationship.[6] The various forms of social oppression all involve exploitation and control. To generate privilege, certain people have to be exploited, and to be exploited they must be controlled—directly or indirectly. The mechanisms of control, ranging from force and violence to legal restrictions to cultural beliefs, ideologies, and modes of socioeconomic integration, are therefore central to an understanding of oppression. Social oppression is a dynamic process by which one segment of society achieves power and privilege through the control and exploitation of other groups, which are *literally* oppressed, that is, burdened and pushed down into the lower levels of the social order.

There is much that is unique and special about racial oppression, but it shares the common elements and dynamics that make up social oppression as a generic phenomenon. In a racial order a dominant group, which thinks of itself as distinct and superior, raises its social position by exploiting, controlling, and keeping down others who are categorized in racial or ethnic terms. When one or more groups are excluded from equal participation in society and from a fair share of its values, other groups not so excluded and dominated are correspondingly elevated in position. The racist restrictions that strike at people of color in America result in a system of special privilege for the white majority. Whether or not particular racist practices are followed *consciously* in order to benefit whites is not the issue. Whatever the intent, the system benefits all strata of the white population, at least in the short run—the lower and working classes as well as the middle and upper classes.

I define privilege in terms of unfair advantage, a preferential situation or systematic "headstart" in the pursuit of social values (whether they be money, power, position, learning, or whatnot). Social privilege is not unique to racist societies. Like hierarchy and exploitation, it is a universal feature of all class societies, including those in which ethnic and racial division are insignificant. The values that people seek are never distributed equally; in the struggle for subsistence and social rewards there are always obstacles that impede some groups more than others. Thus systematic inequality and systematic injustice are built into the very nature of stratified societies. But when these inequities and injustices fall most heavily upon people who differ in color or national origin because race and ethnicity are primary principles upon which people are excluded or blocked in the pursuit of their goals, such a society is in addition racist.

White Americans enjoy special privilege in all areas of existence where racial minorities are systematically excluded or disadvantaged: housing and neighborhoods, education, income, and life style. Privilege is a relative matter, of course, but in racial and colonial systems it cannot be avoided, even by those who consciously reject the society and its privileges![17] The iron law of white privilege gives rise to truly ironic situations. The children of the middle class who have "dropped out" to live in near-poverty conditions always hold in reserve their racial prerogatives when and if they decide to reenter the mainstream. Many of these young cultural rebels have chosen the post office as an occasional means of subsistence, and in doing so they have threatened what has been a relatively protected sanctuary of black employment. And from the civil rights movement to the more recent student demonstrations, the white radicals have received a relatively more benign treatment from the police and the courts than have their third world counterparts.

Though racial privilege pervades all institutions, it is expressed most strategically in the labor market and the structure of occupations. In industrial capitalism economic institutions are central, and occupational role is the major determinant of social status and life style. If there is any one key to the systematic privilege that undergirds a racial capitalist society, it is the special advantage of the white population in the labor market.

As I emphasize in Chapter 2, the white immigrants entered the labor force under considerably more favorable conditions than did the racial minorities. As the European ethnics and their children have moved up in the class structure, the casual, unskilled, low-paying jobs in the economy have been filled in good part through a new form of migration from rural to urban centers within the American continent. The lower stratum of the working class has become predominantly Afro-American, Mexican-American, and Puerto Rican.[8] Suffering high rates of unemployment and marginal employment, third world workers fit Marx's conception of an industrial reserve army, which meets the system's need for an elastic labor pool. When working they tend to be concentrated in jobs that are insecure, dirty, unskilled, and at the bottom of the hierarchy of authority where there is little possibility for advancement. The result is that white workers have a monopoly or a near monopoly on jobs that are secure, clean, highly skilled, involve authority, and provide the possibilities of promotion. This pattern is so consistent that some economists argue that a *dual labor market* exists in many cities, one for whites and one for racial minorities.[9] Moreover, a number of studies summarized recently by Harold Baron show that black workers tend to be concentrated in old industries that are economically stagnant and declining in labor requirements.[10] The most advanced and progressive industries like oil and chemicals typically have all-white labor forces.

The white avoidance of dirty and servile work is a linchpin of colonial labor systems. As of 1960 more Negro men worked as janitors or porters than in any other detailed occupational category in the United States; more black women were employed as private household domestics than in any other line of work.[11] Blacks are either the majority or strikingly overrepresented in the work of cleaning floors and toilets, washing dishes and clothes, shining shoes, and handling the messes of sick people in hospitals and dead bodies in morgues.[12] The white working class elevates its status by protecting itself from the contamination of such unpleasant work and in the bargain increases its share of "good, clean jobs."[13]

White monopoly over the skilled trades has, of course, become a national scandal; the unions have put up the most effective resistance to the general movement against racism. In 1960 only 5 percent of craftsmen and foremen were nonwhite. By 1970 this figure had increased to only 7 percent. In the union-dominated construction industry where blacks have been concentrated in the laborer and other lower-paying trades, there was no increase in the proportion of craftsmen who were nonwhite between 1960 and 1970.[14] A vast number of studies have documented the slowness of employers, public and private, to promote people of color. Although in 1970 blacks made up 15 percent of all federal government employees, they held only 3 percent of the higher grade jobs under the Federal Classification Act, 4 percent of the higher grade positions in the postal service, and less than 10 percent of those blue-collar government jobs paying more than $8,000 a year.[15] In 1960 only 1.5 percent of industrial foremen were nonwhite;[16] by 1970 the proportion had risen to 5 percent.[17] The fact that for Afro-Americans going to work has almost always meant being bossed by whites is one reason why many independent personalities have preferred hustling within the ghetto to conventional employment.[18]

I do not believe that the generally high living standards of white America can be attributed *in toto* to racial oppression and privilege, as the rhetoric of many radicals suggests. Of course, there would be no United States at all without the original colonial conquest. And the contribution of slavery to our economic development was immense. Yet today's widespread affluence is due primarily to the organizational and technological capacities of American capitalism and the historically high productivity of our rural and urban work force. We do not know precisely how much racial privilege has contributed to white living standards. In part because of the multiple variables involved and the lack of satisfactory data, in part because social scientists like other Americans do not face squarely their racial privileges, the problem has only recently begun to receive serious attention. In the most careful analysis to date, based on 1960 census data, Lester Thurow calculates a figure of $15.5 billion as the gain in overall white income that is derived from five areas of racial discrimination: more steady employment, higher wages, more lucrative occupations, greater investment in human capital (that is, education), and labor union monopoly. This averages out to a bonus of $248 a year for every white member of the labor force, and a corresponding loss of $2100 for each nonwhite worker or job-seeker.[19]

Although the figure of $250 per capita appears to be too low, Thurow's findings suggest that a comparative study of racist societies would show an impressive contrast between the traditional colonial situation and that in advanced capitalist societies, like our own. Racial privilege varies from society to society, in both absolute amount and relative degree. In overseas colonialism, Europeans were a minority, either a tiny clique of officials or a more sizable settler population, as in South Africa and Algeria. The impact of racial privilege on white life styles in these colonial situations is suggested by the fact that every European who went overseas to a colonial station in Asia or Africa could afford, and was expected to have, one or more "native" servants. By contrast, in the antebellum South this was generally possible only for plantation owners, and in contemporary urban America only for the upper middle classes. In European colonies white income typically averaged *ten to twenty times* that of the colonized; even for the same work, white employees were paid four to ten times as much in the mines of Rhodesia and South Africa.* By contrast again, when racial

* The African Labour Survey of 1958 cites some typical figures. For Northern Rhodesia in 1956: "in the motor repairing and electrical trades and in the construction industry African wages varied between 5 and 12

wage differentials for the same job were common in American industry, they rarely surpassed 10 to 20 cents an hour. And in recent years the income of blacks has ranged between 50 and 60 percent of that of whites. These impressionistic indicators suggest the likelihood that white privilege, while real and significant, is not as inherently crucial to our economic system and social life styles as it was in classical colonialism. A numerical minority can live off a majority population in a more or less parasitical fashion; it is not possible for a numerical majority to do so. Nevertheless, white Americans tend to be very tenacious in resisting any threats to such privilege, whatever its absolute or relative level.

This may be because the salience of racial privilege is not identical for every segment of the colonizing population. Since white working-class people tend to have little formal education and specialized training, their occupational possibilities are few and tend to overlap with those of the racial minorities, especially when the latter are beginning to move and are challenging their subordination. With relatively low income, white workers have few housing choices and therefore compete more directly with people of color in the effort to improve residential situations. The same point holds for education. Thus the marginal increment that racial privilege contributes to overall life chances may be higher for the white working class than it is for the middle and upper classes. Needless to say, the class privileges of the latter are immeasurably greater.*

---

percent of European wages for what are nominally the same jobs."[20] (Calculations from another source suggest that white workers in the same country's mines earned 16 times that of African workers.)[21] In the engineering industry of Southern Rhodesia, African earnings "as late as 1952 . . . were still on the average less than 7 percent of European employees." And in the mines in the same year the average cash wages for Africans were 6.7 percent of those of whites. In building construction the gap was considerably less.[22] In Kenya the ratio between average earnings of Europeans, Asians, and Africans in 1957 was 100 to 33.45 to 5.37, or a European-African ratio of 19 to 1. In the Belgian Congo in 1954 "the average total remuneration of 1,240,000 indigenous wage earners in 1954 equalled roughly the total remuneration of the 32,000 European employees, which represents a ratio of earning per head of 1 to 40."[23] In the most developed African nation, South Africa, the wages of African men ranged from 20 to 24 percent of those of whites between 1944 and 1954; the overall trend was downward.[24]

* The argument above is supported by another statistical analysis of

Racial privilege is not simply economic. It is a matter of status also. Jefferson Davis understood this when he said that Negro slavery "raises white men to the same general level, that it dignifies and exalts every white man by the presence of a lower race."[27] One hundred years later James Baldwin put the same notion into a more sophisticated analysis when he reasoned that the fluidity and insecurity of the American status order required the Negro—so that white people would know where the bottom is, a fixed point in the system to which they could not sink.[28]

Deplorable and despicable as these ideas are, they are real in terms of social dynamics, the ways in which most white Americans orient their actions. Although race has been a central organizing principle of our class system, racial groups are not economic classes. In Max Weber's terms, they are "status groups," collectivities based on an attempt to monopolize social honor as well as economic advantage. All kinds of social formations—aristocratic and military elites, new religions, ethnic groups—have striven to maximize their relative prestige. The ability of white Europeans to command status in every racially mixed society on the basis of color alone has certainly been the most fateful case of this tendency in modern history.[29] The relevance of race to status illuminates the particular aggressive-

---

the 1960 census. Norvall Glenn examined 179 urbanized areas that differed in the proportion of nonwhites. He found that the occupational status of whites was increased by the presence of nonwhites; where nonwhites were less than 10 percent of the population, 66 percent of the whites held non-manual and skilled jobs; where nonwhites were 30 percent or more, 76 percent of the whites had such occupations. Glenn concluded from his findings (from which I have just given one example) that a majority of the white beneficiaries have intermediate rather than high incomes: "a good many whites may escape poverty, but few seem to receive very high income as the result of the presence and subordination of numerous Negroes." Glenn therefore concluded that his study failed to "support the Marxist view that discrimination against Negroes benefits the 'capitalist class' but hurts white workers."[25] However, a more recent analysis by Michael Reich disputes this thesis, although it does not mention Glenn's research. Reich compared the largest 48 standard metropolitan statistical areas from the same 1960 census and found that a high proportion of nonwhites increased inequality of income *within* the white population, and that "most of the inequality among whites generated by racism was associated with increased income for the richest one percent of white families."[26] Thurow, Glenn, and Reich used different methods, and because of their varied results my argument above must remain hypothetical until more comprehensive research has been carried out.

ness with which whites have defended segregated residential communities and, today, the schools that are rooted in them. The average
person in our society has a very limited opportunity to achieve status
through the social recognition of her or his work or income.* The
concern with status, aggravated by the mass media and the competi-
tive value system of capitalism, centers around home ownership and
the quality and image of the neighborhood in which the home is
located. The sense of community integrity among both white subur-
banites and white ethnic groups in the cities is threatened by the
presence of nonwhite people.[30] The other status concern of Middle
America, the upward mobility of its children, appears endangered by
integrated schools.

Because economic and status privileges are bulwarks of racial
stratification, racism cannot simply be viewed as a set of subjective
irrational beliefs that might be overcome through more and better
contact, communication, and understanding. When such a focus on
prejudice forms the dominant approach to racial conflict—as it does
in America today, even among social scientists—then the fact that
whites, blacks, Chicanos, and other third world groups have distinct objective interests is overlooked. Ethnic and racial groups are first and
foremost interest groups.[31] The Marxian view that "false consciousness" explains the failure of white workers to support racial movements and the nonwhite poor only illuminates one part of a complex
reality. Since racial groups are real in America, the status concerns of
race have a basis in social life. White workers know that they have
something to lose by the elimination of racial privilege.[32]

The fact of racial interest does not belie the importance of
divergent and conflicting interests among different segments of the
same racial groups, divisions that might widen with changing economic
and political circumstances. In American society races and classes in-
terpenetrate one another. Race affects class formation and class in-

* Of course the status of the job itself is affected by its racial cast.
So-called "Negro jobs" are ranked at the bottom of the occupational
prestige scale, the "whitest" positions are at the top. In part, but only in
part, this is an indirect consequence of other factors that account for
occupational placement, such as education and the class one is born into.
Whites have crowded nonwhites out of occupation after occupation, and
historical research would probably indicate that the prestige of such work
then increased.

fluences racial dynamics in ways that have not yet been adequately investigated. The entire relation between racial and class interest (and racial and class privilege) is an exceedingly complicated one that social theorists might well explore in a deeper fashion.[33] It is the most important question that must be faced in constructing a theoretical model of racial capitalist society. But it is by no means only an academic problem, since the relation between class and race in contemporary America has bedeviled radical theorists and movement organizers seeking a strategy for revolutionary politics, as well as liberal policy-makers attempting to promote change within education, welfare, employment, and other urban institutions.

Exploitation and Control

Modern race relations ultimately owe their origins to the exploitative dynamic and expansionist thrust of Western Europe that exploded in the late fifteenth century, ushering in the so-called "Age of Discovery." Purely economic motives predominated in the institution of new systems of domination through which whites appropriated the land, labor, and resources of various non-Western and nonwhite people. Most crucial was the racial division of labor that was established on slave plantations, in the haciendas of Indo-America, and later in the colonies of Asia and Africa (discussed in Chapter 2). Labor and its exploitation must be viewed as the first cause of modern race relations; as we have seen, the main outlines of this division of labor are still reflected in the privileged position of whites within the occupational distribution and economic stratification of present-day multiracial societies.

All forms of labor exploitation—the factory as well as the plantation—require discipline and control. When unpleasant tasks are not integrated into kinship networks or traditional rituals, people have to be induced to do them for a minimal remuneration—especially when others determine the conditions of work and appropriate its results.

The discipline and control over the young proletariat in the early stages of English industry was brutal and heavy handed, as Marx's *Capital* attests. However the problems associated with the control of a working class in capitalist societies are of a lesser order than those generated by a colonial labor system.

The young proletariat under early capitalism resisted exploitation aggressively, through on-the-job actions and wider social movements. As a relatively unassimilated and restive class, the proletariat posed threats to the new economic arrangements and the stability of the larger social order. The capitalists therefore had to institutionalize factory discipline and at the same time contain the specters of anarchy, revolution, and the undermining of culture evoked by the working class and its movements. Both control problems were largely resolved in Western Europe, as well as the United States, through a long period of economic and political conflict. The working classes gained what T. H. Marshall has called *citizenship* in the larger society, with substantive rights and privileges.[34] Mass education, the assimilation of ethnic groups, voting and political parties, and economic mobility contributed to this process. Along with the institutionalization of labor unions, which have been strategic regulators of plant discipline, these developments have brought about the political integration of white working classes in Western capitalist societies. Such citizenship and political integration, made possible by new technology and increasing wealth, characterize the stage of advanced capitalism. Since the white worker no longer threatens the social order, industrial control has become specific to the factory. It is only a means to the ends of more efficient exploitation, stable profits, and the maintenance of the factory system as a paying enterprise. It is not an end in itself.

Crucial to industrial citizenship was the fact that Western proletariats were indigenous, of the same race and bearers of the same traditions as the ruling elites. The existing cultural gap was a product of poverty and economic position—or sometimes national origin, as with the Irish workers in England. But, as variations within European culture, these cultural differences were much smaller than those between Western and non-Western ways of life that racial labor systems institutionalized. Perhaps for this reason the proletariat, although typically stigmatized and deemed inferior, was not viewed as wholly outside the pale of humanity, as irrevocably "the other."

The problem of control was different in racial systems. Originating out of conquest or other forms of physical coercion, the labor force was recruited from societies and cultural traditions that were considered alien. Because of this origin in force and social dislocation, the possibility of resistance and revolt, or at least the fear of them, was greater.[35] Because of the cultural disparities and the colonizer's belief in his racial and cultural superiority, the society had no place

for people of color to fit into the system in the long run as free
citizens and equal competitors. Once such a labor system was established and white supremacy and its packet of privilege became valued
in themselves, people of color had to be controlled and dominated because they were black, Mexican, Indians, or natives—not only because
they were convenient resources for exploitation.* Since the kind of
citizenship that integrated workers into an advanced capitalism was
not a possibility, racial control became an end in itself, despite its
original limited purpose as a means to exploitation and privilege.

Cultural domination may be the most significant mechanism of
such racial control. The expansion of Europe and European peoples
(including white Americans) over the world was motored by economic
forces and by deeply held convictions that Christianity and other core
Western values were superior to non-Western ways of life. In the
course of conquest and consolidating control, the imperial powers
attacked, disrupted, and violated in a thousand ways the original
cultures of the colonized. The depth of white race feeling is intimately
connected with this Western cultural arrogance, the seeming inca-
pacity to appreciate and coexist in a nonaggressive fashion with
diverging modes of organizing society and living in the world.**

The United States was founded on the principle that it was and
would be a white man's country. Nowhere was this insistence expressed more clearly than in the hegemony of Western European
values in the national consciousness and in the symbolic forms that
have expressed this cultural hegemony—institutionalized rituals (such
as the ceremonies of patriotism and holidays), written history, the
curriculum of the schools, and today the mass media. Indian, African,
Asian, and Latin American groups had to adapt to what Harold Cruse
has called "the cultural imperatives" of the white ethnic groups;[37] in

---

* This suggests the irrational element in racial labor systems, in
comparison with the "rationality" of pure capitalist exploitation—for which
the social composition of the industrial labor force is a matter of indifference. Or as Mannoni has expressed it: "North American Negroes may be
less well treated than white workers, but it is not because it is more profitable to treat them in this way: in fact they are ill-treated because they are
treated as Negroes, that is to say in a way which escapes definition in
economic terms."[36]

** This topic is developed further in the Introduction to Part II,
"Racism and Culture."

the process their own cultural contributions were absorbed, obliterated, or ignored. Even the promise of assimilation to those individuals whose adaptations were deemed successful was at bottom a control device, since assimilation weakened the communities of the oppressed and implicitly sanctioned the idea of white cultural superiority. Cultural control over third world minorities has been particularly significant in intellectual life. The very characterization of their existence and group realities and the interpretation of their history and social experience have been dominated by the analyses of white thinkers and writers.

Racial control pervades every institution of American life today. This does not mean that all white people have power, all people of color none. In a bureaucratic capitalist society, even most whites are without effective power, their lives controlled by the decisions of distant bureaucratic structures and the operations of the market. At the same time many individual third world people control some aspects of their own lives and command power over others of their group, as political leaders, employers, professionals, and so on, despite the persistence of the organizational norm that they must not wield authority over whites. Thus I am not making the argument that each person of color is completely powerless, nothing but the pawn of whites who direct and command. The systematic racial control that I am stressing operates on the collective level. Third world communities lack autonomy and self-determination; they are controlled by white economic and political structures. Perhaps the ghetto best illustrates this point.

Today's urban ghettos and barrios, like the legal segregation of the past, are devices for racial control. They reflect the basic contradiction of racial systems, which bring nonwhites into a society to appropriate their land or labor and not to associate with whites as free and equal citizens. The ghettos are the modern "solution" to this insoluble dilemma. They provide walls between the racially oppressed and the mainstream, shield the white majority from the anger and hostility of the confined, and permit the middle class to go about its daily business with a minimal awareness of how basic is racial division to American life. The modern ghetto is not the product of "blind" economic or market forces as many suppose. Rather, it is produced and maintained by deliberate policies of the real estate industry, supported by powerful segments of federal and local government and,

unfortunately, buttressed by majority sentiments of the white population.[38] The police and the national guard are key factors in this
equation. They channel the individual and collective violence that
stems from racial colonialism, keeping it within the ghetto's own
boundaries and containing sporadic tendencies for it to spill over into
"white" areas.

Moreover, the black ghetto and other third world equivalents
further the economic exploitation of the racial minorities. As Reich
summarizes the situation: "Blacks pay higher rents for inferior housing, higher prices in ghetto stores, higher insurance premiums, higher
interest rates in banks and lending companies, travel longer distances
at greater expense to their jobs, suffer from inferior garbage collection and less access to public recreational facilties, and are assessed at
higher property tax rates when they own housing."[39] Racial exploitation is more than economic, however. It is not necessary to argue that
the labor of third world people has become dispensable in an auto-
mating technology and that economic exploitation is no longer a
central underpinning of racism[40] to appreciate Cruse's insight that
cultural exploitation of the Afro-American population takes on a
special importance in the contemporary period. As Cruse emphasizes,
the cultural, economic, and political aspects of oppression are intimately intertwined.[41] Cultural exploitation furthers political control,
which serves to maintain economic subordination. The importance of
subtle cultural manipulation as well as the dialectic between racial
control and exploitation were vividly dramatized in the official national response to the assassination of Martin Luther King.

The death of a national leader is always disorienting. King's
death was particularly disruptive to the precarious racial order of
America, since he was the one black leader who combined a sizable
following among his own people with high status in the country as a
whole. His death was threatening because he was the major spokesman of the traditional civil rights movement and its philosophy of
integration through nonviolence (values shared, at least in principle,
by the liberal establishment)—a bulwark against the developing storms
of nationalism and violence.

For a few days on the symbolic level, the death of King
ironically brought about that integration of black people into American life that the assassinated leader had striven for. The young minister was lionized and elevated into the position of a national hero; it

was clear that he would be the first Afro-American for whom schools, streets, and projects in white neighborhoods were to be named—unlike Booker T. Washington, George Washington Carver, Paul Laurence Dunbar, Frederick Douglass, and others, whose symbolic immortality is confined to segregated ghettos. During the period of national mourning, the mass media, which is virtually the bloodstream of America's body cultural, concentrated almost exclusively on the life and death of King and the problems of his people. It was a concerted attempt to incorporate Afro-American realities as part of the national experience through the creation of a hero and a legend.

Yet, with all the tribute to the fallen leader, the control and exploitation of black America remained the primary imperatives underlying the official reaction, which under close inspection revealed the classic motifs of racism. National leaders and the mass media made a bid to *appropriate* Martin Luther King—just as white America has historically ripped off the economic and cultural products of black life. King was a product of the Southern Negro experience, his viability as a national figure related to the close ties he had maintained with his people. But in his death white establishment power, through the speeches of politicians and the work of television, claimed King as its own, as someone with whom it had always identified, someone it had supported. This did not come from any deep belief that the black leader had been speaking as their leader. Instead it was motivated by a desire to control the black population, to restrain its angry masses from riots and demonstrations, by incorporating them into a national pseudoconsensus of grief and dedication to King's principles. Thus placated by the outpouring of national respect, the black community, through its identification with King, was expected to feel integrated into American society, even though the economic and power arrangements of that society had not changed one whit and were still based on racial oppression.*

But the most important way in which King was exploited in his death was through the distortion of his values and beliefs. Part of the mentality of racism seems to be an unconscious process of distort-

---

* This strategy was advanced by the attendance at the funeral, and its style. With all major politicians present except the President, it became a ceremony for national celebrities rather than a funeral made up of the poor and the blacks who were the murdered man's real constituency.

ing the messages of minority people, particularly when individually or collectively they are acting "out of place," that is, not in accord with conventional stereotypes.* In the case of King the distortion may have been more conscious and calculated. His social philosophy was presented to the nation as centering almost exclusively on nonviolence as an end in itself. Politicians and commentators invoked his strictures against violence and hatred in an attempt to use him to keep the ghettos quiet. Virtually nothing was said about the three major enemies of King's wrath, to which he had devoted his recent efforts and speeches—racism, poverty, and war. Thus the living exploit the dead, and white power exploits black leaders and their philosophies.[42]

The depth of white privilege was revealed by the strange spectacle of television reveling in the life and death of an Afro-American. The commentators and newscasters who introduced us to the dense geography and culture of King's formative years, explained his roots in the Southern Negro religious tradition, and traced his emergence as a civil rights leader were in almost all cases white men. If ever there was an assignment appropriate for a black reporter, this was it. The programs dramatized the fact that the black experience had become a major industry in this country. During the 1960s, racial revolution, protest, and ghetto life with its social, economic, and human problems provide the major news that fills the space on television between the westerns, the ball games, and the old movies. Although many local stations have hired blacks, and many more must be looking for that qualified Negro, the reportage of the King assassination underlined how systematically black men and women have been excluded, on the national level, from profitable careers with the mass media. Exclusion from the desirable values of the society—the best jobs, the best homes and neighborhoods, the best schools—is a basic mechanism of racial domination. The other side of black exclusion is white privilege. This digression into the death of Martin Luther King is intended to illustrate the interconnection of privilege, exploitation, and control in the dynamics of racial oppression.

* This same thing took place with fateful effect as a response to the black power movement. Despite the efforts of black spokesmen to explain the ideas of cultural self-definition and economic and political control, it was only the threat of violence, usually at most only implicit in the tone of the militant's rhetoric, that white journalists and politicians seized upon.

Control of Mobility and the Idea of Place

> If me want for go in a Ebo, Me can't go there!
> Since them tief me from a Guinea, Me can't go there!
>
> If me want to go to a congo, Me can't go there!
> Since them tief me from my tatta, Me can't go there!
>
> If me want for go in a Kingston, Me can't go there!
> Since massa go in a England, Me can't go there!

A Jamaican Slave Song[43]*

In order to control a racially defined people systematically, and so maintain special privilege for the dominant group, limits must be placed on the mobility of the oppressed minority. I refer both to the mobility of individuals in physical space and to collective mobility in socioeconomic status. Restrictions on the freedom of movement, part of the logic of all forms of oppression, are particularly strategic in racial systems. Perhaps this is because the modern racial order emerged from international movements of people, movements that were color patterned.

Exploration, trade, slavery, the settlement of colonies, and industrial development in the capitalist nations were processes that set in motion mass movements of population, which drastically altered the racial ecology of the world. Because expansion was a project of Western Europe and involved to an important extent the land, labor, and resources of non-Western people, this historical transformation intensified the salience of race and color. In the migrations, both voluntary and forced, that brought about the modern era, the primary movers were whites; people of color were, in the main, the moved.

The very essence of slavery is its rigid control over the human impulse to move about, as the Jamaican song expresses so poignantly. In the United States, the decision to maintain the racial order after Emancipation required new devices to constrain the movement and

---

* Reprinted by permission of the publisher from Orlando Patterson's *The Sociology of Slavery*, London: MacGibbon and Kee, Ltd.

mobility of the freedmen. This was accomplished by ensuring their economic dependency, in most cases through tenant farming and sharecropping; by such "legal" devices as vagrancy statutes, pass laws, and jim crow ordinances; and by political intimidation practiced by the Klan and similar groups. For many years the North attracted Afro-Americans because it promised a greater degree of personal freedom; but even in the North restriction of mobility was commonplace.[44]

Other third world groups in the United States experienced limits on individual and collective movement, in large part because they entered as laborers in work situations that were particularly binding: debt servitude, peonage, and agricultural gang systems. Native Americans were, of course, a special and extreme case: their territory was continually constricted; their movements were more and more constrained by federal laws, broken treaties, and settler aggression. The special restrictions that were placed on the immigration of Asian and Latin American groups, including obstacles to attaining citizenship, also contributed to this dynamic. Many Chinese and Mexicans, for example, were able to enter this country only through unofficial or illegal channels, which prevented the possibility of naturalization. The activities of immigration officials in these ethnic communities intimidated citizen and noncitizen alike. European immigrants were favored because they started out as free laborers in industry, were less affected by discriminatory immigration and naturalization laws, and had the advantage of being white. One role of color is to serve as a visible badge of group membership that facilitates this blockage of mobility.*

Thus, systems of racial domination depend ultimately on control over the movements of the oppressed and restriction of their full participation in society. Although this control may be secured by laws, or by violence or the threat of violence, the most common and more stable mechanisms reside in cultural beliefs and psychological adaptations. Here the notion of *place* is central. The idea that there is an appropriate place—or set of roles and activities—for people of color,

---

* Overseas colonial regimes also were based on limiting the free movement of the indigenous peoples. Tribes and individuals became subject to administrative machinery through taxes, pass requirements, and other devices. The white man, however, was able to move freely; in fact, his personal mobility was basic to colonial privilege.

and that other places and possibilities are not proper or acceptable, is a universal element of the racist dynamic.[45] In America, as in the European colonies, white people used to say (and many still do): "The Negro (or native) is all right as long as he stays in his place."

The idea of place has had an infinite variety of expressions. Its classic form was the old-fashioned Southern "etiquette of race relations," patterns of deference and demeanor in interpersonal interaction between the races.[46] Occupationally, it meant that certain jobs were reserved for blacks and, to a degree, for other racial minorities. Its physical manifestation has been the Indian reservation, the Mexican section of town (or barrio), and the ghetto. Because blacks, for example, are supposed to "belong" only in their own neighborhoods, Negroes found in white areas—when they cannot easily be categorized in terms of a conventional racial role—are objects of suspicion and alarm, no matter how legitimate their business. Since police in our society are legally sanctioned to stop people "on suspicion," the practice of law enforcement confines Afro-Americans within the white man's idea of his place.

Central to this dynamic of place is the assumption, at times subconscious, that people of color should be subservient to whites. In the political sphere whites neither expect nor desire to see third world groups acting autonomously, defining their own goals, and controlling the pace of their social movements. The stricture to operate "within the system" along individualistic American lines rather than moving collectively "against" the society reflects the white imperative of overall control. Thus, civil rights activity commanded the support of white liberals as long as blacks were working within the framework of national leadership and accepting the rules and procedures of political decision making in America. The autonomous and aggressive character of the black power thrust was a rejection of this traditional Negro followership role, and many whites therefore cried "unfair."*

Within the national culture, people of color have been prescribed

---

* Others have responded in a more sophisticated fashion, accepting some forms of black power. Here, as Christoffel has argued in his analysis of the Kerner Report, the purpose appears to be "co-optation," using these new currents in order to institutionalize modern forms of domination that are less costly to corporate capitalism.[47] But black power, too, is a diversified movement. I discuss some of these issues in Chapter 3.

distinctive roles. Indians are either romantic figures or the noble savages of our past—or, like the Mexicans, they are ignored, particularly in the contemporary urban condition. Blacks have usually been the group most central to pressing political issues and national obsessions. In the cultural sphere their major role assignment has been that of entertainer. As vaudeville comic, singer, dancer, musician, or athlete, they could make people laugh, cry, or wonder at their exploits; however, they were not to make people think or question their lives, because the roles of intellectual, cultural critic, creator, and political statesman were out of place.

Of course there have always been those who refused to accept "their place" in society. Various Native American tribes carried on armed struggle over a period of three hundred years. In the Southwest the Mexicans who fought Anglocolonialism and racial arrogance were labeled bandits and outlaws. Similarly, the black man who rebelled against white dominance became the "bad nigger," a term that invoked some respect within the Afro-American group. For generations, lynching was the prescribed punishment meted out to "uppity" Negroes who violated the norms of the racial order. It is a general law of colonial racial systems that the oppressing group has a license to kill members of the "inferior" race without serious likelihood of punishment.[48] Legitimizing this ultimate sanction assures control of the oppressed group, because emerging protest movements are checked in their early stages. Even in the recent period, when protest and even rebellion have become commonplace and "bad niggerism" almost an accepted style in race relations, many if not most of the important leaders of the black movement have met violent deaths, and a group such as the Panthers has seen much of its leadership imprisoned or otherwise harassed.

The importance of place and the dynamics of accommodation and resistance explain why racism modifies the forms of social stratification and the processes of social mobility in a racial capitalist society like America. The collective mobility of the racial minorities is reduced because of discrimination in the labor market and at the work place. Some economic gains have taken place, resulting primarily from the movements from rural regions to industrial urban centers and the cyclical swings of the economy. But the pervasiveness of white privilege and blocked movement distorts even this form of individual mobility. Improvements in income and occupation are not easily translated into an overall raising of social status and increase in political effectiveness, as they are for white groups. The symbols and prerequisites by which status is validated—improved residence, neighborhood, and life style—are not available, because the housing market is racist. And political power and the general respect of society lag far behind improvements in group economic position. Finally, the conversion of parental gains into family (intergenerational) mobility is limited by the institutional racism of the schools which thwarts the aspirations and educational achievements of minority children.

In still another way, racial oppression negates the general sorting and sifting processes of social mobility, by which class redistribution takes place in advanced capitalist societies. Studies based on the white population suggest that there is some truth to the old saying, "talent rises to the top." According to this research, the children of the poor and working classes who are above average in intelligence and energy are the ones most likely to attend college and move into the middle classes.[49] But because the institutions that serve as gateways to class placement express the racial oppressiveness of the society, the most sensitive, creative, and energetic youth from minority communities are those most likely to come into conflict with these institutions, challenging the authority of the mediocre functionaries—schoolteachers, policemen, and others—who personally maintain the colonial relationship.[50] The explosion of creative talent and political leadership that has emerged from the prisons and the street corners suggests that the rebellious spirits whose careers have been a cycle of difficulties in school, entanglements with the law, and dropping from the mainstream might have fed the political, economic, and cultural elites of the society had they been born into a nonracist order.* The foremost example is Malcolm X, who achieved greatness through the schools of street hustling, prison, and the Black Muslim movement. Eldridge Cleaver and the late George Jackson exemplify the creative talents locked up in prisons; but these two successful writers and

---

* The above line of reasoning explains in part the weakness of colonized middle classes that Frazier and Fanon dissected for the American and the African contexts.[51] Many of those who achieved status had to do so through compromises that were unacceptable to other creative personalities, who directly or indirectly chose to refuse accommodation to a racist culture.

revolutionary thinkers are only the tip of the iceberg, as the recent political and cultural ferment in state penitentiaries suggests. It is significant that Harold Cruse, perhaps the outstanding theoretician of the black movement in America, developed his scholarship through twenty years in the marginal world of bohemian radicalism rather than in the universities where the leading white social theorists are found. Examples could be multiplied.

One virtue of the poverty program and related special opportunity projects in education and industry is that they have provided a second chance for many of these talented men whom racism had brought to despair or forced to operate outside the system. The demand that poverty organizations hire only indigenous leaders and workers has created a new avenue for the recognition, the use, and the development of these potentials. Even the colleges and the universities, now that they are opening some doors to minority students, are finding that many of the most able are those whom the lower schools had once labeled as unfit for academic pursuits.

In summary, the logic of racial oppression denies members of the subjugated group the full range of human possibility that exists within a society and culture. From this standpoint racism is an historical and social project aimed at reducing or diminishing the humanity or manhood (in the universal, nonrestrictive meaning of the word) of the racially oppressed. All the roles, places, and stereotypes that are forced upon the dominated share a common feature: they function to define the person of color within frameworks that are less than, or opposed to, the status of full adult manhood. The tendency of racism is to convert the colonized into objects or things to be used for the pleasure and profit of the colonizer; the stereotypes and mental imagery of the white population then depict them as animals or children, the better to justify such less than human patterns of relatedness.* This dynamic of racial colonialism has been eloquently expressed by Toynbee:

* The tendency of the West to view people they oppress as animals or children must somehow be related to European culture's psychological denial and repression of both the animality of the human species and the universal presence of the child and his traces in the makeup of the adult. This is what makes people of color such convenient targets for the psychic projection of those character tendencies and desires that Western man has suppressed in himself, in part due to the powerful dualism of the Protestant

When we Westerners call people "Natives," we implicitly
take the cultural colour out of our perceptions of them.
We see them as trees walking, or as wild animals
infesting the country in which we happen to come
across them. In fact, we see them as part of the local flora
and fauna, and not as men of like passions with ourselves, and seeing them thus as something infrahuman,
we feel entitled to treat them as though they did not
possess ordinary human rights. They are merely natives of
the lands which they occupy; and no term of occupancy
can be long enough to confer any prescriptive rights.
Their tenure is as provisional and precarious as that of
the forest trees which the Western pioneer fells or that
of the big game which he shoots down. And how shall
the "civilized" Lords of Creation treat the human game,
when in their own good time they come to take
possession of the land which, by right of eminent domain,
is indefeasibly their own? Shall they treat these "Natives"
as vermin to be exterminated, or as domesticable
animals to be turned into hewers of wood and drawers
of water? No other alternative need be considered, if
"niggers have no souls." All this is implicit in the word
"Natives" as we have come to use it in the English
language in our time.[52]

The Refusal of Racism and the Ambiguous Future

The dehumanization inherent in racial oppression explains why a concern with personal dignity and manhood is central to anticolonial and
antiracist movements. The insistence on affirming these principles lies
at the heart of present-day racial conflict in the United States. What
is new among third world people today, particularly the youth, is a
stubborn unwillingness to compromise the principle of personal
dignity. It is difficult for whites to comprehend how the major institutions in our society (as in others based on a history of racial
colonialism)—the schools, the labor market, welfare, police and the
courts—consistently belittle and diminish the sense of personal worth

---

world view, which sees good–evil, life–death, child–adult, animal–human,
heaven–hell, and so on, as polar opposites rather than as interpenetrating
realities.

and dignity of nonwhite people. In the past the majority of the oppressed adapted to this situation in one way or another; those who could not or would not came into open conflict with institutional authority. Today this numerical balance is shifting.

Therefore the big news in America today is not really racism, the pervasiveness of white domination. Rather, it is the consistent challenge to patterns of racial control that the oppressed are mounting in every area of society. Perhaps the deepest refusal of racial norms has come in the cultural sphere, where entire third world generations are rapidly discarding assumptions about the superiority of white people and Euro-American values. As Franz Schurmann notes, the nationalism of the racial minorities may be viewed as an equivalent of a cultural revolution, which historically tends to precede political and economic revolutions.[53]

People are talking about racism today because race relations are up for grabs. Not since Reconstruction has there been such an extended period of volatility in our racial order. The traditional norms have lost their force as the colonized minorities refuse to be controlled by oppressive institutions. As more and more people of color refuse to play the part of victim of racism, the contradiction between their shifting orientations and white-dominated institutions intensifies. The refusal of racism forces change in education, in employment, in politics, and in other institutions. But because of white privilege and organizational inertia, the changes are too slow for the excluded groups and at the same time too fast for the dominant majority, many of whom have become frightened and confused. Thus, racial awareness and conflict escalate, even if "things are getting better" for at least important segments of nonwhite populations.

Today many of the specific notions of place operate only weakly. Firms hire blacks as door-to-door salesmen in white neighborhoods, and even Wall Street has welcomed its first black-owned brokerage firm. Many institutions have been forced to accept the independent political role of third world caucuses and communities. Television has accelerated the widening of cultural roles, especially for blacks. But breaks in the racial order do not portend its imminent collapse, although they permit the observer to see its outlines more clearly. The specific constellation of the colored man's place in society undergoes change, generally in a less restrictive direction, but the underlying themes reappear in new and unexpected ways.

The thesis that informs this essay and the book as a whole—

that racial division and oppression are leading elements (and probably indispensable ones) in American society and culture as they are presently constituted—is not an optimistic one. Theorists who interpret race within a framework of economic and social class are less pessimistic because they see more explicit promise of progressive social change. The liberal can look forward to eventual integration of, and citizenship for, the racial minorities, like the industrial working class and the ethnic immigrants; the radical Marxist can hold up the prospect of future class-based revolution. But in a racial or colonial capitalist society where the racially oppressed are a numerical minority, how can racism be overcome when the majority of the population gains from it and presumably will defend these privileges as rational and objective interests? Here even the solution reached by victims of classical colonialism, the ejection of the colonizer and the achievement of national independence, does not seem to be a realistic possibility.

If my analysis is correct, the situation is unique and the problems are real and difficult. Yet race is not the only reality of American society, nor its only principle of human oppression. Although I have emphasized in this essay that the racial privileges of the white majority are rooted in objective interests, it is equally important to stress that racial domination is not the only significant interest of white people. The various axes along which people are exploited, manipulated, or otherwise controlled in a capitalist society create potential group interests within the wider population. Workers, employees, consumers, women, old people, youth, and students have specific needs that are not satisfied, and problems that are not resolved, simply by favored position in the racial order. Furthermore, there are interests shared by all people to which racial inequality—and the civil conflict it breeds—is antithetical. These include membership in a social order with at least a minimum of solidarity and community, and a system of cultural values with a modicum of integrity, not one shot through with falsity and contradiction. The political and cultural rebellion of white youth is a symptom of the fact that these crucial human needs are not met by the larger society.[54]

In the long run, the movements of third world people against racial oppression may play a strategic role in creating the conditions for the conversion of these latent nonracial interests into overt challenges to the system. As the civil rights movement made clear, racial protest exposes the contradictions of the larger society and the limits of the possibilities inherent in its political and economic arrangements. In its first stages, such exposure contributes very little to basic social transformation. The majority group responds by resisting change, digging in to maintain its privileges. The so-called "backlash" may represent a more explicit awareness of racial position, a new white consciousness, defensive and reactionary in nature, but, as with all racial consciousness, in large part rational and based on a partial grasp of social reality. As the racial minorities step up the momentum of their demands and white consciousness and racial privilege reveal their limitations as answers to group conflicts, a more complex awareness of the social forces underlying the contemporary crisis should emerge. Third world militancy may play an essential role in the development of a more widespread political consciousness of the oppressive dynamics of racial capitalism. Such a consciousness is a prerequisite for effective mass movements of social transformation.

NOTES

1. Edward Shils, "Color, the Universal Intellectual Community, and the Afro-Asian intellectual," in John Hope Franklin, ed. *Color and Race* (Boston: Beacon, 1968), esp. pp. 1–5.

2. This hypothesis receives some support from a recent survey of race in antiquity. Generalizing from a minute and voluminous examination of works of art, artefacts, and written texts, Frank Snowden found a lively interest in Ethiopians or black people among the Greeks, Romans, and other Mediterranean peoples, without the existence of a racial hierarchy or systematic beliefs as to superiority and inferiority. Frank M. Snowden, Jr., *Blacks in Antiquity* (Cambridge: Harvard University Press, 1971).

3. Winthrop Jordan has described the stereotyped imageries of Africa and black people that existed among Elizabethan Englanders before the slave trade. *White over Black* (Chapel Hill: University of North Carolina Press, 1968), chap. 1.

4. *Random House Dictionary of the English Language,* Unabridged (New York: Random House, 1966).

5. Engels saw the division of labor between men and women as its first historical expression; in his view the shift to a male dominant society set the stage for the emergence of class exploitation.

Frederick Engels, *The Origin of the Family, Private Property, and the State* (New York: International Publishers, 1942), p. 58.

6. Albert Memmi, *The Colonizer and the Colonized* (Boston: Beacon, 1967), pt. 1.

7. The classic discussion is Memmi's essay "The Colonizer Who Refuses," *ibid.*, pp. 19–44.

8. One of the first studies to note that a racially defined "underclass" was in formation was S. M. Lipset and Reinhard Bendix, *Social Mobility in Industrial Society* (Berkeley: University of California Press, 1959), pp. 105–107. Southern whites have also contributed to this migration.

9. Michael J. Piore, "Jobs and Training," in Beer and Barringer, eds., *The State and the Poor* (Boston: Winthrop, 1970); and Harold Baron, "The Web of Urban Racism" in Louis Knowles and Kenneth Prewitt, eds., *Institutional Racism in America* (Englewood Cliffs, N.J.: Prentice-Hall, 1969), pp. 146–149.

10. Harold Baron, "The Demand for Black Labor: Historical Notes on the Political Economy of Racism," *Radical America, 5* (March–April 1971), esp. 34–38, where he describes the dual labor market. The whole article is extremely important.

11. U.S. Census of Population 1960, Bureau of the Census, Department of Commerce, *Occupational Characteristics,* table 3, pp. 21–30.

12. *Ibid.*

13. White workers actively developed these patterns through their own job actions. Symptomatic is the following grievance which was submitted to the management of a Southern textile mill in the 1920s: "We think unstopping Toilets is out of a White Man's Class of Work, it ought to be done by Negroes. You would not unstop Toilets Your Self. You should have the same Respect for Your Employees You have for Your Self." Cited in Liston Pope, *Millhands and Preachers* (New Haven: Yale University Press, 1942), p. 69.

14. *The Social and Economic Status of Negroes in the United States, 1970,* Current Population Reports, series p–23, no. 38, Bureau of the Census, U.S. Department of Commerce (1970), p. 61.

15. *Ibid.*, p. 67.

16. U.S. Census of Population 1960, Bureau of the Census, Department of Commerce, vol. 1, pt. 1, pp. 544–546.

17. *The Social and Economic Status of Negroes* . . . , *op. cit.*, p. 61.
18. The point is documented in Claude Brown's *Manchild in the Promised Land* (New York: Macmillan, 1965). It is a recurring theme in black literature.
19. Lester C. Thurow, *Poverty and Discrimination* (Washington, D.C.: Brookings, 1969), pp. 130–134.
20. International Labour Office, *African Labour Survey* (Geneva: 1958), p. 280.
21. A. L. Epstein, *Politics in an Urban African Community* (Manchester: Manchester University Press, 1958), p. 102.
22. International Labour Office, *op. cit.*, p. 281.
23. *Ibid.*, p. 284.
24. *Ibid.*, p. 687.
25. Norvall Glenn, "White Gain from Negro Subordination," in Gary Marx, ed., *Racial Conflict* (Boston: Little, Brown, 1971), pp. 106–116. See his earlier article also, "Occupational Benefits to Whites from the Subordination of Negroes," *American Sociological Review*, 28 (June 1963), 443–448.
26. Michael Reich, "The Economics of Racism," *Upstart*, 1 (1971), 55–65.
27. Cited in Michael Banton, *Race Relations* (New York: Basic Books, 1967), p. 117.
28. James Baldwin, *Nobody Knows My Name* (New York: Dial, 1969), p. 133: "One cannot afford to lose status on this peculiar ladder, for the prevailing notion of American life seems to involve a kind of rung-by-rung ascension to some hideously desirable state. If this is one's concept of life, obviously one cannot afford to slip back one rung. When one slips, one slips back not a rung but into chaos and no longer knows who he is. And this reason, this fear, suggests to me one of the real reasons for the status of the Negro in this country. In a way, the Negro tells us where the bottom is: *because he is there,* and *where* he is, beneath us, we know where the limits are and how far we must not fall. We must not fall beneath him. We must never allow ourselves to fall that low, and I am not trying to be cynical or sardonic."
29. Everett C. Hughes was one of the first sociologists to emphasize the status aspects of race relations. See E. C. Hughes and Helen M. Hughes, *Where Peoples Meet* (New York: The Free Press, 1952).

30. For convincing reportage on this point from Chicago and Cicero, Illinois, see Gene Marine, "I've Got Nothing Against the Colored, Understand," in Barry N. Schwartz and Robert Disch, eds., *White Racism* (New York: Dell, 1970), pp. 217–228. A particularly sensitive discussion of the importance of home and neighborhood for white ethnic groups is found in Andrew Greeley, *Why Can't They Be Like Us?* (New York: Dutton, 1971), chap. 13.

31. This is well understood by Nathan Glazer, many of whose views on American race relations I quarrel with. See Nathan Glazer and Daniel P. Moynihan, *Beyond the Melting Pot* (Cambridge: M.I.T. and Harvard University Press, 1963).

32. James Boggs puts it much more strongly. He views the white worker as a counterrevolutionary force and the chief enemy of the black movement. *Racism and the Class Struggle* (New York: Monthly Review Press, 1970). This may however be a short-sighted perspective. The resentment of white workers and white ethnics against the rise of racial minorities is in part a recognition that they—and not the rich and the upper middle classes—are being forced to make the major adjustments and pay the largest burden of cost for racial reforms, limited as these have been. There is thus an implicit anticapitalist spirit in the "white backlash" that under certain circumstances could develop into an authentic class consciousness.

33. The concept of interest, so crucial to Marxian theory, is confused and contradictory. For an attempt at clarification, see Isaac D. Balbus, "The Concept of Interest in Pluralist and Marxian Analysis," *Politics and Society*, 1 (February 1971), 151–177.

34. T. H. Marshall, "Citizenship and Social Class," in Marshall, ed., *Class, Citizenship, and Social Development* (Garden City, N.Y.: Doubleday, 1965).

35. On the importance of the slave patrols in the antebellum South, see Kenneth Stampp, *The Peculiar Institution* (New York: Random House, 1956), esp. chaps. 3 and 4.

36. O. Mannoni, *Prospero and Caliban: The Psychology of Colonization* (London: Methuen, 1956), p. 32.

37. Harold Cruse, *The Crisis of the Negro Intellectual* (New York: Morrow, 1967).

38. William K. Tabb, *The Political Economy of the Black Ghetto* (New York: Norton, 1970).

39. Reich, *op. cit.*, p. 57.

40. Sidney M. Willhelm, *Who Needs the Negro?* (Cambridge: Schenkman, 1970).

41. Cruse, *op. cit.*

42. For a discussion of the distorted response to King's death, see Andrew Billingsley, *Black Families in White America* (Englewood Cliffs, N.J.: Prentice-Hall, 1968), pp. 109–110.

43. Orlando Patterson, *The Sociology of Slavery* (London: MacGibbon & Kee, 1967), p. 255. Ebo is an alternate spelling of Ibo, a large group of West African peoples from whom many slaves were taken. Guinea was the term for Africa used by the slaves. Kingston is the principal city and capital of Jamaica.

44. Cf. Leon Litwack, *North of Slavery* (Chicago: University of Chicago Press, 1961).

45. Gunnar Mydral, *An American Dilemma* (New York: Harper & Row, 1944), is a compendium of specifics. A more recent discussion of "the Negro role" appears in Thomas Pettigrew, *A Profile of the Negro American* (New York: Van Nostrand Reinhold, 1964), chap. I.

46. Bertram Doyle, *The Etiquette of Race Relations in the South* (Chicago: University of Chicago Press, 1937).

47. Tom Christoffel, "Black Power and Corporate Capitalism," in Schwartz and Disch, eds., *White Racism, op. cit.*, pp. 333–340.

48. Sithole concludes that "no white man in the whole colonial history of Africa was ever sentenced to death for the murder of an African!" . . . "in perusing the annals of courts in European-ruled Africa, I have failed to discover a single instance where a European was convicted of the murder of an African and sentenced to death, although many cases have been found of Europeans convicted of murder of Europeans and sentenced to death. Many cases of Africans convicted of murder of Europeans and Africans and sentenced to death have also been found." Ndabaningi Sithole, *African Nationalism* (London: Oxford University Press, 1968), p. 139. A similar pattern has existed with respect to other minorities: On the aboriginals of Australia, see A. Grenfell Price, *White Settlers and Native Peoples* (Melbourne: Georgian House, 1949), pp. 107ff.; on American Indians, see W. C. Macleod, *The American Indian Frontier* (London: Routledge & Kegan Paul, 1928); on Mexican-Americans, see Carey McWilliams, *North from Mexico* (Phila-

delphia: Lippincott, 1949), pp. 112 and 273; and on Chinese, see Thomas Chinn, *A History of the Chinese in California* (San Francisco: Chinese Historical Society, 1969). The black case is so notorious that references seem unnecessary.

Whereas Sithole found no deviant cases, Price mentions that the colonial authorities in 1838 hung seven whites who had perpetrated a mass murder of 28 Native Australians; Chinn quotes a report of the Chinese Six Companies of 1862, which noted that only two whites had been convicted and hung out of at least 88 known cases of murdered Chinese; but these exceptions are hard to find in the literature.

49. This research is summarized in Lipset and Bendix, *op. cit.*
50. The mediocrity of colonial functionaries in the classical overseas situation is stressed throughout J. S. Furnivall, *Colonial Policy and Practice* (New York: New York University Press, 1956).
51. E. Franklin Frazier, *Black Bourgeoisie* (New York: The Free Press, 1957), and Frantz Fanon, *The Wretched of the Earth* (New York: Grove, 1968), pp. 149ff.
52. Arnold Toynbee, *A Study in History*, vol. 1 (London: Oxford University Press, 1934), pp. 152–153.
53. Franz Schurmann, "System, Contradictions, and Revolution in America" in Roderick Aya and Norman Miller, eds., *The New American Revolution* (New York: The Free Press, 1971), p. 20.
54. In his *Strategy for Labor*, Andre Gorz integrates such human and spiritual needs into an overall Marxian framework (Boston: Beacon, 1967).

chapter 2
colonized and
immigrant minorities

During the late 1960s a new movement emerged on the Pacific Coast. Beginning at San Francisco State College and spreading across the bay to Berkeley and other campuses, black, Chicano, Asian, and Native American student organizations formed alliances and pressed for ethnic studies curricula and for greater control over the programs that concerned them. Rejecting the implicit condescension in the label "minority students" and the negative afterthought of "nonwhite," these coalitions proclaimed themselves a "Third World Movement."[1] Later, in the East and Middle West, the third world umbrella was spread over other alliances, primarily those urging unity of Puerto Ricans and blacks. In radical circles the term has become the dominant metaphor referring to the nation's racially oppressed people.

As the term *third world* has been increasingly applied to people of color in the United States, a question has disturbed many observers. Is the third world idea essentially a rhetorical expression of the aspirations and political ideology of the young militants in the black, brown, red, and yellow power movements, or does the concept reflect actual sociological realities? Posed this way, the question may be drawn too sharply; neither possibility excludes the other. Life is complex, so we might expect some truth in both positions. Furthermore, social relationships are not static. The rhetoric and ideology of social movements, if they succeed in altering the ways in which groups define their situations, can significantly shape and change social reality. Ultimately, the validity of the third world perspective will be tested in social and political practice. The future is open.

Still, we cannot evade the question, to what extent—in its application to domestic race relations—is the third world idea grounded in firm historical and contemporary actualities? To assess this issue we need to examine the assumptions upon which the concept rests. There are three that seem to me central. The first assumption is that racial groups in America are, and have been, colonized peoples; therefore their social realities cannot be understood in the framework of immigration and assimilation that is applied to European ethnic groups. The second assumption is that the racial minorities share a common situation of oppression, from which a potential political unity is inferred. The final assumption is that there is a historical connection between the third world abroad and the third world within. In placing American realities within the framework of international colonialism, similarities in patterns of racial domination and exploitation are stressed and a common political fate is implied—at least for the long run. I begin by looking at the first assumption since it sets the stage for the main task of this chapter, a comparison and contrast between immigrant and third world experience. I return to the other points at the end of the essay.

The fundamental issue is historical. People of color have never been an integral part of the Anglo-American political community and culture because they did not enter the dominant society in the same way as did the European ethnics. The third world notion points to *a basic distinction between immigration and colonization as the two major processes through which new population groups are incorporated into a nation.* Immigrant groups enter a new territory or society voluntarily, though they may be pushed out of their old country by dire economic or political oppression. Colonized groups become part of a new society through force or violence; they are conquered, enslaved, or pressured into movement. Thus, the third world formulation is a bold attack on the myth that America is the land of the free, or, more specifically, a nation whose population has been built up through successive waves of immigration. The third world perspective returns us to the origins of the American experience, reminding us that this nation owes its very existence to colonialism, and that along with settlers and immigrants there have always been conquered Indians and black slaves, and later defeated Mexicans— that is, colonial subjects—on the national soil. Such a reminder is not pleasant to a society that represses those aspects of its history that do not fit the collective self-image of democracy for all men.

The idea that third world people are colonial subjects is gaining in acceptance today; at the same time it is not at all convincing to those who do not recognize a fundamental similarity between American race relations and Europe's historic domination of Asia and Africa. (I discuss how U.S. colonialism differs from the traditional or classical versions toward the end of the chapter.) Yet the experience of people of color in this country does include a number of circumstances that are universal to the colonial situation, and these are the very circumstances that differentiate third world realities from those of the European immigrants. The first condition, already touched upon, is that of a forced entry into the larger society or metropolitan domain. The second is subjection to various forms of unfree labor that greatly restrict the physical and social mobility of the group and its participation in the political arena. The third is a cultural policy of the colonizer that constrains, transforms, or destroys original values, orientations, and ways of life. These three points organize the comparison of colonized and immigrant minorities that follows.*

Group Entry and Freedom of Movement

Colonialism and immigration are the two major means by which heterogeneous or plural societies, with ethnically diverse populations, develop. In the case of colonialism, metropolitan nations incorporate new territories or peoples through processes that are essentially involuntary, such as war, conquest, capture, and other forms of force or manipulation. Through immigration, new peoples or ethnic groups enter a host society more or less freely. These are ideal-types, the polar ends of a continuum; many historical cases fall in between. In the case of America's racial minorities, some groups clearly fit the criterion for colonial entry; others exemplify mixed types.

Native Americans, Chicanos, and blacks are the third world

* There is another aspect of colonization which I do not deal with in this essay: the experience of being managed and manipulated by outsiders in terms of ethnic status. This is derived from the fact that the lives of colonized people tend to be administered by representatives of the dominant political and legal order. Immigrant groups experienced a considerable degree of such control, but less intensely and for a shorter period of time. They achieved a relative community autonomy earlier and gained power in a wider range of institutions relevant to them. See Chapter 3 for further discussion.

groups whose entry was unequivocally forced and whose subsequent histories best fit the colonial model. Critics of the colonial interpretation usually focus on the black experience, emphasizing how it has differed from those of traditional colonialism. Rather than being conquered and controlled in their native land, African people were captured, transported, and enslaved in the Southern states and other regions of the Western hemisphere. Whether oppression takes place at home in the oppressed's native land or in the heart of the colonizer's mother country, colonization remains colonization. However, the term *internal colonialism* is useful for emphasizing the differences in setting and in the consequences that arise from it.[2] The conquest and virtual elimination of the original Americans, a process that took three hundred years to complete, is an example of classical colonialism, no different in essential features from Europe's imperial control over Asia, Africa, and Latin America. The same is true of the conquest of the Mexican Southwest and the annexation of its Spanish-speaking population.

Other third world groups have undergone an experience that can be seen as part colonial and part immigrant. Puerto Rico has been a colony exploited by the mainland, while, at the same time, the islanders have had relative freedom to move back and forth and to work and settle in the States. Of the Asian-American groups, the situation of the Filipinos has been the most colonial. The islands were colonies of Spain and the United States, and the male population was recruited for agricultural serfdom both in Hawaii and in the States. In the more recent period, however, movement to the States has been largely voluntary.

In the case of the Chinese, we do not have sufficient historical evidence to be able to assess the balance between free and involuntary entry in the nineteenth century. The majority came to work in the mines and fields for an extended period of debt servitude; many individuals were "shanghaied" or pressed into service; many others evidently signed up voluntarily for serflike labor.[3] A similar pattern held for the Japanese who came toward the end of the century, except that the voluntary element in the Japanese entry appears to have been considerably more significant.[4] Thus, for the two largest Asian groups, we have an original entry into American society that might be termed semicolonial, followed in the twentieth century by immigration. Yet the exclusion of Asian immigrants and the restriction acts that followed were unique blows, which marked off the status of the Chinese and Japanese in America, limiting their numbers and potential power. For this reason it is misleading to equate the Asian experience with the European immigrant pattern. Despite the fact that some individuals and families have been able to immigrate freely, the status and size of these ethnic groups have been rigidly controlled.

There is a somewhat parallel ambiguity in the twentieth-century movement from Mexico, which has contributed a majority of the present Mexican-American group. Although the migration of individuals and families in search of work and better living conditions has been largely voluntary, classifying this process as immigration misses the point that the Southwest is historically and culturally a Mexican, Spanish-speaking region. Moreover, from the perspective of conquest that many Mexicans have retained, the movement has been to a land that is still seen as their own. Perhaps the entry of other Latin-Americans approaches more nearly the immigrant model; however, in their case, too, there is a colonial element, arising from the Yankee neo-colonial domination of much of South and Central America; for this reason, along with that of racism in the States, many young Latinos are third world oriented.

Thus the relation between third world groups and a colonial-type entry into American society is impressive, though not perfect or precise. Differences between people of color and Europeans are shown most clearly in the ways the groups first entered. The colonized became ethnic minorities en bloc, collectively, through conquest, slavery, annexation, or a racial labor policy. The European immigrant peoples became ethnic groups and minorities within the United States by the essentially voluntary movements of individuals and families. Even when, later on, some third world peoples were able to immigrate, the circumstances of the earlier entry affected their situation and the attitudes of the dominant culture toward them.

The essentially voluntary entry of the immigrants was a function of their status in the labor market. The European groups were responding to the industrial needs of a free capitalist market. Economic development in other societies with labor shortages—for example, Australia, Brazil, and Argentina—meant that many people could at least envision alternative destinations for their emigration. Though the Irish were colonized at home, and poverty, potato famine, and other disasters made their exodus more of a flight than that of other Europeans, they still had some choice of where to flee.[5] Thus, people of Irish descent are found today in the West Indies, Oceania, and other former British colonies. Germans and Italians moved in large numbers to South America; Eastern Europeans immigrated to Canada as well as to the United States.

Because the Europeans moved on their own, they had a degree of autonomy that was denied those whose entry followed upon conquest, capture, or involuntary labor contracts. They expected to move freely within the society to the extent that they acquired the economic and cultural means. Though they faced great hardships and even prejudice and discrimination on a scale that must have been disillusioning, the Irish, Italians, Jews, and other groups had the advantage of European ancestry and white skins. When living in New York became too difficult, Jewish families moved on to Chicago. Irish trapped in Boston could get land and farm in the Midwest, or search for gold in California. It is obvious that parallel alternatives were not available to the early generations of Afro-Americans, Asians, and Mexican-Americans, because they were not part of the free labor force. Furthermore, limitations on physical movement followed from the purely racial aspect of their oppression, as I stressed in Chapter 1.

Thus, the entrance of the European into the American order involved a degree of choice and self-direction that was for the most part denied people of color. Voluntary immigration .made it more likely that individual Europeans and entire ethnic groups would identify with America and see the host culture as a positive opportunity rather than an alien and dominating value system. It is my assessment that this element of choice, though it can be overestimated and romanticized, must have been crucial in influencing the different careers and perspectives of immigrants and colonized in America, because choice is a necessary condition for commitment to any group, from social club to national society.

Sociologists interpreting race relations in the United States have rarely faced the full implications of these differences. The *immigrant model* became the main focus of analysis, and the experiences of all groups were viewed through its lens.[6] It suited the cultural mythology to see everyone in America as an original immigrant, a later immigrant, a quasi-immigrant or a potential immigrant. Though the black situation long posed problems for this framework, recent developments have made it possible for scholars and ordinary citizens alike to force Afro-American realities into this comfortable schema. Migration from rural South to urban North became an analog of European immigration, blacks became the latest newcomers to the cities, facing parallel problems of assimilation. In the no-nonsense language of Irving Kristol, "The Negro Today Is Like the Immigrant of Yesterday."[7]

The Colonial Labor Principle in the United States

European immigrants and third world people have faced some similar conditions, of course. The overwhelming majority of both groups were poor, and their early generations worked primarily as unskilled laborers. The question of how, where, and why newcomers worked in the United States is central, for the differences in the labor systems that introduced people of color and immigrants to America may be the fundamental reason why their histories have followed disparate paths.

The labor forces that built up the Western hemisphere were structured on the principle of race and color. The European conquest of the Native Americans and the introduction of plantation slavery were crucial beginning points for the emergence of a worldwide colonial order. These "New World" events established the pattern for labor practices in the colonial regimes of Asia, Africa, and Oceania during the centuries that followed. The key equation was the association of free labor with people of white European stock and the association of unfree labor with non-Western people of color, a correlation that did not develop all at once; it took time for it to become a more or less fixed pattern.

North American colonists made several attempts to force Indians into dependent labor relationships, including slavery.[8] But the native North American tribes, many of which were mobile hunters and warrior peoples, resisted agricultural peonage and directly fought the theft of their lands. In addition, the relative sparsity of Indian populations north of the Rio Grande limited their potential utility for colonial labor requirements. Therefore Native American peoples were either massacred or pushed out of the areas of European settlement and enterprise. South of the Rio Grande, where the majority of Native Americans lived in more fixed agricultural societies, they were too numerous to be killed off or pushed aside, though they suffered drastic losses through disease and massacre.[9] In most of Spanish

America, the white man wanted both the land and the labor of the Indian. Agricultural peonage was established and entire communities were subjugated economically and politically. Either directly or indirectly, the Indian worked for the white man.

In the Caribbean region (which may be considered to include the American South),[10] neither Indian nor white labor was available in sufficient supply to meet the demands of large-scale plantation agriculture. African slaves were imported to the West Indies, Brazil, and the colonies that were to become the United States to labor in those industries that promised and produced the greatest profit: indigo, sugar, coffee, and cotton. Whereas many lower-class Britishers submitted to debt servitude in the 1600s, by 1700 slavery had crystallized into a condition thought of as natural and appropriate only to people of African descent.[11] White men, even if from lowly origins and serf-like pasts, were able to own land and property, and to sell their labor in the free market. Though there were always anomalous exceptions, such as free and even slave-owning Negroes, people of color within the Americas had become essentially a class of unfree laborers. Afro-Americans were overwhelmingly bondsmen; Native Americans were serfs and peons in most of the continent.

Colonial conquest and control has been the cutting edge of Western capitalism in its expansion and penetration throughout the world. Yet capitalism and free labor as Western institutions were not developed for people of color; they were reserved for white people and white societies. In the colonies European powers organized other systems of work that were noncapitalist and unfree: slavery, serfdom, peonage. Forced labor in a myriad of forms became the province of the colonized and "native" peoples. European whites managed these forced labor systems and dominated the segments of the economy based on free labor.[12] This has been the general situation in the Western hemisphere (including the United States) for more than three out of the four centuries of European settlement. It was the pattern in the more classical colonial societies also. But from the point of view of labor, the colonial dynamic developed more completely within the United States. Only here emerged a correlation between color and work status that was almost perfect. In Asia and Africa, as well as in much of Central and South America, many if not most of the indigenous peoples remained formally free in their daily work, engaging in traditional subsistence economies rather than working in the plantations, fields, and mines established by European capital. The economies in these areas came within the orbit of imperial control, yet they helped maintain communities and group life and thus countered the uprooting tendencies and the cultural and psychic penetration of colonialism. Because such traditional forms of social existence were viable and preferred, labor could only be moved into the arenas of Western enterprise through some form of coercion. Although the association of color and labor status was not perfect in the classical colonial regimes, as a general rule the racial principle kept white Europeans from becoming slaves, coolies, or peons.

Emancipation in the United States was followed by a period of rapid industrialization in the last third of the nineteenth century. The Civil War and its temporary resolution of sectional division greatly stimulated the economy. With industrialization there was an historic opportunity to transform the nation's racial labor principle. Low as were the condition and income of the factory laborer, his status was that of a free worker. The manpower needs in the new factories and mines of the East and Middle West could have been met by the proletarianization of the freedmen along with some immigration from Europe. But the resurgent Southern ruling class blocked the political and economic democratization movements of Reconstruction, and the mass of blacks became sharecroppers and tenant farmers, agricultural serfs little removed from formal slavery.* American captains of industry and the native white proletariat preferred to employ despised, unlettered European peasants rather than the emancipated Negro population of the South, or for that matter than the many poor white Southern farmers whose labor mobility was also blocked as the entire region became a semi-colony of the North.

The nineteenth century was the time of "manifest destiny," the ideology that justified Anglo expansionism in its sweep to the Pacific.

---

* This pattern was not unique to the United States. The emancipation of slaves in other societies has typically led to their confinement to other forms of unfree labor, usually sharecropping. In this context Kloosterboer cites the examples of the British West Indies, South Africa, the Dutch West Indies, the Dutch East Indies (Java), Portuguese Africa, Madagascar, the Belgian Congo, and Haiti.[13] The great influx of European immigration to Brazil also followed the abolition of slavery, and the new white Brazilians similarly monopolized the occupational opportunities brought by the industrialization that might have otherwise benefited the black masses.[14]

The Texan War of 1836 was followed by the full-scale imperialist conquest of 1846–1848 through which Mexico lost half its territory. By 1900 Anglo-Americans had assumed economic as well as political dominance over most of the Southwest. As white colonists and speculators gained control (often illegally) over the land and livelihood of the independent Hispano farming and ranching villages, a new pool of dependent labor was produced to work the fields and build the railroads of the region.[15] Leonard Pitt sums up the seizure of California in terms applicable to the whole Southwest:

> In the final analysis the Californios were the victims of an
> imperial conquest. . . . The United States, which had
> long coveted California for its trade potential and
> strategic location, finally provoked a war to bring about
> the desired ownership. At the conclusion of fighting, it
> arranged to "purchase" the territory outright, and set
> about to colonize, by throwing open the gates to all
> comers. Yankee settlers then swept in by the tens of
> thousands, and in a matter of months and years
> overturned the old institutional framework, expropriated
> the land, imposed a new body of law, a new language, a
> new economy, and a new culture, and in the process
> exploited the labor of the local population whenever
> necessary. To certain members of the old ruling class
> these settlers awarded a token and symbolic prestige, at
> least temporarily; yet with that status went very little
> genuine authority. In the long run Americans simply
> pushed aside the earlier ruling elite as being irrelevant.[16]

Later, the United States' economic hegemony over a semicolonial Mexico and the upheavals that followed the 1910 revolution brought additional mass migrations of brown workers to the croplands of the region. The Mexicans and Mexican-Americans who created the rich agricultural industries of the Southwest were as a rule bound to contractors, owners, and officials in a status little above peonage. Beginning in the 1850s, shipments of Chinese workmen—who had sold themselves or had been forced into debt servitude—were imported to build railroads and to mine gold and other metals. Later other colonized Asian populations, Filipinos and East Indians, were used as gang laborers for Western farm factories.[17] Among the third world groups that contributed to this labor stream, only the Japanese came from a nation that had successfully resisted Western domination. This may be one important reason why the Japanese entry into American life and much of the group's subsequent development show some striking parallels to the European immigrant pattern. But the racial labor principle confined this Asian people too; they were viewed as fit only for subservient field employment. When they began to buy land, set up businesses, and enter occupations "reserved" for whites, the outcry led to immigration restriction and to exclusion acts.[18]

A tenet central to Marxian theory is that work and systems of labor are crucial in shaping larger social forces and relations. The orthodox Marxist criticism of capitalism, however, often obscures the significance of patterns of labor status. Since, by definition, capitalism is a system of wage slavery and the proletariat are "wage slaves," the varied degrees of freedom within industry and among the working class have not been given enough theoretical attention. Max Weber's treatment of capitalism, though based essentially on Marx's framework, is useful for its emphasis on the unique status of the free mobile proletariat in contrast to the status of those traditional forms of labor more bound to particular masters and work situations. Weber saw "formally free" labor as an essential condition for modern capitalism.[19] Of course, freedom of labor is always a relative matter, and formal freedoms are often limited by informal constraint and the absence of choice. For this reason, the different labor situations of third world and of European newcomers to American capitalism cannot be seen as polar opposites. Many European groups entered as contract laborers,[20] and an ethnic stratification (as well as a racial one) prevailed in industry. Particular immigrant groups dominated certain industries and occupations: the Irish built the canal system that linked the East with the Great Lakes in the early nineteenth century; Italians were concentrated in roadbuilding and other construction; Slavs and East Europeans made up a large segment of the labor force in steel and heavy metals; the garment trades was for many years a Jewish enclave. Yet this ethnic stratification had different consequences than the racial labor principle had, since the white immigrants worked within the wage system whereas the third world groups tended to be clustered in precapitalist employment sectors.[21]

The differences in labor placement for third world and immi-

grant can be further broken down. Like European overseas colonialism, America has used African, Asian, Mexican and, to a lesser degree, Indian workers for the cheapest labor, concentrating people of
color in the most unskilled jobs, the least advanced sectors of the
economy, and the most industrially backward regions of the nation.
In an historical sense, people of color provided much of the hard
labor (and the technical skills) that built up the agricultural base and
the mineral-transport-communication infrastructure necessary for industrialization and modernization, whereas the Europeans worked
primarily within the industrialized, modern sectors.* The initial position of European ethnics, while low, was therefore strategic for
movement up the economic and social pyramid. The placement of
nonwhite groups, however, imposed barrier upon barrier on such
mobility, freezing them for long periods of time in the least favorable
segments of the economy.

Rural Versus Urban

European immigrants were clustered in the cities, whereas the colonized minorities were predominantly agricultural laborers in rural
areas. In the United States, family farming and corporate agriculture
have been primarily white industries. Some immigrants, notably Ger-
man, Scandinavian, Italian, and Portuguese, have prospered through
farming. But most immigrant groups did not contribute to the most
exploited sector of our industrial economy, that with the lowest status: agricultural labor. Curiously, the white rural proletariat of the
South and West was chiefly native born.

Industry: Exclusion from Manufacturing

The rate of occupational mobility was by no means the same for all
ethnics. Among the early immigrants, the stigmatized Irish occupied
a quasi-colonial status, and their ascent into a predominantly middle-
class position took at least a generation longer than that of the Germans. Among later immigrants, Jews, Greeks, and Armenians—urban

---

* I do not imply a perfect correlation between race and industrial
type, only that third world workers have been strikingly overrepresented in
the "primary sector" of the economy. Unlike in classical colonialism, white
labor has outnumbered colored labor in the United States, and therefore
white workers have dominated even such industries as coal mining, non-
ferrous metals, and midwestern agriculture.

people in Europe—have achieved higher social and economic status than Italians and Poles, most of whom were peasants in the old country.[22] But despite these differences, the immigrants as a whole had a key advantage over third world Americans. As unskilled laborers, they worked within manufacturing enterprises or close to centers of industry. Therefore they had a foot in the most dynamic centers of the economy and could, with time, rise to semiskilled and skilled positions.*

Except for a handful of industrial slaves and free Negroes, Afro-Americans did not gain substantial entry into manufacturing industry until World War I,[24] and the stereotype has long existed that Asians and Indians were not fit for factory work. For the most part then, third world groups have been relegated to labor in preindustrial sectors of the nonagricultural economy. Chinese and Mexicans, for example, were used extensively in mining and building railroads, industries that were essential to the early development of a national capitalist economy, but which were primarily prerequisites of industrial development rather than industries with any dynamic future.**

Geography: Concentration in Peripheral Regions

Even geographically the Europeans were in more fortunate positions. The dynamic and modern centers of the nation have been the Northeast and the Midwest, the predominant areas of white immigration. The third world groups were located away from these centers: Africans in the South, Mexicans in their own Southwest, Asians on the Pacific Coast, the Indians pushed relentlessly "across the frontier" toward the margins of the society. Thus Irish, Italians, and Jews went directly to the Northern cities and its unskilled labor market, whereas Afro-Americans had to take two extra "giant steps," rather than the

* Even in the first generation, immigrants were never as thoroughly clustered in unskilled labor as blacks, Mexicans, and Chinese were in their early years. In 1855, when New York Irishmen dominated the fields of common labor and domestic service, there were sizable numbers (more than a thousand in each category) working as blacksmiths, carpenters, masons, painters, stonecutters, clerks, shoemakers, tailors, food dealers and cartmen.[23]

** Of course some Europeans did parallel labor in mining and transportation construction. But since they had the freedom of movement that was denied colored laborers, they could transfer the skills and experience gained to other pursuits.

immigrants' one, before their large-scale arrival in the same place in the present century: the emancipation from slavery and migration from the underdeveloped semicolonial Southern region. Another result of colonized entry and labor placement is that the racial groups had to go through major historical dislocations within this country before they could arrive at the point in the economy where the immigrants began! When finally they did arrive in Northern cities, that economy had changed to their disadvantage. Technological trends in industry had drastically reduced the number of unskilled jobs available for people with little formal education.[25]

Racial Discrimination

To these "structural" factors must be added the factor of racial discrimination. The argument that Jews, Italians, and Irish also faced prejudice in hiring misses the point. Herman Bloch's historical study of Afro-Americans in New York provides clear evidence that immigrant groups benefited from racism. When blacks began to consolidate in skilled and unskilled jobs that yielded relatively decent wages and some security, Germans, Irish, and Italians came along to usurp occupation after occupation, forcing blacks out and down into the least skilled, marginal reaches of the economy.[26] Although the European immigrant was only struggling to better his lot, the irony is that his relative success helped to block the upward economic mobility of Northern blacks. Without such a combination of immigration and white racism, the Harlems and the South Chicagos might have become solid working-class and middle-class communities with the economic and social resources to absorb and aid the incoming masses of Southerners, much as European ethnic groups have been able to do for their newcomers. The mobility of Asians, Mexicans, and Indians has been contained by similar discrimination and expulsion from hard-won occupational bases.[27]

Our look at the labor situation of the colonized and the immigrant minorities calls into question the popular sociological idea that there is no fundamental difference in condition and history between the nonwhite poor today and the ethnic poor of past generations. This dangerous myth is used by the children of the immigrants to rationalize racial oppression and to oppose the demands of third world people for special group recognition and economic policies—thus the folk beliefs that all Americans "started at the bottom" and most have been able to "work themselves up through their own efforts." But the racial labor principle has meant, in effect, that "the bottom" has by no means been the same for all groups. In addition, the cultural experiences of third world and immigrant groups have diverged in America, a matter I take up in the next section.

Culture and Social Organization

Labor status and the quality of entry had their most significant impact on the cultural dynamics of minority people. Every new group that entered America experienced cultural conflict, the degree depending on the newcomers' distance from the Western European, Anglo-Saxon Protestant norm. Since the cultures of people of color in America, as much as they differed from one another, were non-European and non-Western, their encounters with dominant institutions have resulted in a more intense conflict of ethos and world view than was the case for the various Western elements that fed into the American nation. The divergent situations of colonization and immigration were fateful in determining the ability of minorities to develop group integrity and autonomous community life in the face of WASP ethnocentrism and cultural hegemony.

Voluntary immigration and free labor status made it possible for European minorities to establish new social relationships and cultural forms after a period of adjustment to the American scene. One feature of the modern labor relationship is the separation of the place of work from the place of residence or community. European ethnics were exploited on the job, but in the urban ghettos where they lived they had the insulation and freedom to carry on many aspects of their old country cultures—to speak their languages, establish their religions and build institutions such as schools, newspapers, welfare societies, and political organizations. In fact, because they had been oppressed in Europe—by such imperial powers as England, Tsarist Russia, and the Hapsburg Monarchy—the Irish, Poles, Jews, and other East Europeans actually had more autonomy in the New World for their cultural and political development. In the case of the Italians, many of their immigrant institutions had no counterpart in Italy, and a sense of nationality, overriding parochial and regional identities, developed only in the United States.[28]

But there were pressures toward assimilation; the norm of "Anglo-conformity" has been a dynamic of domination central to

American life.[29] The early immigrants were primarily from Western Europe. Therefore, their institutions were close to the dominant pattern, and assimilation for them did not involve great conflict. Among later newcomers from Eastern and Southern Europe, however, the disparity in values and institutions made the goal of cultural pluralism attractive for a time; to many of the first generation, America's assimilation dynamic must have appeared oppressive. The majority of their children, on the other hand, apparently welcomed Americanization, for with the passage of time many, if not most, European ethnics have merged into the larger society, and the distinctive Euro-American communities have taken on more and more of the characteristics of the dominant culture.

The cultural experience of third world people in America has been different. The labor systems through which people of color became Americans tended to destroy or weaken their cultures and communal ties. Regrouping and new institutional forms developed, but in situations with extremely limited possibilities. The transformation of group life that is central to the colonial cultural dynamic took place most completely on the plantation. Slavery in the United States appears to have gone the farthest in eliminating African social and cultural forms; the plantation system provided the most restricted context for the development of new kinds of group integrity.[30]

In New York City, Jews were able to reconstruct their East European family system, with its distinctive sex roles and interlocking sets of religious rituals and customs. Some of these patterns broke down or changed in response, primarily, to economic conditions, but the changes took time and occurred within a community of fellow ethnics with considerable cultural autonomy. The family systems of West Africans, however, could not be reconstructed under plantation slavery, since in this labor system the "community" of workers was subordinated to the imperatives of the production process. Africans of the same ethnic group could not gather together because their assignment to plantations and subsequent movements were controlled by slaveholders who endeavored to eliminate any basis for group solidarity. Even assimilation to American kinship forms was denied as an alternative, since masters freely broke up families when it suited their economic or other interests.* In the nonplantation context, the

---

* I do not imply here that African culture was totally eliminated, nor

disruption of culture and suppression of the regrouping dynamic was less extreme. But systems of debt servitude and semifree agricultural labor had similar, if less drastic, effects. The first generations of Chinese in the United States were recruited for gang labor; they therefore entered without women and children. Had they been free immigrants, most of whom also were male initially, the group composition would have normalized in time with the arrival of wives and families. But as bonded laborers without even the legal rights of immigrants, the Chinese were powerless to fight the exclusion acts of the late nineteenth century, which left predominantly male communities in America's Chinatowns for many decades. In such a skewed social structure, leading features of Chinese culture could not be reconstructed. A similar male-predominant group emerged among mainland Filipinos. In the twentieth century the migrant work situation of Mexican-American farm laborers has operated against stable community life and the building of new institutional forms in politics and education. However, Mexican culture as a whole has retained considerable strength in the Southwest because Chicanos have remained close to their original territory, language, and religion.

Yet the colonial attack on culture is more than a matter of economic factors such as labor recruitment and special exploitation. The colonial situation differs from the class situation of capitalism precisely in the importance of culture as an instrument of domination.[31] Colonialism depends on conquest, control, and the imposition of new institutions and ways of thought. Culture and social organization are important as vessels of a people's autonomy and integrity; when cultures are whole and vigorous, conquest, penetration, and certain modes of control are more readily resisted.[32] Therefore, imperial regimes attempt, consciously or unwittingly, either to destroy the cultures of colonized people or, when it is more convenient, to exploit them for the purposes of more efficient control and economic profit. As Mina Caulfield has put it, imperialism exploits the cultures of the colonized as much as it does their labor.[33] Among America's third

---

that Afro-Americans have lived in a cultural vacuum. A distinctive black culture emerged during slavery. From the complex vicissitudes of their historical experience in the United States, Afro-American culture has continued its development and differentiation to the present day, providing an ethnic content to black peoplehood. For a full discussion, see Chapter 4.

world groups, Africans, Indians, and Mexicans are all conquered peoples whose cultures have been in various degrees destroyed, exploited, and controlled. One key function of racism, defined here as the assumption of the superiority of white Westerners and their cultures and the concomitant denial of the humanity of people of color, is that it "legitimates" cultural oppression in the colonial situation.

The present-day inclination to equate racism against third world groups with the ethnic prejudice and persecution that immigrant groups have experienced is mistaken. Compare, for example, intolerance and discrimination in the sphere of religion. European Jews who followed their orthodox religion were mocked and scorned, but they never lost the freedom to worship in their own way. Bigotry certainly contributed to the Americanization of contemporary Judaism, but the Jewish religious transformation has been a slow and predominantly voluntary adaptation to the group's social and economic mobility. In contrast, the U.S. policy against Native American religion in the nineteenth century was one of all-out attack; the goal was cultural genocide. Various tribal rituals and beliefs were legally proscribed and new religious movements were met by military force and physical extermination. The largest twentieth-century movement, the Native American Church, was outlawed for years because of its peyote ceremony.[34] Other third world groups experienced similar, if perhaps less concerted, attacks on their cultural institutions. In the decade following the conquest, California prohibited bullfighting and severely restricted other popular Mexican sports.[35] In the same state various aspects of Chinese culture, dress, pigtails, and traditional forms of recreation were outlawed. Although it was tolerated in Brazil and the Caribbean, the use of the drum, the instrument that was the central means of communication among African peoples, was successfully repressed in the North American slave states.[36]

American capitalism has been partially successful in absorbing third world groups into its economic system and culture. Because of the colonial experience and the prevalence of racism, this integration has been much less complete than in the case of the ethnic groups. The white ethnics who entered the class system at its lowest point were exploited, but not colonized. Because their group realities were not systematically violated in the course of immigration, adaptation, and integration, the white newcomers could become Americans more or less at their own pace and on their own terms. They have moved up, though slowly in the case of some groups, into working-class and middle-class positions. Their cultural dynamic has moved from an initial stage of group consciousness and ethnic pluralism to a present strategy of individual mobility and assimilation. The immigrants have become part of the white majority, partaking of the racial privilege in a colonizing society; their assimilation into the dominant culture is now relatively complete, even though ethnic identity is by no means dead among them. In the postwar period it has asserted itself in a third-generation reaction to "overassimilation"[37] and more recently as a response to third world movements. But the ethnic groups have basically accepted the overall culture's rules of "making it" within the system, including the norms of racial oppression that benefit them directly or indirectly.

The situation and outlook of the racial minorities are more ambiguous. From the moment of their entry into the Anglo-American system, the third world peoples have been oppressed as groups, and their group realities have been under continuing attack. Unfree and semifree labor relations as well as the undermining of non-Western cultures have deprived the colonized of the autonomy to regroup their social forms according to their own needs and rhythms. During certain periods in the past, individual assimilation into the dominant society was seen as both a political and a personal solution to this dilemma. As an individual answer it has soured for many facing the continuing power of racism at all levels of the society. As a collective strategy, assimilation is compromised by the recognition that thus far only a minority have been able to improve their lot in this way, as well as by the feeling that it weakens group integrity and denies their cultural heritage. At the same time the vast majority of third world people in America "want in." Since the racial colonialism of the United States is embedded in a context of industrial capitalism, the colonized must look to the economy, division of labor, and politics of the larger society for their individual and group aspirations. Both integration into the division of labor and the class system of American capitalism as well as the "separatist" culture building and nationalist politics of third world groups reflect the complex realities of a colonial capitalist society.*

* These two poles of the pendulum, integration and nationalism, have long been recognized as central to the political dynamics of American

The colonial interpretation of American race relations helps illuminate the present-day shift in emphasis toward cultural pluralism and ethnic nationalism on the part of an increasing segment of third world people. The building of social solidarity and group culture is an attempt to complete the long historical project that colonial domination made so critical and so problematic. It involves a deemphasis on individual mobility and assimilation, since these approaches cannot speak to the condition of the most economically oppressed, nor fundamentally affect the realities of colonization. Such issues require group action and political struggle. Collective consciousness is growing among third world people, and their efforts to advance economically have a political character that challenges longstanding patterns of racial and cultural subordination.

Conclusion: The Third World Perspective

Let us return to the basic assumptions of the third world perspective and examine the idea that a common oppression has created the conditions for effective unity among the constituent racial groups. The third world ideology attempts to promote the consciousness of such common circumstances by emphasizing that the similarities in situation among America's people of color are the essential matter, the differences less relevant. I would like to suggest some problems in this position.

Each third world people has undergone distinctive, indeed cataclysmic, experiences on the American continent that separate its history from the others, as well as from whites. Only Native Americans waged a 300-year war against white encroachment; only they were subject to genocide and removal. Only Chicanos were severed from an ongoing modern nation; only they remain concentrated in the area of their original land base, close to Mexico. Only blacks went through a 250-year period of slavery. The Chinese were the first people whose presence was interdicted by exclusion acts. The Japanese were the one group declared an internal enemy and rounded up in concentration camps. Though the notion of colonized minorities points to a

---

blacks. As early as 1903 in *The Souls of Black Folk* W. E. B. Du Bois analyzed the existential "twoness" of the American Negro experience which lies behind this dilemma. However it is a general phenomenon applicable to all third world people in the United States, to the extent that their history has been a colonial one.

similarity of situation, it should not imply that black, red, yellow, and brown Americans are all in the same bag. Colonization has taken different forms in the histories of the individual groups. Each people is strikingly heterogeneous, and the variables of time, place, and manner have affected the forms of colonialism, the character of racial domination, and the responses of the group.

Because the colonized groups have been concentrated in different regions, geographical isolation has heretofore limited the possibilities of cooperation.* When they have inhabited the same area, competition for jobs has fed ethnic antagonisms. Today, as relatively powerless groups, the racial minorities often find themselves fighting one another for the modicum of political power and material resources involved in antipoverty, model-cities, and educational reform projects. Differences in culture and political style exacerbate these conflicts.

The third world movement will have to deal with the situational differences that are obstacles to coalition and coordinated politics. One of these is the great variation in size between the populous black and Chicano groups and the much smaller Indian and Asian minorities. Numbers affect potential political power as well as an ethnic group's visibility and the possibilities of an assimilative strategy. Economic differentiation may be accelerating both between and within third world groups. The racial minorities are not all poor. The Japanese and, to a lesser extent, the Chinese have moved toward middle-class status. The black middle class also is growing. The ultimate barrier to effective third world alliance is the pervasive racism of the society, which affects people of color as well as whites, furthering division between all groups in America. Colonialism brings into its orbit a variety of groups, which it oppresses and exploits in differing degrees and fashions; the result is a complex structure of racial and ethnic division.[38]

The final assumption of the third world idea remains to be considered. The new perspective represents more than a negation of the immigrant analogy. By its very language the concept assumes an essential connection between the colonized people within the United States and the peoples of Africa, Asia, and Latin America, with re-

* The historical accounts also indicate a number of instances of solidarity. A serious study of the history of unity and disunity among third world groups in America is badly needed.

spect to whom the idea of *le tiers monde* originated. The communities of color in America share essential conditions with third world nations abroad: economic underdevelopment, a heritage of colonialism and neocolonialism, and a lack of real political autonomy and power.[39]

This insistence on viewing American race relations from an international perspective is an important corrective to the parochial and ahistorical outlook of our national consciousness. The economic, social, and political subordination of third world groups in America is a microcosm of the position of all peoples of color in the world order of stratification. This is neither an accident nor the result of some essential racial genius. Racial domination in the United States is part of a world historical drama in which the culture, economic system, and political power of the white West has spread throughout virtually the entire globe. The expansion of the West, particularly Europe's domination over non-Western people of color, was the major theme in the almost five hundred years that followed the onset of "The Age of Discovery." The European conquest of Native American peoples, leading to the white settlement of the Western hemisphere, and the African slave trade, were the two leading historical events that ushered in the age of colonialism.* Colonial subjugation and racial domination began much earlier and have lasted much longer in North America than in Asia and Africa, the continents usually thought of as colonial prototypes. The oppression of racial colonies within our national borders cannot be understood without considering worldwide patterns of white European hegemony.

The present movement goes further than simply drawing historical and contemporary parallels between the third world within and the third world external to the United States. The new ideology implies that the fate of colonized Americans is tied up with that of the colonial and former colonial peoples of the world. There is at least impressionistic evidence to support this idea. If one looks at the place of the various racial minorities in America's stratified economic and social order, one finds a rough correlation between relative internal status and the international position of the original fatherland. According to most indicators of income, education, and occupation, Native Americans are at the bottom. The Indians alone lack an inde-

---

* The other major event was instituting trade with India.

pendent nation, a center of power in the world community to which they might look for political aid and psychic identification. At the other pole, Japanese-Americans are the most successful nonwhite group by conventional criteria, and Japan has been the most economically developed and politically potent non-Western nation during most of the twentieth century. The transformation of African societies from colonial dependency to independent statehood, with new authority and prestige in the international arena, has had an undoubted impact on Afro-Americans in the United States; it has contributed both to civil rights movements and to a developing black consciousness.*

What is not clear is whether an international strategy can in itself be the principle of third world liberation within this country. Since the oppression, the struggle, and the survival of the colonized groups have taken place within our society, it is to be expected that their people will orient their daily lives and their political aspirations to the domestic scene. The racial minorities have been able to wrest some material advantages from American capitalism and empire at the same time that they have been denied real citizenship in the society. Average levels of income, education, and health for the third world in the United States are far above their counterparts overseas; this gap will affect the possibility of internationalism. Besides which, group alliances that transcend national borders have been difficult to sustain in the modern era because of the power of nationalism.

Thus, the situation of the colonized minorities in the United States is by no means identical with that of Algerians, Kenyans, In-

* In the early 1970s Pan-Africanism seems to be gaining ground among black American militants and intellectuals. The most celebrated spokesman has been Stokely Carmichael who has virtually eschewed the struggle in the United States. The *Black Scholar* devoted its February and March (1971) issues to Pan-Africanism. Afro-American organizations have been challenging the South African involvements of U.S. business and government, as, for example, in the action of black employees against the Polaroid Corporation. Chicano groups have been taking an active political interest in Mexico and Latin America. On some university campuses Asian militants have taken the lead in protesting American imperialism and genocide in Southeast Asia. Whereas only recently black and brown nationalists tended to see antiwar protest as a white middle-class "trip," the third world perspective has led to an aggressive condemnation of the war in Indochina and a sense of solidarity with the Vietnamese people.

donesians, and other nations who suffered under white European rule. Though there are many parallels in cultural and political developments, the differences in land, economy, population composition, and power relations make it impossible to transport wholesale sociopolitical analyses or strategies of liberation from one context to another. The colonial analogy has gained great vogue recently among militant nationalists—partly because it is largely valid, partly because its rhetoric so aggressively condemns white America, past and present. Yet it may be that the comparison with English, French, and Dutch overseas rule lets our nation off too easily! In many ways the special versions of colonialism practiced against Americans of color have been more pernicious in quality and more profound in consequences than the European overseas varieties.

In traditional colonialism, the colonized "natives" have usually been the majority of the population, and their culture, while less prestigious than that of the white Europeans, still pervaded the landscape. Members of the third world within the United States are individually and collectively outnumbered by whites, and Anglo-American cultural imperatives dominate the society—although this has been less true historically in the Southwest where the Mexican-American population has never been a true cultural minority.[40] The oppressed masses of Asia and Africa had the relative "advantage" of being colonized in their own land.* In the United States, the more total cultural domination, the alienation of most third world people from a land base, and the numerical minority factor have weakened the group integrity of the colonized and their possibilities for cultural and political self-determination.

Many critics of the third world perspective seize on these differences to question the value of viewing America's racial dynamics within the colonial framework. But all the differences demonstrate is

---

* Within the United States, Native Americans and Chicanos, in general, retain more original culture than blacks and Asians, because they faced European power in their homelands, rather than being transported to the nation of the colonized. Of course the ecological advantage of colonization at home tends to be undermined to the extent to which large European settlements overwhelm numerically the original people, as happened in much of Indo-America. And in much of the Americas a relative cultural integrity among Indian peoples exists at the expense of economic impoverishment and backwardness.

that colonialisms vary greatly in structure and that political power and group liberation are more problematic in our society than in the overseas situation. The fact that we have no historical models for decolonization in the American context does not alter the objective realities. Decolonization is an insistent and irreversible project of the third world groups, although its contents and forms are at present unclear and will be worked out only in the course of an extended period of political and social conflict.

NOTES

1. For accounts of this movement at San Francisco State, see James McEvoy and Abraham Miller, eds., *Black Power and Student Rebellion* (Belmont, Calif.: Wadsworth, 1969), especially the articles by Barlow and Shapiro, Gitlin, Chrisman, and the editors; and Bill Barlow and Peter Shapiro, *An End to Silence* (New York: Pegasus Books, Division of Bobbs-Merrill), 1971.

2. In addition to its application to white-black relations in the United States—see for example, Stokely Carmichael and Charles Hamilton, *Black Power* (New York: Vintage, 1967), esp. chap. 1—the concept of internal colonialism is a leading one for a number of students of Indian–white and Indian–mestizo relations in Latin America. Representative statements are Pablo Gonzalez Casanova, "Internal Colonialism and National Development," Rodolfo Stavenhagen, "Classes, Colonialism, and Acculturation," and Julio Cotler, "The Mechanics of Internal Domination and Social Change in Peru," *Studies in Comparative International Development*, vol. 1, 1965, no. 4, vol. 1, 1965, no. 6, vol. 3, 1967–1968, no. 12. The Stavenhagen and Cotler papers are found also in Irving L. Horowitz, ed., *Masses in Latin America* (New York: Oxford University Press, 1970). See also André Gunder Frank, *Capitalism and Underdevelopment in Latin America* (New York: Monthly Review Press, 1967), and Eugene Havens and William Flinn, eds., *Internal Colonialism and Structural Change in Colombia* (New York: Praeger, 1970).

3. Gunther Barth, *Bitter Strength, A History of the Chinese in the United States, 1850–1870* (Cambridge: Harvard University Press, 1964).

4. Harry H. L. Kitano, *Japanese-Americans: The Evolution of a Subculture* (Englewood Cliffs, N.J.: Prentice-Hall, 1969).
5. Oscar Handlin, *Boston's Immigrants* (Cambridge: Harvard University Press, 1959), chap. 2.
6. A crucial treatment of the model of immigration and assimilation is Oscar Handlin, *The Uprooted* (New York: Grosset & Dunlap, 1951).
7. *New York Times Magazine* (September 11, 1966), reprinted in Nathan Glazer, ed., *Cities in Trouble* (Chicago: Quadrangle, 1970), pp. 139–157. Another influential study in this genre is Edward Banfield, *The Unheavenly City* (Boston: Little, Brown, 1970). For a critical discussion of this thesis and the presentation of contrary demographic data, see Karl E. Taueber and Alma F. Taueber, "The Negro as an Immigrant Group: Recent Trends in Racial and Ethnic Segregation in Chicago," *American Journal of Sociology,* 69 (1964), 374–382. The Kerner Report also devotes a brief chapter to "Comparing the Immigrant and Negro Experience," *Report of the National Advisory Commission on Civil Disorders* (New York: Bantam, 1968), chap. 9.
8. W. C. Macleod, *The American Indian Frontier* (London: Routledge & Kegan Paul, 1928).
9. For a discussion of these differences in ecological and material circumstances, see Marvin Harris, *Patterns of Race in America* (New York: Walker, 1964), esp. chaps 1–4. Compare also John Collier, *The Indians of the Americas* (New York: Mentor, 1947), pp. 100–103.
10. H. Hoetink, *The Two Variants of Race Relations in the Caribbean* (London: Oxford University Press, 1967), presents a strong argument on this point.
11. For an historical account of this development, see Winthrop Jordan, *White over Black* (Chapel Hill: University of North Carolina Press, 1968), chap. 2.
12. Pedro Carrasco, cited in Sidney W. Mintz, "The Plantation as a Socio-Cultural Type," in Pan American Union, "Plantation Systems of the New World," *Social Science Monographs,* 7 (1959), 52–53.

It is an equally regular feature of the absorption of colonial peoples into the wider capitalistic system, that such absorption has often been limited to the introduction of the minimum changes necessary for production of staples required by the Western economy, while otherwise leaving practically untouched the non-capitalistic economic system prevalent in the colonial areas. The sharp separation of worker and employer classes and the colonial status of plantation areas, that is, the limited social and political absorption of plantation populations are the usual correlates of the limited economic absorption.

The systems of labor by which these colonial populations come to participate in the world capitalist system are usually described in terms of a dichotomy of compulsory versus free labor which generally results in a typological and developmental continuum: slavery, forced or conscripted labor of subject populations, various forms of contract labor with elements of compulsion such as indentured labor or peonage, and finally free labor.

Also see W. Kloosterboer, *Involuntary Labour Since the Abolition of Slavery* (Leiden: Brill, 1960), for a general account and a specific analysis of 13 different societies. This survey found the racial principle to be the prevailing rule with the following exceptions: the forced labor camps in the Soviet Union during the Stalin era, the peonage of white laborers by Maine lumber companies around 1900, and two situations where people of African descent oppressed unfree black labor, Haiti and Liberia. In addition, Portuguese have at times served as semifree agricultural workers in Brazil and the Caribbean.

13. *Ibid.*
14. F. Fernandes, "The Weight of the Past," in John Hope Franklin, ed., *Color and Race* (Boston: Beacon, 1969), pp. 283–286.
15. See Carey McWilliams, *The Mexicans in America, A Student's Guide to Localized History* (New York: Teacher's College, Columbia University Press, 1968), for a summary discussion.
16. Leonard Pitt, *The Decline of the Californios, A Social History of the Spanish-Speaking Californians, 1846–1890* (Berkeley and Los Angeles: University of California Press, 1970), p. 296.
17. Carey McWilliams, *Factories in the Fields* (Boston: Little, Brown, 1934), and *Ill Fares the Land* (Boston: Little, Brown, 1942). See also McWilliams, *North from Mexico* (Philadelphia: Lippincott, 1948). Recently two papers have applied the colonial model to Mexican-Americans. See Joan W. Moore, "Colonialism: The

Case of the Mexican Americans," *Social Problems*, 17 (Spring 1970), 463–472; and Mario Barrera, Carlos Muñoz, and Charles Ornelas, "The Barrio as Internal Colony," in Harlan Hahn, ed., *Urban Affairs Annual Review*, 6 (1972).

18. Roger Daniels and Harry Kitano, *American Racism* (Englewood Cliffs, N.J.: Prentice-Hall, 1970), pp. 45–66. See also R. Daniels, *The Politics of Prejudice* (Berkeley and Los Angeles: University of California Press, 1962). The most comprehensive study of American racist attitudes and practices toward the Chinese is Stuart Miller, *The Unwelcome Immigrant: The American Image of the Chinese, 1785–1882* (Berkeley and Los Angeles: University of California Press, 1969).

19. Max Weber, *General Economic History* (New York: The Free Press, 1950), p. 277.

20. John Higham, *Strangers in the Land* (New York: Atheneum, 1969), pp. 45–52.

21. In a provocative paper which contains a comparison of black and European immigrant experience, Melvin Posey argues that Afro-Americans were never permitted to enter the nation's class system. "Toward a More Meaningful Revolution: Ideology in Transition," in McEvoy and Miller, eds., *Black Power and Student Rebellion*, *op. cit.*, esp. pp. 264–271.

    A contrast between Mexican and European immigrant patterns of work and settlement, and their consequences for social mobility is found in Leo Grebler, Joan W. Moore, and Ralph C. Guzman, *The Mexican-American People* (New York: The Free Press, 1970), chap. 5.

22. Analyzing early twentieth-century data on European immigrant groups, Stephen Steinberg has found significant differences in occupational background, literacy, and other mobility-related factors. The Jews were consistently advantaged on these points, Catholic ethnic groups such as Poles and Italians disadvantaged. S. Steinberg, "The Religious Factor in Higher Education," Doctoral dissertation, Department of Sociology, University of California, Berkeley (1971).

23. Robert Ernst, *Immigrant Life in New York City, 1825–1863* (Port Washington, N.Y.: Friedman, 1965), pp. 214–217.

24. Robert Starobin, *Industrial Slavery in the Old South* (New York: Oxford University Press, 1970), and Leon Litwack, *North of*

Slavery (Chicago: University of Chicago Press, 1961). For a recent interpretation, see Harold M. Baron, "The Demand for Black Labor: Historical Notes on the Political Economy of Racism," *Radical America,* 5 (March–April 1971), 1–46.

25. *Report of the National Advisory Commission on Civil Disorders, op. cit.*

26. Herman Bloch, *The Circle of Discrimination* (New York: New York University Press, 1969), esp. pp. 34–46. That discrimination in the labor market continues to make a strong contribution to income disparity between white and nonwhite is demonstrated in Lester Thurow's careful study, *Poverty and Discrimination* (Washington, D.C.: Brookings, 1969).

27. As far as I know no study exists that has attempted to analyze industrial and occupational competition among a variety of ethnic and racial groups. Such research would be very valuable. With respect to discrimination against Asians and Mexicans, Pitt, for example, describes how white and European miners were largely successful in driving Chinese and Mexican independent prospectors out of the gold fields. *The Decline of the Californios, op. cit.,* chap. 3.

28. Humbert S. Nelli, *Italians in Chicago 1880–1930: A Study in Ethnic Mobility* (New York: Oxford University Press, 1970).

29. Milton Gordon, *Assimilation in American Life* (New York: Oxford University Press, 1964).

30. Beltran makes the point that the plantation system was more significant than enforced migration in affecting African cultural development in the new world. "This system, which had created institutionalized forms of land tenure, work patterns, specialization of labor, consumption and distribution of produce, destroyed African economic forms by forceably imposing Western forms. . . . Negro political life along with African social structure, was in a position of subordination." Gonzalo Aguirre Beltran, "African Influences in the Development of Regional Cultures in the New World," in Pan American Union, *Plantation Systems of the New World, op. cit.,* p. 70.

31. According to Stokely Carmichael, capitalism exploits its own working classes, while racist systems colonize alien peoples of color. Here colonization refers to dehumanization, the tendency toward the destruction of culture and peoplehood, above and be-

yond exploitation. S. Carmichael, "Free Huey," in Edith Minor, ed., *Stokely Speaks* (New York: Vintage, 1971).

32. An historical study of Brazilian coffee plantations illustrates how African cultural institutions were the focal point for the slave's resistance to intensified exploitation. Stanley Stein, *Vassouras* (Cambridge: Harvard University Press, 1957), pt. 3.

33. Mina Davis Caulfield, "Culture and Imperialism: Proposing a New Dialectic," in Dell Himes, ed., *Reinventing Anthropology* (New York: Pantheon, 1972).

34. Collier, *op. cit.*, pp. 132–142.

35. Pitt, *The Decline of the Californios, op. cit.*, pp. 196–197.

36. Janheinz Jahn, *Muntu* (New York: Grove, n.d.), p. 217:

> The peculiar development of African culture in North America began with the loss of the drums. The Protestant, and often Puritan, slave owners interfered much more radically with the personal life of their slaves than did their Catholic colleagues in the West Indies or in South America. . . . And to forbid the drums was to show a keen scent for the essential: for without the drums it was impossible to call the orishas, the ancestors were silent, and the proselytizers seemed to have a free hand. The Baptists and Methodists, whose practical maxims and revivals were sympathetic to African religiosity quickly found masses of adherents.

> Thus the long-term interest of many Afro-American youth in the playing of drums, as well as the more recent and general embracing of African and black cultural forms, might be viewed as *the return of the repressed*—to borrow a leading concept from Freudian psychology.

> For a discussion of the attack on culture in the context of classical colonialism, see K. M. Panikkar, *Asia and Western Dominance* (New York: Collier, 1969); H. Alan C. Cairns, *The Clash of Cultures: Early Race Relations in Central Africa* (New York: Praeger, 1965), originally published in England as *Prelude to Imperialism,* and my brief introduction to Part 2 of this book.

37. The standard discussion of this phenomenon is Will Herberg, *Protestant-Catholic-Jew* (Garden City, N.Y.: Doubleday, 1955).

38. The ethnic and racially "plural society" is another characteristic colonial phenomenon. See J. S. Furnivall, *Colonial Policy and Practice* (New York: New York University Press, 1956), and

M. G. Smith, *The Plural Society in the British West Indies* (Berkeley and Los Angeles: University of California Press, 1965).

39. The connection has been cogently argued by Dale L. Johnson, "On Oppressed Classes and the Role of the Social Scientist in Human Liberation," in Frank Cockcroft and Dale Johnson, eds., *The Political Economy of Underdevelopment in Latin America* (Garden City, N.Y.: Doubleday, 1971), and by William K. Tabb, *The Political Economy of the Black Ghetto* (New York: Norton, 1970), esp. chap. 2.

However, the international perspective on American racial problems is by no means new. W. E. B. Du Bois was one of its early exponents, and in more recent years Malcolm X placed domestic racism and strategies of liberation in a worldwide context. For a discussion of the internationalizing of Malcolm's politics, see Robert L. Allen, *Black Awakening in Capitalist America* (Garden City, N.Y.: Doubleday, 1969), pp. 31–34.

40. McWilliams, *North From Mexico, op. cit.*

chapter 3
internal colonialism
and ghetto revolt*

During the late 1950s identification with African nations and other colonial or formerly colonized peoples grew in importance among black militants.[1] As a result the United States was increasingly seen as a colonial power, and the concept of domestic colonialism was introduced into the political analysis and rhetoric of militant nationalists. During the same period Afro-American theorists began developing this frame of reference for American realities. As early as 1962, Harold Cruse characterized race relations in this country as *domestic colonialism*.[2] Two years later in *Youth in the Ghetto* Kenneth Clark demonstrated how the political, economic, and social structure of Harlem was essentially that of a colony.[3] Finally, in 1967 a comprehensive discussion of *internal colonialism* provided the theoretical framework for Stokely Carmichael and Charles Hamilton's widely read *Black Power*.[4] The following year the colonial analogy gained currency and new "respectability" when Eugene McCarthy habitually referred to black Americans as a colonized people during his campaign. While the rhetoric of internal colonialism was catching on,

* An earlier version of this chapter appeared in *Social Problems, 16,* no. 4 (Spring 1969), 393–408. Published by the Society for the Study of Social Problems. At the time of writing this article, unfortunately, I did not have available Robert L. Allen's *Black Awakening in Capitalist America* (Garden City, N.Y.: Doubleday, 1969), which analyzes ghetto revolts in terms of a conception of internal colonialism similar to my own. Allen, however, deals much more thoroughly with the history and the dynamics of the black movement, class divisions in the black community, and the neocolonial strategies of corporate capitalism.

other social scientists began to raise questions about its appropriateness as a scheme of analysis.

The colonial interpretation has been rejected as obscurantist and misleading by scholars who point to the significant differences in history and sociopolitical conditions between our domestic patterns and what took place in Africa and Asia. Colonialism traditionally refers to the establishment of domination over a geographically external political unit, most often inhabited by people of a different race and culture, where this domination is political and economic and the colony exists subordinated to and dependent upon the mother country. Typically, the colonizers exploit the land, the raw materials, the labor, and other resources of the colonized nation; a formal recognition is given to the difference in power, autonomy, and political status, and various agencies are set up to maintain this subordination. Seemingly the model must be stretched beyond utility if the American case is to be forced into its mold. For here we are talking about group relations within a society; the geographical separation between mother country and colony is absent. Although whites certainly colonized the territory of the original Americans, internal colonization of Afro-Americans did not involve the settlement of whites in a land that was unequivocally black. Unlike the classical situation, there has been no formal recognition of differences in power, outside the South, since slavery was abolished. Traditional colonialism involves the control and exploitation of the majority of a nation by a minority of outsiders, whereas in America the oppressed black population is a numerical minority and was, originally, the "outside" group.

This conventional critique of internal colonialism is useful in pointing to the differences between our domestic patterns and the overseas situation. At the same time its bold attack tends to lose sight of common experiences that have historically been shared by the subjugated racial minorities in America and nonwhite peoples in other parts of the world. These common core elements—which make up a complex I shall call *colonization*—may be more important for understanding the most significant developments in the recent racial scene than the undeniable divergences between the two contexts.

The common features ultimately relate to the fact that classical colonialism of the imperialist era and American racism both developed out of the same historical situation and reflected a common world economic and power stratification. The slave trade preceded the imperialist partition and economic exploitation of Africa; in fact it may have been a necessary prerequisite for colonial conquest, since it helped deplete and pacify Africa, undermining resistance to direct occupation. Slavery contributed one of the basic raw materials for the textile industry, which provided much of the capital for the West's industrial development and economic expansionism. The essential condition for both American slavery and European colonialism was the political domination and the technological superiority of the Western world in relation to peoples of non-Western and nonwhite origins. This objective supremacy in technology and military power buttressed the West's sense of cultural superiority, laying the basis for racist ideologies that were elaborated to justify control and exploitation of nonwhite people. Because classical colonialism and America's internal colonialism developed out of similar technological, cultural, and power relations, a common *process* of social oppression characterized the racial patterns in the two contexts—despite the variations in political and social structure.

There appear to be four basic components of the colonization complex.* The first component is the mode of entry into the dominant society. Colonization begins with a forced, involuntary entry. Second, there is the impact on culture. The effects of colonization on the culture and social organization of the colonized people are more than the results of such "natural" processes as contact and acculturation. The colonizing power carries out a policy that constrains, transforms, or destroys indigenous values, orientations, and ways of life. Third is a special relationship to governmental bureaucracies or the legal order. The lives of the subordinate group are administered by representatives of the dominant power. The colonized have the experience of being managed and manipulated by outsiders who look down on them.

The final component of colonization is racism. Racism is a principle of social domination by which a group seen as inferior or different in alleged biological characteristics is exploited, controlled, and oppressed socially and psychically by a superordinate group. The systems of colonialism that have been most central to the modern era

---

* Perhaps a fifth should be added: the separation in labor status between the colonized and the colonizers. I develop this theme in Chapter 2, which was written after the main outlines of the present essay had been drafted.

have involved the subjugation of nonwhite Asian, African, and Latin American peoples by the white European powers, although imperial nations have colonized people who were technically considered to be of the same race; examples of such colonization are the British dominion over Ireland, the Hapsburg oppression of Central and Eastern European nationalities, and the Japanese suzerainty in Southeast Asia, which was ended by defeat in World War II. Even in these examples the link between colonialism and racism is indicated by the tendency of the ruling powers to view their subjects as inherently alien, culturally degenerate, and biologically inferior.*

The concept of colonization stresses the enormous fatefulness of the manner in which a minority group becomes a part of the dominant society.[6] The crucial difference between the colonized Americans and the ethnic immigrant minorities is that the latter have always been able to operate fairly competitively within the relatively open spaces of the capitalist class order. They came voluntarily in search of a better life. They have worked predominantly as free laborers; therefore their movements in society have been less controlled. Finally, as white Europeans they could achieve a sense of membership in the larger society by making minor modifications in their ethnic institutions.

In present-day America, a major device of black colonization is the powerless ghetto. As the Haryou Report describes the situation:

> Ghettoes are the consequence of the imposition of ex-
> ternal power and the institutionalization of powerlessness.
> In this respect, they are in fact social, political, educational,
> and above all—economic colonies. Those confined
> within the ghetto walls are subject peoples. They are
> victims of the greed, cruelty, insensitivity, guilt and fear
> of their masters. . . .

* In stressing a general racist dynamic, I do not imply that the specific racial patterns of colonial societies have been identical in all historical and contemporary contexts. In fact, much research on slavery and colonialism has been devoted to the study of differences in the intensity of racial feeling, the definition of the subordinate races, the nature of inter-racial contacts, and strategies of control between one historical setting and another. Such variation, the importance of which remains a lively area of scholarly debate, has, however, existed within a situation of universal white dominance and belief in European cultural superiority.[5]

The community can best be described in terms of the
analogy of a powerless colony. Its political leadership is
divided, and all but one or two of its political leaders
are shortsighted and dependent upon the larger political
power structure. Its social agencies are financially precarious and dependent upon sources of support outside
the community. Its churches are isolated or dependent. Its
economy is dominated by small businesses which are
largely owned by absentee owners, and its tenements and
other real property are also owned by absentee landlords.
Under a system of centralization, Harlem's schools are
controlled by forces outside the community. Programs and
policies are supervised and determined by individuals
who do not live in the community. . . .[7]

Many ethnic groups in America have lived in ghettos. What
makes the black ghettos an expression of colonized status are three
special features. First, the ethnic ghettos arose more through voluntary
choice: the choice to immigrate to America and the choice to live
among fellow ethnics. Second, the immigrant ghettos of the inner city
were one- or two-generation phenomena—way stations along the
road of acculturation and assimilation. When ethnic communities
persist, they tend to reflect voluntary decisions to live among one's
fellows and maintain group institutions, as in the case of the so-called
"gilded ghettos" of the Jewish suburban middle class. The black ghettos
on the other hand have been more permanent, though their boundaries
expand and change and some individuals do escape them. But most
relevant is the third point, that black communities are, to a great extent, controlled from the outside. For many Europeans—the Poles,
Italians, and Jews, for example—there was only a brief period, often
less than a generation, during which their residential buildings, commercial stores, and other enterprises were owned by outsiders. Afro-
Americans are distinct in the extent to which their segregated communities have remained under outside control: economic, political, and
administrative.

When we speak of Negro social disabilities under
capitalism . . . we refer to the fact that he does not own
anything—*even what is ownable in his own community.*
Thus to fight for black liberation *is to fight for his right*

to own. The Negro is politically compromised today because he owns nothing. He has little voice in the affairs of state because he owns nothing. The fundamental reason why the Negro bourgeois-democratic revolution has been aborted is because American capitalism has prevented the development of a black class of capitalist owners of institutions and economic tools. To take one crucial example, Negro radicals today are severely hampered in their tasks of educating the black masses on political issues because Negroes do not own any of the necessary means of propaganda and communication. The Negro owns no printing presses, he has no stake in the networks of the means of communication. Inside his own communities he does not own the houses he lives in, the property he lives on, nor the wholesale and retail stores from which he buys his commodities. He does not own the edifices in which he enjoys culture and entertainment or in which he socializes. In capitalist society, an individual or group that does not own anything is powerless.[8]

And what is true of business is true also for the other social institutions that operate within the ghetto. The educators, policemen, social workers, politicians, and others who administer the affairs of ghetto residents are typically whites who live outside the black community. Thus the ghetto plays a strategic role as the focus for that outside administration which in overseas colonialism is called "direct rule."

The colonial status of the Negro community goes beyond the issue of ownership and decision making within black neighborhoods. Despite the fact that blacks are numerically superior to many other interest groups, the Afro-American population has very little influence on the power structure and institutions of most of the larger cities. A recent analysis of policy making in Chicago estimates that "Negroes really hold less than one percent of the effective power in the Chicago metropolitan area. (Negroes are 20 percent of Cook County's population.) Realistically the power structure of Chicago is hardly less white than that of Mississippi."[9]

Although the Chinese-American experience has not yet been adequately studied, it may be worthwhile to consider briefly how

"Chinatowns" relate to the two ideal types, the voluntary ethnic community and the involuntary racial ghetto. Like the blacks, the Chinese have faced intense color prejudice and a racist housing market. However, a major divergence from the Afro-American pattern is suggested by the estimate that the "income of Chinese-Americans from Chinese-owned businesses is in proportion to their numbers 45 times as great as the income of Negroes from Negro-owned businesses."[10] The strength of Chinese business and community institutions appears to be related to the fact that traditional ethnic culture and social organization, in which entrepreneurial values were strong, were not destroyed by slavery; it may also be that the group's relatively small numbers made systematic oppression less central to American capitalism. Yet these facts in and of themselves do not prove the absence of colonization. Chinese middlemen played a major role in the exploitation of the masses of their own group: Chinese contractors supplied and managed the indentured laborers that worked in the mines and on the railroads. The Chinatowns of America may be viewed as neocolonial enclaves in which a business class has been able to gain wealth and political power within the ethnic community. In the larger society, however, the Chinese are ultimately powerless, controlled by outside political and economic arrangements.*

* In a criticism of an earlier version of this chapter, Nathan Glazer argues that I exaggerate the differences between Afro-American and immigrant ghettos by overstating the coercive and dependent character of the former, while minimizing the constraints and disabilities experienced by the latter. I have no quarrel with his reminder that many white ethnics also were policed and taught in the schools by people of other, more assimilated nationalities. Nevertheless, this pattern was not as uniform and monolithic for the ethnics; they were able to make inroads into some institutions and thus escape a situation of total domination by outsiders. I am less impressed with his response to my first point; the fact that one-sixth of New York Negroes were West Indian immigrants a generation ago makes little impact on the overall character of black entry into American life; nor does the fact that many Afro-Americans prefer to live in black communities (just as the European groups did) alter the predominant reality that they have had little choice in the matter. The most profound point raised by Professor Glazer is the ambiguity of the time and regional reference of the colonial interpretation. If one views the black situation from the limited time span of their large-scale migration to *Northern* cities, then the possibility is always open that a century from now they will have appeared to have followed a pattern of mobility and assimilation not dissimilar from the

Colonization outside of a traditional colonial structure has its own special conditions. In America the group culture and social structure of the colonized are less developed and less autonomous; the colonized are a numerical minority; and they are ghettoized more totally, yet are more dispersed geographically, than people under classic colonialism. All these realities affect the magnitude and direction of reaction by the colonized. But it is my basic thesis that the most important expressions of protest in the black community during the recent years reflect the colonized status of Afro-America. Riots, programs of separation, politics of community control, black revolutionary movements, and cultural nationalism each represents a different strategy of attack on domestic colonialism in America. Let us now examine some of these movements from this perspective.

Riot or Revolt?

The so-called riots are being increasingly recognized as a preliminary if primitive form of mass rebellion against colonial status. There is still a tendency to absorb their meaning within the conventional scope of assimilation-integration politics; some commentators stress the material motives involved in looting as a sign that the rioters want to join America's middle-class affluence just like everyone else. That motives are mixed and often unconscious; that black people want good furniture and television sets like whites is beside the point. The guiding impulse in most major outbreaks has not been integration with American society, but an attempt to stake out a sphere of control by moving against that society and destroying the symbols of its oppression.

In my critique of the McCone Report (see Chapter 6), I observe that the rioters "were asserting a claim to territoriality, making an unorganized and rather inchoate attempt to gain control over their community turf." In succeeding disorders also the thrust of the action has been toward ridding the community of the alien presence of white officials, rather than killing white people, as in a conventional race riot. The main attacks have been directed at the property of white businessmen and at the police who operate in the black community "like an army of occupation," protecting the interests of outside ex-

---

European one. Unlike Glazer I do not think it is possible to restrict one's time perspective and avoid a national approach to American racial realities by drastically separating the Southern and Northern black experiences.[11]

ploiters and maintaining the domination over the ghetto of the central metropolitan power structure.[12] The Kerner Report misleads when it attempts to explain riots in terms of integration: "What the rioters appear to be seeking was fuller participation in the social order and the material benefits enjoyed by the majority of American citizens. Rather than rejecting the American system, they were anxious to obtain a place for themselves in it."[13] More accurately, the revolts pointed to alienation from the system on the part of many poor, and some not-so-poor, blacks. Again as I argue with respect to Los Angeles: the sacredness of private property, that unconsciously accepted bulwark of our social arrangements, was rejected. People who looted—apparently without guilt—generally remarked that they were taking things that "really belonged" to them anyway.* Obviously the society's bases of legitimacy and authority have been attacked. Law and order has long been viewed by Afro-Americans as the white man's law and order; but now this characteristic perspective of a colonized people is out in the open. The Kerner Report's own data question how well ghetto rebels have been buying the system: In Newark only 33 percent of self-reported rioters said they thought this country was worth fighting for in the event of a major war; in the Detroit sample the figure was 55 percent.[15]

One of the most significant consequences of the process of colonization is a weakening of the individual and collective will to resist oppression. It has been easier to contain and control black ghettos because communal bonds and group solidarity have been weakened through divisions among leadership, failures of organization, and a general dispiritment that accompanies social oppression. The riots were a signal that the will to resist had broken the mold of accommodation. In some cities they represented nascent movements toward community identity. The outbursts stimulated new organizations and movements in several riot-torn ghettos. If it is true that the riot phenomenon of 1964–1968 has passed its peak, its historical import may be more for the "internal" organizing momentum that

---

* This kind of attitude has a long history. During slavery, blacks used the same rationalization to justify stealing from their masters. Appropriating things from the master was viewed as "*taking* part of his property for the benefit of another part;" whereas stealing referred to appropriating something from another slave, an offense that was not condoned.[14]

was generated than for any profound "external" response by the larger society in facing underlying causes.

Despite the appeal of Frantz Fanon to young black revolutionaries, America is not Algeria. It is difficult to foresee how rioting in our cities can function in a manner similar to the situation of overseas colonialism where such outbursts were an integral phase in a movement for national liberation. By 1968 some militant groups (for example, the Black Panther Party in Oakland) had concluded that ghetto riots were self-defeating for black people in the present balance of organization and gunpower—endangering their lives and their interests—though they had served to stimulate both black consciousness and white awareness of the depths of racial crisis. Such militants have been influential in "cooling" their communities during periods of high riot potential. Theoretically-oriented black radicals see riots as spontaneous mass behavior, which must be replaced by a revolutionary organization and consciousness. Despite the differences in objective conditions, violence seems to have served the same psychic function for young ghetto blacks in the 1960s as it did for the colonized of North Africa described by Fanon and Albert Memmi—the assertion of dignity and manhood.[16]

In the past few years riotlike political action appears to have shifted from the urban ghetto streets to more limited and focused institutional settings. One has been the high schools and colleges where a white European cultural system carries out the psychic and intellectual colonization of people of color. The second has been the prisons, whose inmates are disproportionately black, brown, and lower class. In confining within its walls a significant segment of those who have reacted against racial and colonialism overtly and aggressively, although not always with political consciousness, the prison is a concentrated essence of the colonial relationship. It is therefore not surprising that it has become a new breeding ground for nationalist and revolutionary organization.

Cultural Nationalism
Cultural conflict is generic to the colonial relation because colonization involves the domination of Western technological values over the more communal cultures of non-Western peoples. Colonialism played havoc with the national integrity of the peoples it brought under its sway. Of course, all traditional cultures are threatened by industrial-

ism, the city, and modernization in communication, transportation, health, and education. What is special to colonialism is that political and administrative decisions are made by colonizers toward the end of managing and controlling the colonized peoples. The boundaries of African colonies, for example, were drawn to suit the political conveniences of the European nations without regard to the social organization and cultures of African tribes and kingdoms. Nigeria as blocked out by the British included the Yorubas and the Ibos. The recent civil war was at least partially a by-product of the colonialist's disrespect for the integrity of indigenous cultures.*

The most total destruction of culture took place not in traditional colonialism but in America. As E. Franklin Frazier stressed, the integral cultures of the diverse African peoples who furnished the slave trade were destroyed because slaves from different tribes, kingdoms, and linguistic groups were purposely separated to maximize domination and control. Language, religion, and national loyalties were lost in North America much more completely than in the Caribbean countries and Brazil, where slavery developed somewhat differently. On this key point America's internal colonization has been more total and extreme than classic colonialism. The British in India and the European powers in Africa were simply not able—as outnumbered minorities—to destroy the national and tribal cultures of the colonized. Recall that American slavery lasted 250 years and its racist aftermath has lasted another 100. Colonial dependency in British Kenya and French Algeria lasted only 77 and 125 years, respectively. In the wake of this more drastic uprooting and destruction of culture and social organization, much more powerful agencies of social, political, and psychological domination developed in America.

> Colonial control of many peoples inhabiting the colonies
> was more a goal than a fact, and at Independence there
> were undoubtedly fairly large numbers of Africans
> who had never seen a colonial administrator. The gradual
> process of extension of control from the administrative
> center on the African coast contrasts sharply with the
> total uprooting involved in the slave trade and the

* For a discussion of the colonial territorial frontier and administrative boundary drawing in Africa, see Peter Worsley, *The Third World* (London: Weidenfeld and Nicolson, 1964), pp. 66–68.

totalitarian aspects of slavery in the United States. Whether or not Elkins is correct in treating slavery as a total institution, it undoubtedly had a far more radical and pervasive impact on American slaves than did colonialism on the vast majority of Africans.[17]

Yet a similar cultural process unfolds in both contexts of colonialism. To the extent that they are involved in the larger society and economy, the colonized are caught up in a conflict between two cultures. Fanon has described how the assimilation-oriented schools of Martinique taught him to reject his own culture and blackness in favor of Westernized, French, and white values.[18] Both the colonized elites under traditional colonialism and perhaps the majority of Afro-Americans today experience a parallel split in identity, cultural loyalty, and political orientation.[19]

The colonizers use their culture to socialize the colonized elites (intellectuals, politicians, and middle class) into an identification with the colonial system. Because Western culture has the prestige, the power, and the key to the limited opportunity available to a minority of the colonized, the first reaction seems to be an acceptance of the dominant values. Call it brainwashing, as the Black Muslims put it; call it identifying with the aggressor, if you prefer Freudian terminology; call it a natural response to the hope and belief that integration and democratization can really take place, if you favor a more commonsense explanation; however the process is defined, this initial acceptance crumbles in time on the realities of racism and colonialism. The colonized, seeing that his success within colonialism is at the expense of his group and his own inner identity, moves radically toward a rejection of the Western culture and develops a nationalist outlook that celebrates his people and their traditions. As Memmi describes it:

> Assimilation being abandoned, the colonized's liberation must be carried out through a recovery of self and of autonomous dignity. Attempts at imitating the colonizer required self-denial; the colonizer's rejection is the indispensable prelude to self-discovery. That accusing and annihilating image must be shaken off; oppression must be attacked boldly since it is impossible to go around it. After having been rejected for so long by the colonizer, the day has come when it is the colonized who must refuse the colonizer.[20]

Memmi's book, *The Colonizer and the Colonized*, is based on his experience as a Tunisian Jew in a marginal position between the French and the colonized Arab majority. The uncanny parallels between the North African situation he describes and the course of black–white relations in our society is the best impressionist argument I know for the thesis that we have a colonized group and a colonizing system in America. His discussion of why the most radical French anticolonialist cannot participate in the struggle of the colonized is directly applicable to the situation of the white liberal and radical vis-à-vis the black movement.* His portrait of the colonized is as good an analysis of the psychology behind black power and black nationalism as anything that has been written in the United States.

> Considered *en bloc* as *them, they* or *those,* different from every point of view, homogeneous in a radical heterogeneity, the colonized reacts by rejecting all the colonizers *en bloc.* The distinction between deed and intent has no great significance in the colonial situation. In the eyes of the colonized, all Europeans in the colonies are de facto colonizers, and whether they want to be or not, they are colonizers in some ways. By their privileged economic position, by belonging to the political system of oppression, or by participating in an effectively negative complex toward the colonized, they are colonizers. . . . They are supporters or at least unconscious accomplices of that great collective aggression of Europe.[21]

* During the early civil rights campaigns many whites had the illusion that they could disassociate themselves from racist privilege by participating in the movement for racial equality. Memmi shows how racism is a universal and inevitable part of the mentality of all members of the dominant group in a racially oppressive society. Out of their own experience this understanding came to black activists and led to the position that liberation could only develop out of "a black thing." The black power movement led also to a new reading of American racism as a colonial question. Confronted by this shift in perspective, white activists felt disoriented, left "out in the cold." Many former advocates of "Negro rights" not only turned against the black nationalist trend, but reversed their formerly "positive" orientation toward the Afro-American community as a whole, much in the manner of Memmi's left colonizer's reaction to the "excesses" of the anticolonial struggle. The recent third world movement seems to have aggravated this response: Black indifference is bad enough, but collective exclusion is intolerable!

> The same passion which made him admire and absorb
> Europe shall make him assert his differences; since those
> differences, after all, are within him and correctly consti-
> tute his true self.[22]

> The important thing now is to rebuild his people, whatever
> be their authentic nature; to reforge their unity, com-
> municate with it, and to feel that they belong.[23]

Cultural revitalization movements play a key role in anticolonial movements. They follow an inner necessity and logic of their own that comes from the effects of colonialism on groups and personal identities; they are also essential to provide the solidarity that the political or military phase of the anticolonial revolution requires. In the United States an Afro-American culture has developed out of the ingredients of African world views, the experiences of slavery, migration, and the Northern lower-class ghettos—and, most importantly, the political history of the black population in its struggle against racism. That Afro-Americans are moving toward cultural consciousness in a period when ethnic loyalties tend to be weak (and perhaps on the decline) in this country is another confirmation of the unique colonized position of the black group.

The Movement for Ghetto Control

The call for black power unites a number of varied movements and tendencies.[24] Although agreement on a unified program has not yet emerged, the most important emphasis seems to be on the movement for control of the ghetto. Black leaders and organizations are increasingly concerned with owning and controlling those institutions that exist within or impinge upon their community. The colonial model provides a key to the understanding of this movement; indeed, advocates of ghetto control have increasingly invoked the language of colonialism in pressing for local home rule. The framework of anti-colonialism explains why the struggle to put poor people in control of poverty programs has in many cities been more important than the content of these programs and why it has been crucial to exclude whites from leadership positions in black organizations.

The key institutions that anticolonialists want to take over or control are business, social services, schools, and the police. Though many spokesmen have advocated the exclusion of white landlords and small businessmen from the ghetto, the idea has evidently not caught

fire among the blacks, and little concrete movement toward economic
expropriation has as yet developed. Welfare recipients have organized
in many cities to protect their rights and gain a greater voice in the
decisions that affect them. Larry Jackson observes that "there is no
organizational structure in the black community which can equal (on
a national level) the number of troops that the National Welfare
Rights Movement can politically engage in literally hundreds of cities
across the country."[25] However, because the problems of welfare do
not cut across class lines, whole communities have not mounted direct
action against this form of colonialism. Thus, schools and the police
have been the crucial issues of ghetto control politics.

The Schools

In many cities during the late 1960s educational priorities shifted from
integration to community control, New York and Brooklyn being the
most publicized examples. Afro-Americans demanded their own school
boards, with the power to hire and fire principals and teachers and to
construct a curriculum that would be relevant to the special needs and
culture of ghetto youth. Black students across the country have been
active in high schools and colleges, protesting in behalf of incorporating black power and black culture into the education system. Consider
how similar the spirit behind these developments is to the attitude of
the colonized North African toward European education:

> He will prefer a long period of educational mistakes to
> the continuance of the colonizer's school organization. He
> will choose institutional disorder in order to destroy the
> institutions built by the colonizer as soon as possible.
> There we see, indeed a reactive drive of profound protest.
> He will no longer owe anything to the colonizer and will
> have definitely broken with him.[26]

Protest and institutional disorder over the issue of school control in New York City came to a head in 1968. The procrastination in
the Albany State legislature, the several crippling strikes called by the
teachers' union, and the almost frenzied response of Jewish organizations made it clear that decolonization of education faces the resistance of powerful vested interests. Funding for the experimental
school districts was ended after one year, and the limited autonomy
that had been granted these districts was incorporated into a more

general plan of decentralization. The defeat of "community control" in New York may have contributed to its failure to spread rapidly to other major cities.[27]

The movement reflected some of the problems and ambiguities that stem from colonization within the borders of the "mother country." The Afro-American community is not parallel in structure to the communities of colonized nations under traditional colonialism. The significant difference here is the lack of fully developed indigenous institutions other than the church. Outside of some areas of the South there is really no black economy, and most Afro-Americans are inevitably caught up in the larger society's structure of occupations, education, and mass communications. Thus the ethnic nationalist orientation, which reflects the reality of colonization, exists alongside an integrationist orientation, which reflects the reality that the institutions of the larger society are much more developed than those of the incipient nation.[28] As would be expected, the movement for school control reflected both orientations. The militant leaders who spearhead such local movements may be primarily motivated by the desire to gain control over the community's institutions—they are anticolonialists first and foremost. Many parents who support them may share this goal, but the majority are probably more concerned about creating a new education that will enable their children to "make it" in the society and the economy as a whole; they know that the present school system fails ghetto children and does not prepare them for participation in American life.

In many communities black leaders are now struggling for measures that fall between the poles of integration and community autonomy: for example, control over special programs, ethnically oriented curricula, and "alternative schools" within a racially heterogeneous institution or district. And by 1971 the ways and means of achieving integration had reappeared as a major national controversy as the Nixon administration backtracked on the busing issue. As more cities and school systems move toward black majorities, however, demands for community control are likely to emerge again.

The Police

There has been a growing recognition that law enforcement is particularly crucial in maintaining the colonized status of black Americans. Of all establishment institutions, police departments probably include the highest proportion of individual racists. This is no accident, since central to the workings of racism are attacks on the humanity and dignity of the subject group. The police constrict Afro-Americans to black neighborhoods by harassing and questioning them when they are found outside the ghetto; without provocation they break up groups of youths congregated on corners or in cars; and they continue to use offensive and racist language no matter how many seminars on intergroup understanding have been built into the police academy. They also shoot to kill ghetto residents for alleged crimes such as car thefts and running from officers of the law. According to a recent survey:

> In the predominantly Negro areas of several large cities, many of the police perceive the residents as basically hostile, especially the youth and adolescents. A lack of public support—from citizens, from courts, and from laws—is the policeman's major complaint. But some of the public criticism can be traced to the activities in which he engages day by day, and perhaps to the tone in which he enforces the "law" in the Negro neighborhoods. Most frequently he is "called upon" to intervene in domestic quarrels and break up loitering groups. He stops and frisks two or three times as many people as are carrying dangerous weapons or are actual criminals, and almost half of these don't wish to cooperate with the policeman's efforts.[29]

Thus the police enforce the culturally repressive aspects of middle-class American values against the distinctive ethnic orientations of Afro-American and other minority subcultures. It has been observed that few whites are arrested for gambling despite its popularity in a variety of forms; blacks, however, are arrested unduly for this offense and similar crimes like making noise in public. The Detroit officer David Senak as described by John Hersey[30] well exemplifies how individual policemen can become moral crusaders against "deviant behavior" and how the black community is particularly vulnerable to such cultural aggression.*

* In the trial of Huey Newton, the definition of the widely used expression "pig" became germane to the case. As a number of witnesses

Police are key agents in the power equation as well as in the dramas of dehumanization and cultural repression. In the final analysis they do the dirty work for the larger system by restricting the striking back of black rebels to skirmishes inside the ghetto, thus deflecting energies and attacks from the communities and institutions of the larger power structure. In an historical review, Gary Marx notes that since the French revolution, police and other authorities have killed large numbers of demonstrators and rioters; the rebellious "rabble" rarely destroys human life. The same pattern has been repeated in America's recent revolts.[31] Journalistic accounts suggest that police see themselves as defending the interests of white people against a tide of black insurgence; the majority of whites appear to view "blue power" in this same light.[32] There is probably no other opinion on which the races are today so far apart as they are on the question of attitudes toward the police.

Set off in many cases by a confrontation between an officer and a black citizen, the ghetto uprisings have dramatized the role of law enforcement and the issue of police brutality. In their aftermath, movements have arisen to contain police activity. One of the first was the Community Alert Patrol in Los Angeles, a group organized to police the police in order to keep them honest and constrain their violations of personal dignity. This was the first tactic of the Black Panther Party, which originated in Oakland—perhaps the most significant group to challenge the police role in maintaining the ghetto's colonized status. The Panthers' later policy of openly carrying guns (a legally protected right) and their intention of defending themselves against police aggression brought on a series of confrontations with the Oakland police department. In 1968 when I first drafted this chapter I wrote: "All indications are that the authorities intend to destroy the Panthers by shooting, framing up, or legally harassing their leadership—diverting the group's energies away from its primary purpose of self-defense and organization of the black community to that of legal defense and gaining support in the white community." Within

---

testified, in the language of the ghetto the term connotes a spectrum much wider than that of policeman. As one man put it succinctly, a pig is any outsider who comes into an oppressed community to direct the lives and activities of people whose feelings and culture he neither understands nor respects.

three years all these "indications" had materialized into hard fact. The Panthers have suffered critical losses to their leadership and organizational unity, and their cofounder Huey Newton has publicly criticized his party for isolating itself from the problems and concerns of the black community.

There are three major answers to "police colonialism," which correspond to reformist and more radical approaches to the situation. The most elementary, and most superficial, focuses on the fact that ghettos are overwhelmingly patrolled by white rather than by black officers. Therefore, the first proposal—supported today by many police departments—is to increase the numbers of blacks on local forces to something like their distribution in the city, making it possible to reduce the use of white cops in the ghetto.[33] This reform should be supported for a variety of obvious reasons, but it does not get to the heart of the role of the police as agents of colonization.

The Kerner Report documents the fact that in some cases black policemen can be as brutal as their white counterparts. I have not found data on who polices the ghetto, but statistics showing the proportion of blacks on the overall force are available for many cities. In most places the disparity is so striking that white police must predominate in patrolling black neighborhoods. Among the 30 cities listed by *Ebony* magazine, in the modal case the proportion of blacks in the population was three to four times as great as their proportion on the police force; for many cities this ratio was 5, 10, and even 20 times. In Oakland 34.5 percent of the population was black; only 4.7 percent of the policemen were black. For Boston the percentages were 16 and 2, for Cleveland 39 and 5, Dallas 25 and 2, Birmingham, 42 and 2! There were only five cities where the ratio was less than 2 to 1, that is, where the proportion of black cops was slightly more than one-half their percentage in the town as a whole: Gary, Washington, D.C., Atlanta, Philadelphia, and Chicago.[34] These figures suggest that both the extent and the pattern of colonization may vary from one city to another. It would be useful to study how black communities differ in degree of control over internal institutions as well as in economic and political power in the metropolitan area.

A second more radical demand is that the police must live in the communities where they work. The idea is that black officers who lived in the ghetto would have to be accountable to the community; if they came on like white cops then "the brothers would take care of business" and make their lives miserable. In many cities large numbers of policemen, like other public employees, reside in adjacent suburbs; they have resisted the demand of political leaders and pressure groups that they live where they work on the grounds that it singles out their occupation for discriminatory treatment.

The third, or maximalist, position is based on the premise that the police play no positive role in the ghettos. It calls for the withdrawal of metropolitan officers from black communities and the substitution of an autonomous indigenous force that would maintain order without oppressing the population. The precise relation between such an independent police, a ghetto governing body that would supervise and finance it, the city and county law enforcement agencies, and the law itself is as yet unclear. It is unlikely that any major city will soon face these problems as directly as New York did in the case of its schools. Of all the programs of decolonization, police autonomy will be most resisted. It gets to the heart of the way the state controls and contains the black community by delegating the legitimate use of violence to police authority.*

The various black power programs that are aimed at gaining control of individual ghettos—buying up property and businesses, running the schools through community boards, taking over antipoverty programs and other social agencies, diminishing the arbitrary power of the police—can serve to revitalize the institutions of the ghetto and build up an economic, professional, and political power base. These programs seem limited; we do not know at present whether they are enough in themselves to end colonized status.[35] But they are certainly a necessary first step.

---

* As far as I know the only locale where these problems have been at least considered is Berkeley, California. In April 1971 a measure to divide the police department into autonomous units, each controlled by one of the city's three major social areas (the white middle-class "hills," the predominantly black South and West sides, and the youth-oriented campus section), was placed on the ballot. The plan received about 32 percent of the vote in the city as a whole. It did not receive the support of black Berkeley, where not a single precinct was carried. In my judgment this was because the project did not arise out of the experience and politics of the black community, but was chiefly engineered and organized by the white left and students. Others have stressed the middle-class character of Berkeley's minority population and the sophistication and liberal image of its police force.

Yet they have dangers and pitfalls. Just as the limitation of a riot "strategy" became apparent, and just as the cultural movement bears a potential tendency toward antipolitical withdrawal that would have little impact on the condition of the poor and dispossessed, so ghetto control politics—indeed "black power" itself—faces the possibility that its programs and political thrust could be co-opted by the larger system of power. A number of radical political analysts already see a new stage of neocolonialism in which Afro-American leaders, under the black power banner, exercise a form of "indirect rule" over their internal communities, whose people are then more efficiently exploited and controlled by an ever-flexible corporate capitalism.[36] While this eventuality is not to be discounted, I do not look for such a pat and facile solution to what Franz Schurmann has called a key contradiction of American capitalism—that between the emerging black cities and the white suburbs.[37]

The Role of Whites

What makes the Kerner Report a less-than-radical document is its superficial treatment of racism and its reluctance to confront the colonized relation between black people and the larger society. The report emphasizes the attitudes and feelings that make up white racism, rather than the system of privilege and control, which is the heart of the matter. With all its discussion of the ghetto and its problems, it never faces the question of the stake that white Americans have in racism and ghettoization.

It is not a simple question, but this chapter should not end with the impression that police are the major villains. As I have argued in Chapter 1, all white Americans gain privilege and advantage from the colonization of black communities. The majority of whites also lose something from this oppression and division in society. Serious research should be directed to the ways in which white individuals and institutions are tied into the ghetto. Let me in closing suggest some possible parameters.

1. It is my guess that only a small minority of whites make a direct economic profit from ghetto colonization. This is hopeful, in that the ouster of white businessmen may become politically feasible. Much more significant, however, are the private and corporate interests in the land and residential property of the black community;

their holdings and influence on urban decision making must be exposed and combatted.[38]

2. A much larger minority of whites have occupational and professional interests in the present arrangements. The Kerner Commission reports that 1.3 million nonwhite men would have to be upgraded occupationally in order to make the black job distribution roughly similar to that for whites. The commission advocates such upgrading without mentioning that 1.3 million specially privileged white workers would lose in the bargain.[39] In addition, there are those professionals who carry out what Lee Rainwater has called the "dirty work" of administering the lives of the ghetto poor: the social workers, the schoolteachers, the urban development people, and of course the police.[40] The social problems of the black community will ultimately be solved only by people and organizations from that community; the emphasis within these professions must shift toward training such a cadre of minority personnel. Social scientists who study and teach courses on problems of race and poverty likewise have an obligation to replace themselves by bringing into the graduate schools and college faculties men and women of color who will become the future experts in these areas. For cultural and intellectual imperialism is as real as welfare colonialism, although it is currently screened behind such unassailable shibboleths as universalism and the objectivity of scientific inquiry.

3. Without downgrading the vested interests of profit and profession, the real nitty-gritty elements of the white stake are political power and bureaucratic security. Although few whites have much understanding of the realities of race relations and ghetto life, I think most give tacit or at least subconscious support for the containment and control of the black population. And whereas most whites have extremely distorted images of black power, many—if not most—would be frightened by actual black political power. Racial groups and identities are real in American life; white Americans sense they are on top, and they fear possible reprisals or disruptions were power to be more equalized. There seems to be in the white psyche a paranoid fear of black dominance; the belief that black autonomy would mean unbridled license is so ingrained that such reasonable outcomes as black political majorities and independent black police forces will be bitterly resisted.

On this level the major bulwark of colonization is bureaucratic security, which allows the middle classes to go about life and business in peace and quiet. The black militant movement is a threat to the orderly procedures by which bureaucracies and suburbs manage their existence, and I think today there are more people who feel a stake in conventional procedures than there are who gain directly from racism. In their fight for institutional control, the colonized are not playing by the white rules of the game. These administrative rules have kept them down and out of the system; therefore blacks are not committed to running institutions in the image of the white middle class.*

The liberal, humanist value that violence is the worst sin cannot be defended today if one is committed squarely against racism and for self-determination. Some violence is almost inevitable in the decolonization process; unfortunately racism in America has been so effective that the greatest power Afro-Americans wield today is the power to disrupt.** If we are going to swing with these revolutionary times and at least respond positively to the anticolonial movement, we shall have to learn to live with conflict, confrontation, constant change, and what may be either real or apparent chaos and disorder.

A positive response from the white majority needs to be in two major directions at the same time. First, community liberation movements should be supported in every way by pulling out white instruments of direct control and exploitation and substituting technical assistance to the community when this is asked for. But it is not enough to relate affirmatively to the nationalist movement for ghetto control without at the same time radically opening doors for full participation in the institutions of the mainstream. Otherwise the liberal and radical position is little different from the traditional segregationist position. Freedom in the special conditions of American colonization means that the colonized must have the choice between participating in the larger society and in independent structures of their own.

* Some, of course, will recreate "white" forms, as happened in a number of formerly colonial nations after independence, and as has been the pattern of "the black Anglo-Saxons." My point is that today the opposite tendency is on the rise.

** This is because racism has fractionated the black population, making unity of political action difficult. A unified people and movement would have power to implement its goals and force changes on the society that would go far beyond disruption.

NOTES

1. Nationalism, including an orientation toward Africa, is no new development. It has been a constant tendency within Afro-American politics. See Harold Cruse, *Rebellion or Revolution* (New York: Morrow, 1968), esp. chaps. 5–7.

2. This was five years before the publication of *The Crisis of the Negro Intellectual* (New York: Morrow, 1967), which brought Cruse into prominence. Thus, the 1962 article was not widely read until its reprinting in Cruse's essays, *Rebellion or Revolution, op. cit.*

3. Kenneth Clark, *Youth in the Ghetto* (New York: Haryou Associates, 1964). Clark dropped the colonial metaphor from his *Dark Ghetto* (New York: Harper & Row, 1965), although much of the data and analysis are the same.

4. Stokely Carmichael and Charles Hamilton, *Black Power* (New York: Random House, 1967).

5. For a treatment of this universal aspect, along with an approach to the analysis of variation, see Georges Balandier, "The Colonial Situation: A Theoretical Approach," in Immanuel Wallerstein, ed., *Social Change: The Colonial Situation* (New York: Wiley, 1966), pp. 34–61. Some of the many studies that have focused on comparative patterns of slavery and colonialism include Frank Tannenbaum, *Slave and Citizen* (New York: Knopf, 1947); Stanley M. Elkins, *Slavery* (Chicago: University of Chicago Press, 1959); David B. Davis, *The Problem of Slavery in Western Culture* (Ithaca: Cornell University Press, 1966); Herbert S. Klein, *Slavery in the Americas* (Chicago: University of Chicago Press, 1967); H. Hoetink, *The Two Variants of Race Relations in the Caribbean* (London: Oxford University Press, 1967); J. S. Furnivall, *Colonial Policy and Practice* (New York: New York University Press, 1948); and Immanuel Wallerstein, *Africa, The Politics of Independence* (New York: Random House, 1961).

   The link between colonization and racism may be questioned from still another standpoint. In his provocative study, *Rebels in Eden* (Boston: Little, Brown, 1970), Richard Rubenstein has expanded the concepts of internal colonialism and colonization to encompass the major subordinated strata—regardless of color and racism—in American history. Rubenstein views the social movements of farmers in the eighteenth century, of the working class in the nineteenth and early twentieth centuries, and of contemporary students—as well as those of the ethnic immigrants and racial minorities—as attempts to gain or defend a measure of local autonomy vis-à-vis alien and dominant power hierarchies. Rubenstein's analysis of ghetto revolt in the 1960s and his approach to decolonization today is in very close agreement with the theses of the present chapter; unfortunately his book did not come to my attention in time to give it the consideration it deserves.

6. As Eldridge Cleaver reminds us, "Black people are a stolen people held in a colonial status on stolen land, and any analysis which does not acknowledge the colonial status of black people cannot hope to deal with the real problem." "The Land Question," *Ramparts* (May 1968), 51. Reprinted in Cleaver, *Post-Prison Writings and Speeches* (New York: Vintage, 1969).

7. Clark, *Youth in the Ghetto, op. cit.* pp. 10–11, 79–80.

8. Harold Cruse, "Behind the Black Power Slogan," in Cruse, *Rebellion or Revolution, op. cit.*, pp. 238–239. A business association which primarily serves black communities (The National Association of Market Development) has only 131 black-owned firms out of a total of 407. Andrew Brimmer, "The Negro in the National Economy," in John P. Davis, ed., *The American Negro Reference Book* (Englewood Cliffs, N.J.: Prentice-Hall, 1966), p. 297, as cited in Louis Knowles and Kenneth Prewitt, eds., *Institutional Racism in America* (Englewood Cliffs, N.J.: Prentice-Hall, 1969), p. 16.

   For a convincing critique of black capitalism as a strategy for liberation, see Earl Ofari, *The Myth of Black Capitalism* (New York: Monthly Review Press, 1970).

9. Harold M. Baron, "Black Powerlessness in Chicago," *Trans-Action* (November 1968), 27–33.

10. Nathan Glazer and Daniel P. Moynihan, *Beyond the Melting Pot* (Cambridge: M.I.T. and Harvard University Press, 1963), p. 37.

11. Nathan Glazer, "Blacks and Ethnic Groups: The Difference, and the Political Difference It Makes," in Nathan I. Huggins, Martin Kilson, and Daniel M. Fox, eds., *Key Issues in the Afro-American Experience* (New York: Harcourt Brace Jovanovich, 1971), pp. 193–211.

12. "The police function to support and enforce the interests of the

dominant political, social, and economic interests of the town" is a statement made by a former police scholar and official, according to A. Neiderhoffer, *Behind the Shield* (Garden City, N.Y.: Doubleday, 1967), as cited by Gary T. Marx, "Civil Disorder and the Agents of Control," in Marx, ed., *Racial Conflict* (Boston: Little, Brown, 1971), pp. 286–306.

13. *Report of the National Advisory Commission on Civil Disorders* (New York: Bantam, 1968), p. 71.

14. Kenneth Stampp, *The Peculiar Institution* (New York: Vintage, 1956), p. 127.

15. *Report of the National Advisory Commission on Civil Disorders*, *op. cit.*, p. 178.

16. Frantz Fanon, *Wretched of the Earth* (New York: Grove, 1963); Albert Memmi, *The Colonizer and the Colonized* (Boston: Beacon, 1967).

17. Robert Wood, "Colonialism in Africa and America: Some Conceptual Considerations," unpublished paper (December 1967), Department of Sociology, University of California, Berkeley, California.

18. Frantz Fanon, *Black Skins, White Masks* (New York: Grove, 1967).

19. Harold Cruse has described how these two themes of integration with the larger society and identification with ethnic nationality have struggled within the political and cultural movements of Negro Americans. *The Crisis of the Negro Intellectual, op. cit.*

20. Memmi, *op. cit.*, p. 128.

21. *Ibid.*, p. 130.

22. *Ibid.*, p. 132.

23. *Ibid.*, p. 134.

24. Scholars and social commentators, black and white alike, disagree in interpreting the black power movement. The issues concern whether this is a new development in black protest or an old tendency revived; whether the movement is radical, revolutionary, reformist, or conservative; and whether this orientation is unique to Afro-Americans or essentially a black parallel to other ethnic group strategies for collective mobility. For an interesting discussion of black power as a modernized version of Booker T. Washington's separatism and economism, see Harold Cruse, *Rebellion or Revolution, op. cit.*, pp. 193–258.

Other sources and interpretations are found in Floyd Barbour, ed., *The Black Power Revolt* (Boston: Porter Sargent, 1968); Nathan Wright, *Black Power and Urban Unrest* (New York: Hawthorn, 1967); Robert L. Scott and Wayne Brockriede, *The Rhetoric of Black Power* (New York: Harper & Row, 1969); Julius Lester, *Look Out Whitey, Black Power's Gon' Get Your Mama* (New York: Dial, 1969); Raymond Franklin, "The Political Economy of Black Power," in James Geschwender, ed., *The Black Revolt* (Englewood Cliffs, N.J.: Prentice-Hall, 1971); and Joel D. Aberbach and Jack L. Walker, "The Meanings of Black Power: A Comparison of White and Black Interpretations of a Political Slogan," in John Bracey, August Meier, and Elliott Rudwick, eds., *Conflict and Competition* (Belmont, Calif.: Wadsworth, 1971), pp. 157–191.

25. Larry R. Jackson, "Welfare Mothers and Black Liberation," *Black Scholar*, 1, no. 5 (April 1970), 35.

26. Memmi, *op. cit.*, pp. 137–138.

27. Major documents in the school controversy, various viewpoints and analyses are included in Maurice R. Berube and Marilyn Gittell, eds., *Confrontation at Ocean Hill-Brownsville* (New York: Praeger, 1969).

28. This split in the politics and psyche of the black American was poetically described by W. E. B. Du Bois in his *Souls of Black Folk* (New York: Crest, 1972), and more recently analyzed by Harold Cruse in *The Crisis of the Negro Intellectual, op. cit.*

29. Peter Rossi, *et al.*, "Between Black and White—The Faces of American Institutions in the Ghetto," in *Supplemental Studies for the National Advisory Commission on Civil Disorders* (July 1968), 114.

30. John Hersey, *The Algiers Motel Incident* (New York: Bantam, 1968).

31. "In the Gordon Riots of 1780 demonstrators destroyed property and freed prisoners, but did not seem to kill anyone, while authorities killed several hundred rioters and hung an additional 25. In the Rebellion Riots of the French Revolution, though several hundred rioters were killed, they killed no one. Up to the end of the summer of 1967, this pattern had clearly been repeated, as police, not rioters, were responsible for most of the more than 100 deaths that have occurred. Similarly, in a related context, the

more than 100 civil rights murders of recent years have been matched by almost no murders of racist whites." G. Marx, "Civil Disorders and the Agents of Social Control," *op. cit.*

32. Jerome H. Skolnick, ed., *The Politics of Protest* (New York: Ballantine, 1969), esp. chap. 7, "The Police in Protest."

33. Thus, a United Press dispatch from Detroit notes that the police department has announced plans "to increase the percentage of black policemen on the force from 13 percent to 45 percent by 1980 to match the city's current racial composition." *San Francisco Chronicle* (July 24, 1971). Even if this were achieved by their formula of recruiting five blacks out of every eight new members, the personnel department has evidently failed to consider what the black proportion of Detroit's population will be by 1980.

34. *San Francisco Sunday Examiner and Chronicle* (May 9, 1971), sec. A, p. 19, summarizing "The Dilemma of the Black Policeman," *Ebony* (May 1971). Comparing the 1971 figures with the 1968 data reported in the Kerner Report (p. 321) shows very little change in the overall pattern. Some cities made absolute and relative gains in police integration; others, including two of the "leaders," Philadelphia and Chicago, lost ground.

That black officers nevertheless would make a difference is suggested by data from one of the supplemental studies to the Kerner Report. They found Negro policemen working in the ghettos considerably more sympathetic to the community and its social problems than their white counterparts. Peter Rossi, *et al.*, "Between Black and White—The Faces of American Institutions in the Ghetto," *op. cit.*, chap. 6.

35. Eldridge Cleaver has called this first stage of the anticolonial movement *community* liberation in contrast to. a more long-range goal of *national* liberation, "Community Imperialism," Black *Panther Party Newspaper*, 2, no. 3 (May 18, 1968).

36. See for example, Earl Ofari, *The Myth of Black Capitalism, op. cit.*; Robert Allen, *Black Awakening in Capitalist America* (Garden City, N.Y.: Doubleday, 1969); Martin Oppenheimer, *The Urban Guerilla* (Chicago: Quadrangle, 1969); William K. Tabb, *The Political Economy of the Black Ghetto* (New York: Norton, 1970); and Jan Dizard and David Wellman, "I Love Ralph Bunche But I Can't Eat Him for Lunch: Corporate Liberalism,

Racism, and Reform—Emerging Strategies for Ghetto Control," *Leviathan*, 1 (Summer 1969), 46–53.

37. Franz Schurmann, "System, Contradictions, and Revolution in America," in Roderick Aya and Norman Miller, eds., *The New American Revolution* (New York: The Free Press, 1971).

38. On the network of interests in the ghetto, see Harold Baron, "The Web of Urban Racism," in Knowles and Prewitt, eds., *Institutional Racism, op. cit.*

39. *Report of the National Advisory Commission on Civil Disorders, op. cit.*, pp. 253–256.

40. Lee Rainwater, "The Revolt of the Dirty-Workers," *Trans-Action, 5*, no. 1 (November 1967), 2, 64.

part II
racism and
culture

A central idea in this book is the antagonistic yet intimate
relation between racism and culture. As stated earlier, cultural domination is a major instrument of racial control, and oppression has
a negative, weakening effect on the cultures of dominated groups.
During the colonial experience the many dimensions of racism in its
relation to culture were highlighted. European rule caused acute
conflicts between Western societies and non-Western peoples,
conflicts that were exacerbated by the white man's deep sense of
racial superiority. At the same time, colonialism's attack on nonwhite
cultures—and the color line it institutionalized—set into motion
new movements of race consciousness, cultural revitalization, and
political nationalism, movements that contributed to the emergence
of new nations and group identities. Whereas racism tends to
undermine culture, its special intensity in certain societies appears
to be linked to an existing weakness in the integration of the
national heritage. Racism fills a void and ironically helps cement
the oppressor's culture. The essays in Part II deal with the impact
of white racism on the cultures of Afro-Americans and Mexican-
Americans; the remarks that follow in this introduction suggest a
more general approach to the topic.

Racism as the Negation of Culture
Racism can be defined as a propensity to categorize people who are
culturally different in terms of noncultural traits, for example, skin
color, hair, structure of face and eye. Obviously the human failing
of imputing social significance to these differences—a failing
Western Europeans have had to an extreme—underlies the
fatefulness of race in recent history. By its very logic racial thinking
emphasizes the variations between groups rather than the things they
have in common. Further, it tends either to ignore the existence of
culture or social heritage or, more often, to minimize its importance in
accounting for real differences. Since virtually every nation, tribe,
or ethnic group defines its uniqueness in terms of culture—its history, religion, ritual, art, philosophy or world view—rather than
in terms of "blood," racism as a view of reality violates the
autonomy and self-determination of peoples. It rejects their own
definition of themselves and substitutes one based on the framework
of the oppressor.

One tradition of British colonials was to call all indigenous
people of color "niggers" despite the incredible diversity in history

and culture among the Africans, Indians, Burmese, and Chinese who received this appellation.[1] In England today West Indians, Africans, Pakistani, and East Indians are lumped together as "blacks." In a similar manner American GI's in "police actions" in Asia have used the term "gook" to refer, successively, to Koreans, Chinese, and Vietnamese. These racial definitions have permitted whites to order a universe of unfamiliar peoples without confronting their diversity and individuality, which are products of rich and distinct cultural traditions. Such a propensity to excessive categorization is fundamental to racism; another example is the tendency to view members of the same minority in global generalized terms when the group may be quite differentiated in a variety of ways.

More important than such mental mechanisms have been the actions of white Europeans as they colonized the world, and the objective consequences of their acts. Especially in the early period, the colonial powers set out to weaken the cultures of the colonized. Missionaries, often the advance guard of Western expansion, were fortified by an almost fanatical belief in the virtues of European religion, morality, and customs. Such an ingrained sense of moral rectitude was responsible for the inability of many Europeans to comprehend other ways of life and led to barbaric attacks on pagan artifacts and social institutions. In Goa and a number of other Asian cities, for example, Western missionaries destroyed Hindu temples, shrines, and priceless works of art.[2] In Central Africa they attempted to outlaw the *lobala,* an exchange of cattle in the betrothal ceremony, on the grounds that it was a bride-purchase, a mercenary custom that profaned the marriage sacrament. The *lobala* was the institution around which the entire social organization of these cattle-raising tribes revolved; its elimination would have meant a total breakdown in social order.[3]* Every competent survey of Western colonialism reveals countless similar examples.[5]**

---

* There is a parallel here to our own interdiction of the plains Indians' sun dance.[4]

** According to a study of cultural contact in Central Africa, the missionaries assumed "that the inferiority of African culture, self-evident to Britons, was equally obvious to Africans" and that "their cultures, inchoate and fragmentary, need not be regarded as serious barriers to the introduction of social change." They based their ignorance of tribalism on "the implicit assumption that there was really nothing to study. . . .

The depreciation of the cultural integrity of non-Western people appears to be a result of specific values and emphases within the Western ethos, not just a matter of ignorance, arrogance, and ill will. The leading concepts of Western culture, intensified in Protestantism, include control and dominance, property and appropriation, competition and individualism. These values have worked well in support of racial oppression and cultural domination: equalitarian and democratic themes have been weak countertrends at best. Particularly important has been the conflict between the Western technological orientation or engineering mentality and the more organic, harmonious notions of the relation between man and nature that were held by the societies dominated by colonialism. The aggressive implementation of such an exploitative attitude toward the external world often disrupted non-Western ways of life and contributed to the white man's depreciation of people of color.

For the European mentality "the apparent inability of the African to dominate his environment provided perhaps the basic proof of his backwardness. . . . Nothing, as Lord Bryce remarked, was more surprising to the European than the fact that savages left 'few marks of their presence' on their physical environment. . . . The savage, he argued, had 'no more right to claim that the land was made for him than have the wild beasts of the forest who roar after their prey and seek their meat from God.' Bryce's view was standard."[10] Similar arguments belittling the Native Americans' claim to their continent were popular in the United States. Englishmen evaluated other cultures primarily in terms of their mastery of nature—but the mastery had to be achieved in the British manner. African footpaths were winding and therefore objects

---

Tribalism did not represent a way of life in any significant sense, but simply a generalized category of inferior attainment."[6]

Considering such attitudes it is no surprise that the missionary effort in Asia and Africa was a colossal failure. Cairns concludes that there were very few converts to show for the decades of missionary effort in Central Africa during the nineteenth and early twentieth centuries.[7] Panikkar cites a Robert Morrison who arrived in Canton in 1807; though aided by several associates, he converted only 16 Chinese in 25 years.[8] The more impressive success of Islam in Africa, with its easy adaptation to indigenous ways of life, is instructive.[9] And Catholics, especially the Jesuits, were generally more successful than Protestants; the most striking example being the conversion of Indian populations in the Americas.

of ridicule: "the straight line, a man-made construct, was indica-
cative of order and environmental control."[11]

The Tension Between Race and Ethnicity

Systems of racial oppression tend to undermine ethnic groups and
ethnicity as a principle of social organization. One of the most
profound consequences of colonialism was its creation of races and
racism through weakening the relevance of other human distinctions.
The extreme case was slavery in the New World.

It is an error to assume that slave traders and plantation
owners always saw their captives as an undifferentiated mass of
black Africans. In North America, as well as in the Caribbean and
Brazil, a crude working knowledge of African tribal diversity and
social character existed. Thus some West African peoples were
viewed as good workers, whereas others were considered less desirable because it was believed that they were more likely to rebel,
escape, fall ill, or even commit suicide in the state of bondage.[12]
Yet the logic of slavery had to weaken, if it did not necessarily
eliminate, the long run significance of ethnic ties. Cultural groups
were broken up, in part because it was the more convenient administrative arrangement, in part because traders and planters were
aware that tribal fragmentation would reduce the ability of slaves
to communicate and resist. With time it became "natural" to treat
the bondsmen as a more or less homogeneous mass of Africans.
This took place earlier and more thoroughly in the United States
because favorable economic conditions made it possible to reproduce
the slave population through natural increase, which ended the need
for new imports from Africa. In Brazil and the Caribbean, slaves
were more typically worked to death; continuous replenishment
through the slave trade maintained the relevance of African ethnicity
much longer.[13]

The slave system created the "New World Negro" out of a
mélange of distinct cultural groups. In a similar fashion, racial
practices common to the European powers in Africa—despite their
different colonial policies—created the identities of Negro and African
and a corresponding sense of Blackness and African-ness among the
disparate populations south of the Sahara. Sithole quotes a saying
of the Ndau-speaking people of Rhodesia: " 'Muyungu ndiye ndiye'—
'the white man is the same the world over.' By this they mean to say

that the white man the world over likes to rule and humiliate the black man."[14] It is important to stress that race awareness and racial thinking of this type were almost nonexistent in Africa before white rule.[15] A critical consequence of Western colonialism has been to bring racial divisions and racial thinking to parts of the world and to social groups where they previously held little sway. This cannot be dismissed as false consciousness, a purely mental trip, for to the extent that the West introduced systems of labor and social organization in which color rather than kinship or ethnic group determined social position, race became a socioeconomic reality at the expense of cultural definitions.

It was not possible to override ethnic and cultural differences in the classical situation of overseas colonialism. Ethnic groups were rooted in the land and the natural clusterings of people. Western cultural domination had relatively little direct effect on the traditional ways of life of the Asian and African masses. It was the "assimilated" elites, taught in missionary schools or other centers of Western education, for whom ethnic loyalties became less than central. Furthermore, the Western powers often fostered ethnic divisions and exacerbated cultural conflict by importing non-indigenous peoples to serve certain functions. The British policy of indirect rule was based on maintaining the traditional authority of tribal chieftains as long as they remained subservient to colonial power. The French used militia and policemen from one colony, for example Senegal, to put down disturbances in other territories. The English brought East Indians to their colonies in the West Indies, Africa, and Asia to work as laborers and to fulfill administrative and business roles; people from the Middle East often became small traders in African and Asian colonies.[16]

In addition to races, racism, cultural pluralism, and ethnic conflict, nations and nationalism were further unanticipated consequences of Western colonial rule. Movements of reaction against the colonial cultural attack were especially significant for emerging national consciousness. The first and most characteristic cultural resistance was the maintaining of values and ways of life in the face of Westernization. Where disruption of culture did take place, new religious movements and cults often emerged, based on some combination of old and new, but carrying within them an overt or covert attack on white domination and values.* Such religious developments were followed by politically oriented and often race-conscious movements such as *négritude*, which sought to restore the validity and dignity of the cultural heritages impugned by Western racism and to challenge its cultural domination. These forms of cultural resistance contributed to the developing abilities of colonized people to organize for national independence.

Race replaced ethnicity most completely in slave and postslavery societies, above all, in the United States. Many of the ambiguities of American race relations stem from the fact that two principles of social division, race and ethnicity, were compressed into one. With their own internal ethnic differences eliminated, people of African descent became a race in objective terms, especially so in the view of the white majority. Afro-Americans became an ethnic group also, one of the many cultural segments of the nation. The ethnicity of Afro-America, however, is either overlooked, denied, or distorted by white Americans, in part because of the historic decision to focus on the racial definition, in part because of the racist tendency to gainsay culture to people of color beyond what they may have assimilated directly from the European tradition. This merging of ethnicity with race, in the eyes of people of color as well as of whites, made it inevitable that racial consciousness among blacks would play a central part in their historic project of culture building, and that their institutions, politics, and social character would be misinterpreted in a restricted racial paradigm.

For those Africans who escaped the slave trade and remained at home, ethnic realities have persisted. Because the colonialists drew their boundaries in disregard for cultural facts, ethnic groups are major social forces in the internal differentiation of African nations today. A paradox of the colonial encounter with culture lies in the fact that the stronger ethnicity in the classical situation has resulted in a weakening of the national unity of many new independent states—though cultural continuity has undoubtedly strengthened

* Examples of such prepolitical or protopolitical movements are the Ghost Dance religions of the North American Indians, the Ethiopian and Messianistic Churches in South and Central Africa, the Ras Tafari movement in Jamaica, Pentecostalism among Mexicans in the U.S. Southwest, and the famous Cargo Cults of Melanesia.

social institutions and personal identities—whereas in the United
States the more complete development of the racial basis of collective
identity among Afro-Americans, which weakened group and individual
integrity, ironically created the conditions for a more unified regrouping and a new sense of peoplehood unimpaired by ethnic division.*

Up to now I have focused on racism's impact on the cultures
of the oppressed. How racism relates to the oppressor's culture is
another crucial, though relatively unexplored, issue. It is plausible
to assume that the finding of modern psychology that people who
are least secure and integrated in personality structure have the greatest
need for racist and other distorted belief systems might apply also
to nations and their cultures. The special intensity of racial feeling
among settler populations and in the cultures of new societies that
develop by fragmentation from older national traditions[18] seems to
confirm this insight. The new society is characterized by a weakness
in cultural identity, a lack of great tradition, an absence of a sense
of distinctiveness. Winthrop Jordan has suggested that racist thought
contributed to the resolution of such cultural problems among the
white American settlers who used African people as "contrast
conceptions" to help define themselves.[19] ** The fear of chaos, even

* The major ethnic group within the American black population has
been the West Indian. Significant conflicts between West Indian and
American-born blacks existed in the first half of the century;[17] they appear
to be relatively unimportant today. The absence of internal ethnicity
among Afro-Americans is a reflection of their greater participation in the
larger culture, for American ethnic groups have less holistic and distinctive
ways of life than do the ethnic groups in such societies as Java, India,
Nigeria, or Kenya.

** The general point also applies "in reverse," that is, to "racism"
or intense racial feeling on the part of oppressed racial groups. It has been
frequently noted that the négritude movement, with its high level of race
consciousness, was in part a reaction to the assimilation experience of those
French-speaking Africans and Antilleans who developed its special outlook
and literature. Such a parallel movement did not develop in British Africa
where traditional cultural attachments remained stronger. In the United
States aggressive racial ideologies have been most prominent in the North
and among the middle classes where ethnic culture tends to be weaker, less
prominent in the South and among the lower classes. On the basis of very
impressionistic observations, I have been struck by apparent differences in
the degree of antiwhite sentiments among third world people in the United
States—the groups and the individuals with the strongest sense of ethnic
culture seem to have the least need for antiwhite feelings.

of reversion to barbarism, that comes from the weakness of civil constraints in frontier situations is dealt with by projecting all the undesirable (but dangerously appealing) possibilities associated with savagery and uncivilized animal existence on a scapegoat race.[20] The colonial society of overseas Europeans was even less integrated culturally than the new society in America; in such a context racism and obsessive denigration of the native population became the single most important unifying thread in the lives of the white group. Racial oppressors, in the process of attacking the cultural realities of the oppressed, are engaged in fortifying their own precarious cultures; this tradeoff is another example of the exploitative thrust of white Europe in its historical encounter with peoples of color. Those who believe that racial oppression is on its way out, or can be readily eliminated in American life through reforms that guarantee greater equality in living standards and political participation, fail to reckon with the "integrating" role that racism performs for the society and the depths to which it has penetrated the national culture.

Cultural Development as a Response to Racism: Two Studies

The two essays that follow focus on the interplay of racism and culture within the United States in the case of our largest racial minorities, Chicano and Afro-American. The essays illustrate some of the general themes developed in this introduction. The conquest and absorption of the Mexican population is an example of classical colonialism, in contrast to the "internal colonialism" that has followed black enslavement.[21] The Mexican experience suggests that cultural penetration is less effective and extreme when a people are colonized within their original territory. Yet a racist deprecation exists—and perhaps an even greater ignorance of group history and culture than in the case of the Afro-Americans.

In both these domestic instances—as well as in other colonial settings—the colonizer usurps from the colonized control over his history, cultural development, and definition of group realities. Therefore, much of the material in these essays documents the process of cultural imperialism, and criticizes the viewpoints and interpretations of white scholars which have become "standard knowledge." In the case of both the Afro-Americans and the Mexicans, movements of decolonization have arisen for which the first priority is to regain control over cultural life.

Chapter 4 was written originally as a response to the sociologist Bennett Berger who in a review of Charles Keil's *Urban Blues* had questioned the reality of an Afro-American culture. I titled that earlier essay "Black Culture: Myth or Reality." The fact that traces of it remain after much rewriting explains why so many references to Berger and Keil are found in the present chapter. In 1967, the time of first writing, a vigorous defense of the sociological realities of black ethnicity was unusual in the literature. Since then, movements for Afro-American studies and other events may have increased the awareness of many readers to a point where some of my analysis may appear to be old-hat today.

The central thesis is the unique cultural experience of Afro-Americans in the United States and the pivotal position of the struggle against racism in the development of black ethnicity. I focus also on the workings of the white racial mentality: how American racism has systematically distorted the facts of black culture; how Africa and its heritage have been stigmatized and ignored; how Americans have consistently overlooked or minimized the weight of the contributions that Africa and its American-born descendants have made to the nation as a whole; and how the ethnic quality of Afro-American life has been denied as an authentic and independent reality. And yet, paradoxically, the racist organization of American society has provided the crucial context for the distinctive cultural development of the black community.

Friendly critics of the original essay suggested that I had a responsibility to spell out in detail the contents and themes of black culture. I felt it was important enough to analyze the sociological processes through which Afro-American ethnicity has developed and the ways in which racism has blocked our understanding of it. A valid delineation of this culture would be delivered only by black writers and social scientists. Writing today in 1972 I am less rigid on this point. I would not want to dictate who should study what. Yet I continue to feel that the attempt to depict and interpret a culture that is not one's own is inauthentic, in the least, and is likely to result in missing its essence, nuances, and inner complexity. This is especially true when the analyst is a member of the oppressing group, for his imagery of the oppressed culture is inevitably colored by preconceptions and unconscious fantasies. Such reservations haunt me even more strongly with respect to the Chicano experience. Their group realities have been the most systematically maligned by white scholars, whose work is drawn up in an objective conceptual language that only veils the racist tendency to reduce a culture to stereotypes. This explains why Chapter 5 ventures into literary criticism, an apparently strange form for a sociologist. By reviewing important new developments in Chicano writing, I attempt to convey a sense of the complexities of the Mexican-American experience from the perspective of the group's own creative spokesmen. I believe that literature and art are especially likely to capture faithfully the preoccupations of a group and the inner core of a culture. Opportunism also motivated this essay. In acquainting a wider audience with these artists and their works, I could be trying my hand at literary analysis and, at the same time, be tacking on my own sociological observations on the different manner in which the white racial mentality relates to the Mexican presence as compared with the black.

Elizabeth Martinez has remarked: "The United States today crawls with writers who feed themselves by probing, 'analyzing' and then writing about people unlike themselves—people now at last considered worthy of note and of publishers' contracts. The days of this journalistic parasitism should have passed. There are few publishers left who would contract a white writer to do a book on the black movement and for that matter, few editors who would commission a white reviewer to deal with a black writer's book. Apparently Chicanos, on the other hand, haven't become scarey enough yet."[22] The point is well stated, except that Martinez is wrong to assume that this kind of literary and theoretical colonialism has stopped in the case of the black movement and black writers. It hasn't.[23]

NOTES

1. George Orwell's character, Ellis, in his novel *Burmese Days* is an excellent depiction of this mentality (1934; reprint ed., New York: New American Library, 1963).
2. K. M. Panikkar, *Asia and Western Dominance* (London: Allen and Unwin, 1953).
3. H. Alan C. Cairns, *The Clash of Cultures: Early Race Relations in Central Africa* (New York: Praeger, 1965); published in Eng-

land under the title *Prelude to Imperialism* (London: Routledge & Kegan Paul, 1965), pp. 176–178.

4. John Collier, *Indians of the Americas* (New York: Mentor, 1947), pp. 135–137.

5. The best study of the moral arrogance of Europeans in relation to non-Western societies is V. G. Kiernan, *The Lords of Human Kind* (London: Weidenfeld and Nicholson, 1969).

6. Cairns, *op. cit.*, pp. 163–166.

7. *Ibid.*, pp. 181–188.

8. Panikkar, *op. cit.*, p. 423.

9. Cairns, *op. cit.*, pp. 214–218; and M. G. Smith, *The Plural Society in the British West Indies* (Berkeley and Los Angeles: University of California Press, 1965), chap. 6.

10. Cairns, *op. cit.*, pp. 77–79.

11. Cairns, *op. cit.*, p. 78.

12. "The purchase of slaves called for a business sense and shrewd discrimination. An Angolan Negro was proverbial for worthlessness; Coromantines (Ashantis) from the Gold Coast were good workers but too rebellious; Mandingoes (Senegal) were too prone to theft; the Eboes (Nigeria) were timid and despondent; the Pawpaws or Whydahs (Dahomey) were the most docile and best-disposed." Eric Williams, *Capitalism and Slavery* (New York: Russell, 1961), pp. 37–38. See also Stanley Stein, *Vassouras* (Cambridge: Harvard University Press, 1957), pp. 70–71.

13. See Eugene D. Genovese, "The Treatment of Slaves in Different Countries: Problems in the Application of the Comparative Method," in Laura Foner and E. Genovese, *Slavery in the New World* (Englewood Cliffs, N.J.: Prentice-Hall, 1969), pp. 202–210, for a general discussion of these differences. On Brazil, see David B. Davis, *The Problem of Slavery in Western Culture* (Ithaca, N.Y.: Cornell University Press, 1966), chap. 8, and Stanley Stein, *op. cit.* The significance of African ethnicity until late in the nineteenth century is discussed in Stein, *ibid.* for Brazil, and by Orlando Patterson in *The Sociology of Slavery* (London: MacGibbon & Kee, 1967) for Jamaica. Stein notes that the contraband slave trade continued to supply Brazil through the 1860s; and Patterson calculates that almost a quarter of Jamaican slaves were African born at the time of emancipation (1838).

14. Ndabaningi Sithole, *African Nationalism* (London: Oxford University Press, 1968), p. 68.

15. *Ibid.*

16. Some general works on colonialism and plural societies that discuss these issues are Rupert Emerson, *From Empire to Nation* (Boston: Beacon, 1962); Stewart Easton, *The Rise and Fall of Western Colonialism* (New York: Praeger, 1964); J. S. Furnivall, *Colonial Policy and Practice* (New York: New York University Press, 1956); Immanuel Wallerstein, *Social Change: The Colonial Situation* (New York: Wiley, 1966), and *Africa, The Politics of Independence* (New York: Random House, 1961); and M. G. Smith, *The Plural Society in the British West Indies, op. cit.*

17. Gilbert Osofsky, *Harlem: The Making of a Ghetto* (New York: Harper & Row, 1965), pp. 131–135; and Harold Cruse, *The Crisis of the Negro Intellectual* (New York: Morrow, 1967), pp. 115–146.

18. The concepts of new societies and fragmentation are borrowed from Louis Hartz, *The Founding of New Societies* (New York: Harcourt Brace Jovanovich, 1964).

19. Winthrop Jordan, *White over Black* (Chapel Hill: University of North Carolina Press, 1968), and Lewis Copeland, "The Negro as a Contrast Conception," in Edgar T. Thompson, ed., *Race Relations and the Race Problem* (Durham, N.C.: Duke University Press, 1939), pp. 152–179.

20. Joel Kovel, *White Racism: A Psychohistory* (New York: Random House, 1970).

21. This distinction has been questioned recently by three Chicano political scientists who have interpreted the relation between the Mexican-American community and the larger society in terms of the framework of internal colonialism. See Mario Barrera, Carlos Muñoz, and Charles Ornelas, "The Barrio as Internal Colony," in Harlan Hahn, ed., *Urban Affairs Annual Review, 6* (1972). Barrera suggests that the granting of legal equality to a colonized people and absorption within the boundaries of the colonizing nation are the distinguishing features of internal colonialism (personal communication—September, 1971).

22. Elizabeth Martinez, "An Exchange on La Raza," *New York Review of Books* (February 12, 1970), 37.

23. On the topic of whites reviewing books by black authors, see June Meyer, "Spokesmen for the Blacks," *Nation* (December 4, 1967), 597–599.

chapter 4
black
culture*

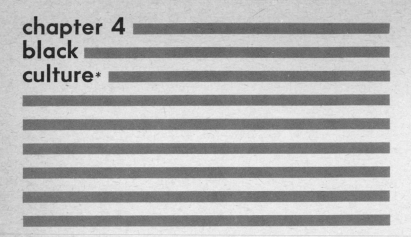

During the 1960s the black communities of the nation became increasingly concerned with culture. Afro-Americans aggressively substituted their own ethnic alternatives for dominant standards of beauty, behavior, and value, many of which were rejected as "white" and "middle-class." Although the emphasis on blackness was largely a project of a younger generation, it pervaded the group as a whole and affected the entire society. The mass media and the publishing houses began to replace the word *Negro* with *black*. For Stokely Carmichael the criterion of being black was a realization and an acceptance of one's African-ness; indeed, a renewed interest in Africa, its politics, and cultural traditions developed in Afro-American communities. The shift away from integration as the central goal of the organized liberation movement brought with it a reevalution of black cultural entities and social institutions and a commitment to their development, within both the ghetto and the mainstream. A characteristic expression of this trend was the black studies movement, a struggle within education for the recognition of the Afro-American experience. All in all, an impressive cultural ferment has been taking place with respect to the black American's heritage and identity and his relation to American society, a ferment that has informed public and private discourse, political and personal action, and art and literature.

The emergence of this movement of cultural revitalization[1]

* An earlier version of this chapter appeared as "Black Culture: Myth or Reality," in *Afro-American Anthropology*, by Norman Whitten and John Szwed (New York: The Free Press, 1970).

poses an intellectual dilemma for analysts of American society. The black culture development upsets basic assumptions upon which social scientists and liberal intellectuals have constructed the nation's official "enlightened" attitudes toward race relations and black people. The primary tenet is that Negroes—unlike other minority groups—have no ethnic culture because the elimination of African ancestral heritages brought about total acculturation. A second related assumption attributes the apparently distinctive styles of the ghetto to lower-class conditions rather than to ethnic or national traditions. (The middle-class orientations of most federal programs for the minority poor follow from this.) In this essay, I attempt to make sense of these recent trends by questioning the standard sociological position on the ethnic character of Afro-Americans.

The view that black people lack any characteristics of a distinctive nationality, that they are only Americans and nothing else, has become almost a dogma of liberal social science. Gunnar Myrdal and his great book *An American Dilemma* set the tone for the present outlook.[2] In this influential and voluminous work there is no chapter on Afro-American culture and only a sketchy treatment of the black community. Furthermore, Myrdal's statement that the Negro is "an exaggerated American" and that his values are "pathological" elaborations on general American values has been widely quoted for a generation.[3] As recently as 1963 another influential study of ethnic groups in New York took a similar position. "It is not possible for Negroes to view themselves as other ethnic groups viewed themselves," wrote Glazer and Moynihan, "because—and this is the key to much in the Negro world—the Negro is only an American and nothing else. He has no values and culture to guard and protect."[4]

It is misleading to give the impression that the standard position has been advanced only by white liberal sociologists. On this point, E. Franklin Frazier was at least as influential as Myrdal. Perhaps the leading black sociologist of his generation, Frazier took issue with the anthropologist Melville Herskovits, who in his *Myth of the Negro Past* had imputed African origins to many, if not most, Afro-American social and cultural patterns.[5] Frazier's view was published in 1957 in the revised edition of his comprehensive work, *The Negro in the United States:*

As a racial or cultural minority the Negro occupies a

unique position. He has been in the United States longer
than any other racial or cultural minority with the
exception, of course, of the American Indian. Although
the Negro is distinguished from other minorities by his
physical characteristics, unlike other racial or cultural
minorities the Negro is not distinguished by culture from
the dominant group. Having completely lost his ancestral
culture, he speaks the same language, practices the same
religion, and accepts the same values and political ideals
as the dominant group. Consequently, when one speaks
of Negro culture in the United States, one can
only refer to the folk culture of the rural Southern Negro
or the traditional forms of behavior and values which
have grown out of the Negro's social and mental isolation.
Moreover, many of the elements of Negro culture which
have grown out of his peculiar experience in America,
such as music, have become a part of the general
American culture.

Since the institutions, the social stratification, and the
culture of the Negro minority are essentially the same as
those of the larger community, it is not strange that the
Negro minority belongs among the assimilationist rather
than the pluralist, secessionist or militant minorities. It is
seldom that one finds Negroes who think of themselves as
possessing a different culture from whites and that their
peculiar culture should be preserved.[6]

Despite this prevailing point of view, the studies of Southern
towns and Northern ghettos undertaken from the 1930s through the
1950s are rich in evidence of distinctive institutions and unique ways
of looking upon life and society that read very much like descriptions
of ethnic cultures.[7] Yet, until recently, the positive assertion of black
culture has been confined to nationalist and political circles; it has not
been defended in academic research. During the 1960s, the recognition of Afro-American ethnicity finally crept into the social sciences.
One of the first instances was the anthropological study *Urban Blues*.
Charles Keil used the blues singer and his audience as the raw materials to outline the distinctive traits and ethos of black American
culture, the core of which he located in the ideology of *Soul*. The

importance of the Soul idea to Keil is its suggestion that "Negroes have a dearly bought experiential wisdom, a 'perspective by incongruity,'" that provides black Americans a unique outlook on life that cannot be shared by whites.[8]

Urban Blues evoked an incisive critique by the sociologist Bennett Berger. In the context of a generally positive review, Berger attacked Keil's major thesis at three pivotal points. First, he asserted that Soul theorists·romanticize Negro life and thereby lose sight of the fact that "black culture" is at bottom only an American Negro version of lower-class culture. Second, because this culture has no future, analytical appreciation of it may be misplaced. Lower-class culture in America is no basis for the development of a national consciousness and ethnic solidarity. Since it has no appeal to the socially mobile, it can only interfere with progress toward integration and equality. Finally, Berger argued that black cultural spokesmen are only confusing the intellectual atmosphere and obstructing the road to Negro progress and racial harmony. As intellectuals and political men they have the obligation to specify clearly what in Afro-American culture is to be affirmed, so that everyone can see whether anything solid or meaningful is involved. But, speaking so generally if not demagogically, black spokesmen have failed in their obligation, Berger noted.[9]

With unusual cogency, Berger has expressed a position that is held by many people today, including scholarly experts in the study of race relations. In the pages that follow I argue that this perspective is based on a number of misconceptions about culture and ethnicity in modern American society. It reflects a restricted usage of the idea of culture and, even more important, a mechanical application of the model of immigrant assimilation to the very different cultural experience of black people in America. I argue further that the inability to perceive the realities of Afro-American ethnicity is related to the complexity of black culture, its diverse and paradoxical elements, as well as to a failure to grasp the fact that racism and its legacy, black political history, are central to this cultural dynamic. In addition, the position is based on a static, deterministic approach to cultural development, one that minimizes its open-ended quality and therefore underplays the role of consciousness and culture building in affecting that development. And finally, the conventional sociological position is yet another reflection—albeit in liberal form—of the ideological imperative of a racist society, which ignores, discredits, or depreciates the cultural realities of people of color. Let us examine each of these issues in turn.

The Unique Cultural Process

The premise that informs Kenneth Stampp's history of slavery—"that the slaves were merely ordinary human beings, that innately Negroes *are,* after all, only white men with black skins, nothing more, nothing less"—is plausible to a degree.[10] As Frazier stressed, the manner in which North American slavery developed—in contrast to Caribbean and South American slavery—eliminated the most central African traits, those elements of ethnicity that European and Asian immigrants brought to this country: language, dress, religion and other traditional institutions, and a conscious identification with an overseas homeland. Scholars of postslavery societies concur that "Africanisms" are least apparent in the United States. The cultural critic Janheinz Jahn concluded that the American Negro novel was the only stream of black literature outside the African or neo-African tradition.[11] But the African heritage approach to black ethnicity can be misleading. Its proponents typically assume that there is only one generic process— the model of European ethnic assimilation—through which nationality cultures and the dominant American ethos have interacted. What must be understood is that the Afro-American historical experience and the experiences of other third world peoples have unique features that suggest a cultural development that has reversed the path traveled by the European ethnics.

Howard Brotz has observed that the "no Negro culture" argu-ment rests on the assumption that an ethnic group must possess three attributes—a distinctive language, a unique religion, and a national homeland.[12] This position is derived from the classic anthropological conception, or *holistic view,* of culture, which points to an integrated way of life and system of customs, institutions, beliefs, and values that fit together into some organic whole, perhaps dominated by a central ethos. This idea of culture was developed from the study of primitive peoples and contributed to the overemphasis on social integration that characterizes *functionalist theory* in the social sciences. Yet it does point up the unity of the heritages that the various immigrant groups brought to America.[13] The parallel holistic cultures of the African peoples were destroyed in America because groups of slaves from the diverse tribes, kingdoms, and linguistic groups were consciously broken up so that language, religion, and national loyalties were lost.* But ethnic cultures as organic, holistic ways of life did not last very long for the immigrant nationalities either, and in fact the idea of a holistic culture is less and less applicable to any group in a modern urban society. Today when we characterize Jews, Italians, or Greeks as ethnic groups, we are referring to a different notion of culture, one that locates ethnicity in certain distinctive values, orientations to life and experience, and shared memories that coexist within the framework of general American life styles and allegiances. Most sociologists and laymen find little difficulty in calling American Jews an ethnic group despite the fact that in most of their institutional and cultural behavior Jews are eminently American and middle class. Still, there are distinctive cultural orientations—a peculiarly ethnic style of humor, for example—that come from a common historical and social experience.

Let us look more closely at the model of ethnic group assimilation that dominates sociological thinking about nationalities. The holistic way of life was introduced with the immigrant group's first entry or, more accurately, early in the peak period of its immigration. It soon gave way to the demands of the American environment and the competition of domestic ways of life. Typically, after one generation an ethnic culture developed out of old-country elements, American ways, and original adaptations to the immigrant's situation. Such a culture was more fragmented and full of normative and value conflicts than the traditional one; yet it still provided some round of life and center of community for the group. As time went on the number of people involved in the more traditional holistic cultures declined, and the emerging ethnic-American cultures took on more and more characteristics of the larger society. Assimilation meant modifying or giving up certain ethnic institutions and culturally distinct values as the generations followed one another. The process tended to be one-way and nonreversible, from immigrant extra-national status to ethnic group to assimilation, though Will Herberg has noted that ethnic identity is sometimes reasserted by the third generation.[14] The means

* But, as I discuss below, the underlying ethos or world view that cut across many West African societies and is expressed in aesthetics and philosophy was not destroyed.

that move this process forward are occupational mobility and the ethnic group's increasing contact with dominant institutions, especially education.

Very little of this fits the cultural experience of Afro-Americans.* How a minority group enters the host society has fateful—if not permanent—consequences. The very manner in which Africans became Americans undermined original culture and social organization. The slave-making operation vitiated the meaning and relevance of the traditional, specific African identities. On the other hand, black people did not enter this country with the group identity of Negro. As Singer has pointed out, blacks at first constituted a sociolegal *category,* rather than a group in sociological terms.[15] Therefore the cultural process could not be one of movement from ethnic group to assimilation, since blacks were not an ethnic group. What took place was not acculturation but an incorporation into a legal status that did not permit the collective autonomy, nor the social and economic progress, that accompanied assimilation for other minorities. It was a forced deculturation, a spurious assimilation. At the same time, beginning with slavery,[16] the group- and culture-building process began among the black population, and the development of an ethnic group identity and distinctive culture has been going on ever since. But this cultural process is infinitely more complex than that for the immigrant groups. One reason is the general reversal in direction. But it is not a simple one-way process in the opposite direction, from "assimilation" to ethnic group; the black cultural experience is more like an alternating than a direct current. The movement toward ethnicity and distinctive consciousness has been paralleled by one toward becoming more "American" in action and identity. Sometimes these conflicting vectors characterize different time periods; sometimes they reflect different segments of the large and diversified black minority; sometimes both contradictory cultural tendencies have been present simultaneously and within the psyche and social orientations of a single individual. Underlying these phenomena are the many and varied historical and social conditions that have produced Afro-American culture. Black culture cannot be understood in terms of the model that is reasonably satisfactory for the European ethnic groups.

* And certainly not the Native Americans! The model does not fit the Mexican case either, although here immigration in the present century has produced some common experiences. See Chapter 2 and Chapter 5.

The Diverse Sources of Afro-American Culture

The idea of black culture meets resistance because the term itself contains a number of ambiguities. To many liberals, the term *black culture* appears unacceptable and even racist because it threatens the distinction between race and culture—a distinction that is a basic principle of the modern scientific outlook, the special contribution of anthropology to that outlook. But if it is understood that in this context black refers to ethnic realities and experiences and not to color per se, the grounds for this objection disappear.* A further problem is that black culture has several connotations. The two most common usages are conflicting, to a degree. On the one hand, the term refers to the totality of the culture that is lived and possessed by black Americans. On the other hand, it connotes those traditions, symbols, and meanings that are specially associated with black people and their experience. The culture of black Americans (first meaning) and Afro-American ethnic culture (second meaning) are not identical, though the two overlap. The relation between these two referents must be clarified to avoid confusion.

Those who deny the reality of black culture argue that people of African descent in America live and think much like other Americans. This is true, for the culture of Afro-Americans is in some ways like that of all human beings in the world; in other ways it is specific to the concerns and values of all Americans; in still other ways it is considerably diversified by differences in region, social class, age, and sex. It is also uniquely ethnic in some other ways. But to argue that black people must think and feel alike and that the culture of a group must be in every way different from that of other groups in order to qualify as cultural is to set up a standard for black culture that would disallow the cultural realities of all peoples! Jahn makes this point tellingly with respect to African culture:

> If in places the reader is inclined to object that what we are expounding as an aspect of African culture plays a part also in other cultures, that the meaning of life is also stressed in European culture, that the spoken word has the greatest significance also in other cultures, above all

* Perhaps this confusion suggests that Afro-American culture is the more precise term. Black people prefer to use both, however, and the shorter expression the more frequently.

in illiterate ones, that rhythm has its functions among
all peoples, that even in the Christian middle ages the
picture has also functioned as a symbol, ideogram, and
sensory image, and that therefore all these so emphatically
African matters are not after all so original—then let him
recollect that all human cultures resemble one another
up to a point, that different cultures only value their
common elements differently, in so far as one puts the
accent here, another there, and that it is the ordering, the
relation of the elements to one another that determines the
difference between the cultures.[17]

Just as the culture of black Americans consists in part of life
styles and values that were originally Euro-American, Afro-American
ethnic culture is also to a considerable degree part of the larger American cultural panoply. Building from the base of their special oppressed
situation, blacks have contributed much (in relation to reward and
recognition, overcontributed) to the language, lore, art, and styles that
are today available to Americans of every ethnic origin. It is this
mutual interaction and interpenetration between the Euro-American
and the Afro-American streams that make the question of black culture so paradoxical and therefore impervious to precise analysis.

The poetry of Melvin Tolson, based upon the integration and
striking concatenation of thematic materials from the African,
European, American, and Afro-American traditions, abounds with
these paradoxes. Consider the following passage from *A Harlem Gallery*:[18]

> Frog Legs Lux and his Indigo Combo
>   let go
>   with a wailing pedal point
>   that slid into
>   Basin Street Blues
>   `like Ty Cobb stealing second base:
> Zulu, King of the Africans,
> arrives on Mardi Gras morning;
> the veld drum of Baby Dodds'
> great-grandfather in Congo Square
> pancakes the first blue note
> in a callithump of the USA.

And now comes the eve of Ash Wednesday.
Comus on parade!
All God's children revel
like post-Valley Forge
charivari in Boston celebrating the nuptials of
a gay-old-dog minuteman with a lusty maid.

And when Tolson introduces an ethnic metaphor suddenly into a "universal" discussion of aesthetics, the effect is powerful:

An artist makes what he can;
every work of art asserts,
  "I am that I am."
  So leave the rind to the pedant
and the bone to The Hamfat Man.*

In the present essay I focus primarily on Afro-American ethnicity, though I do move back and forth at times between the two major referents of black culture. I attempt some broad generalizations about the historical and contemporary conditions that have given rise to distinctive cultural orientations. The special target of my wrath is the view that the ways of life of black people in America is primarily a class, namely, a lower-class, phenomenon. Poverty is only one source of black culture, and, as I shall attempt to prove, even the lower-class traits and institutions have been modified by strictly ethnic values. Among the other sources of the culture are Africa, the South, slavery, Emancipation and Northern migration, and, above all, racism. That racial oppression provides the basis for a more elaborate and more ethnic cultural response than does class exploitation and lower-class status is central to my thesis.

The African Heritage

In *The Myth of the Negro Past*, Melville Herskovits places emphasis on the continuity between African and American black life styles. His thesis has been too easily dismissed as exaggeration, in part because his own conception of culture as specific institutions and traits undermined the power of his argument and evidence. Only a modicum of

* Reprinted by permission of Twayne Publishers, Inc., *A Harlem Gallery* by Melvin Tolson.

such specific practices could be maintained in the slave condition. But if the essence of culture is viewed instead as the more subtle human orientations to the problems of existence, as ways of being in the world, as ethos or philosophy of life, then the entire matter of the African-ness of black Americans must be reviewed once again. Sociology and anthropology may have misread these realities because they are expressed more profoundly in literature and art than in the conventional data of the social scientist. The close fit between African cultural assumptions and the world view that is called Soul in the United States, between African aesthetics and the themes underlying Negro American music and literature, suggests that those black nationalists who have for generations insisted on the relevance of the African heritage may have grasped a significant truth.[19] As Toynbee noted in his *Study of History*, modern scholars assume that Asian societies have been westernized because so much of "our" material culture—our techniques and products—has been widely diffused. He argues that the souls of these civilizations, where the people really live, have not been seriously penetrated or transformed.[20] Thus, because we have viewed culture primarily in its material and behavioral aspects rather than in the spiritual life of a people, we may have exaggerated the westernization of Afro-Americans in the United States.*

Without doubt, the salience of African culture for Afro-American ethnicity was reduced by the fact that these orientations and ways of thought were transmitted for the most part subliminally, rather than through conscious awareness and identification. We can assume that the slaves and later the freedmen who created and sang new musical forms, expressed themselves in *nonstandard (Black) English,* moved about in distinct fashions, and worshipped in their own way did not know that they were behaving according to African linguistic, aesthetic, and theological precepts—as contemporary scholars are now discovering.[21] The black community's revived interest in Africa—a product of that continent's anticolonial movements and the emergence of independent nations there, as well as of the domestic struggle—is stimulating serious research by both black and white scholars, which in time should provide a clearer understanding of how

---

* The central thesis of the idea of Soul is precisely that Afro-Americans have always maintained their unique spiritual life.

African cultural values interacted with, and were modified by, specific American conditions.

From the beginning Africa's role was consistently obscured by the frenzied racist imageries of the continent as a cesspool of savagery and barbarism.* The Western nations have until recently assumed that Africa had no history and that consequently blacks were people without a past.[24] The stigmatization of Africa was evidently more pronounced among Protestant nations. Though racist in their own way, such countries as Brazil and Cuba have officially recognized African contributions to their national cultures.** North Americans only on rare occasions acknowledge the Indian influences on our culture and history; at other times the importance of the Negro to our society may be referred to—but *never* the impact of *Africa* and its cultures. This phenomenon must have been important in alienating Afro-Americans from a sense of their own past, including a partly self-imposed tendency to deny and reject the bond with Africa.[26]

The South as Neo-African
Our society's repression of Africa has distorted—in racist fashion—the realities of cultural influence in the nation as a whole. Thus, we say that many Negroes speak with "a Southern accent," and the im-

---

* Omnipresent racism notwithstanding, the West has generally appreciated the cultures of Asia far more than those of Africa. Even Toynbee omits African societies from the civilizations he interprets in his 11-volume *Study*.[22] The same practice is continued in one of the more recent syntheses of world history, which discusses Africa only marginally. The neglect is apparently justified by a view that this continent was peripheral to the mainstream of cultural and political developments from ancient times to the modern period![23]

** Gilberto Freyre's masterwork, *The Masters and the Slaves*, was widely hailed in Brazil as the outstanding historical interpretation of the national culture when it was published in the 1930s. A constant theme of Freyre is the contribution of Africans to Brazilian society and culture. Indeed he saw the slaves as the superior cultural and biological element among the three major population components. He notes the impact of Africa on almost all aspects of Brazilian life, including language. One gets the impression that Africans from different regions and tribes were not as readily lumped together in Brazil as in the United States. Freyre also notes numerous African place-names, something that is missing in North America. Having said all this, Freyre's great study is still notorious for the paternalism that underlies his approach to people of color.[25]

plicit assumption is that, in their imitating ways, blacks picked up this slow, modulated drawl from the whites—when the fact is that Southerners in general, whites as well as blacks, speak with *African accents.*

In the future, the pioneering studies of the American South will be based on research into the ways in which the distinctive patterns and ethos of the region were shaped by the culture of Africa and the black presence. Even such classic interpreters of the inner essence of Southern culture as Wilbur Cash and James Agee paid very little attention to the Afro-American influence.[27] When the neo-African character of the South has been properly recognized, then this region can be viewed as the black analog to the European immigrant's old country, and in the South we will find also the roots of the two additional criteria of ethnic peoplehood: language and religion, the distinctiveness of which has been overlooked because of the surface similarities to white counterparts. Ralph Ellison and Calvin Hernton have pointed out how much the black man's attitudes and cultural styles reflect the patterns of this region, for the Southern heritage has been carried to the Northern cities and is constantly refurbished through visiting and new migration.*[28] Obviously much of black religion, "soul food," music, and language overlaps with Southern poor white culture. Undoubtedly there was mutual interaction; yet it is likely that the African was the more vigorous cultural influence.

The Culture of Slavery

Slavery may be viewed as the third great source of black American culture. Here, under seriously restricting conditions, Afro-Americans began developing their own communities and codes of conduct.[30] Many persisting themes in the black experience emerged from the situation of servitude: the search for freedom and self-determination, ambivalence toward the white master class and white people in general, the centrality of religion, and the special role of the woman in the family. To slavery also more negative adaptations and character types owe their origins—for example, the submission, timidity, fear,

---

* Blacks also assimilated some of the values and styles of the Southern ruling classes, though they were not always in a position to emulate them. Ellison has attributed the general aristocratic flavor of ghetto life styles to this origin, as well as the American Negro's apparent lack of passion for business entrepreneurship.[29]

and manipulation embedded in the "Uncle Tom" orientation. It is these kinds of cultural adaptations that many nationalist leaders have been trying to stamp out in their attacks on "the slave mentality."

Because racist ideology blotted out the significance of African realities for black life and for the culture of the South, slavery came to be viewed as the be-all-and-end-all of the social heritage of American Negroes. Such a view of the black experience and its corollary that an Afro-American culture is nonexistent, or at best a cruel joke, is well expressed by a leading literary figure:

> I think I know why the Jews once wished to survive
> (though I am less certain as to why they still do) : they
> not only believed that God had given them no choice, but
> they were tied to a memory of past glory and a dream
> of imminent redemption. What does the American Negro
> have that might correspond to this? His past is a stigma,
> his color is a stigma, and his vision of the future is the
> hope of erasing the stigma by making color irrelevant,
> by making it disappear as a fact of consciousness.[31]

Emancipation and Migration

A further source was Emancipation: the promises, the betrayals, and the frustrations that followed upon release from bondage. Because slavery restricted free movement to the ultimate, a period of great mobility followed in its wake.[32] The promise of the North, the attractions of industry, and the push from a depressed Southland, set the stage for ghetto life in the urban North. This is the source of black culture that is most clearly tied to poverty and lower-class existence. And yet the black ghetto is different from the ethnic ghettos of the Irish, Jews, or Italians because it comes out of a different history, that of slavery, Southern jim crow, and a Northern migration that only in part parallels a transoceanic search for a better life. Whereas the immigrant ghettos allowed ethnic cultures to flower for a period, in the long term they functioned as way stations on the road to acculturation and assimilation.[33] But the black ghetto has served as a central fixture of American racism's strong resistance to the assimilation of black people. Thus the ghetto's permanence has made it a continuing crucible for ethnic development and culture building.[34]

The Lower-Class Component

The black ghettos are overwhelmingly made up of people with low incomes, and poverty is the first fact of life. This has encouraged the view that the ghetto subculture is lower-class culture, or the "culture of poverty" to use Oscar Lewis's now fashionable phrase. Such an interpretation is based on the liberal assumption that Afro-Americans lack distinctive ethnic or national characteristics and the social science discovery that lower-class groups in America share somewhat deviant orientations and ways of life, or a subculture.[35] Since black Americans are overwhelmingly in the low-income population, then whatever appears to be distinctive in the ghetto must be due to class status rather than ethnicity.

Although Charles Keil did not deal explicitly with the analytical problem of class and ethnic contributions in his *Urban Blues*, his critic Bennett Berger based a rebuttal on the premise that ghetto culture is essentially lower-class in character. I think Berger found Keil's emphasis on Soul very convenient to his position, since this elusive and yet real cultural symbol does contain many of the values, orientations, and virtues that have been historically attributed to the poor and downtrodden. Berger (drawing from Keil) interprets Soul as a stereotype that flatters the oppressed black lower class and thus can serve as a compensation, an ideological palliative for its discontents:

> . . . strong emotions and feelings, especially when shared
> with others; something pure, nonmachined; staying power
> and wisdom through suffering; telling it like it is, being
> what you are, and believing in what you do. The concept
> suggests further a tight intermingling of sex, love,
> and reciprocal responsiveness which constitute the pattern
> of Negro Dionysianism, manifest in the swing of the
> blues-jazz-gospel musical milieu and in the brilliant,
> moving, linguistic innovations which spring from it. The
> pattern emphasizes the erotic, the frenetic, and the
> ecstatic—a pattern which when made ideological constitutes
> a claim to emotional depth and authenticity. . . .[36]

As this capsule summary suggests, there are many themes in ghetto life that can be identified in other lower-class groups, among the Latin American poor described by Lewis, for example, or in the immigrant ghettos of the Irish and the Poles. Some of these themes are expressive of a present-oriented style of life, characterized by minimal planning and organization. Religion is a dominant value and release; crime, hustling, rackets, and other forms of "deviance" are commonplace. Economic pressures strain the family, and "matriarchal" trends are visible. Aggression and violence are more everyday occurrences than in middle-class neighborhoods—at least in their public expression. Personal releases that some sociologists label "immediate rather than deferred gratifications"—sex, drinking, drugs, music—are emphasized in the life organizations of individuals. A sense of fatalism, or apathy, a quasi-paranoid outlook (the "world is against me") pervade the streets, where the public life of the lower-class subculture is set.

That the black ghetto shares these realities with other lower-class milieus and that these themes flow primarily from the condition of poverty I do not doubt. But that is not the whole story. Even the class-based characteristics gain an ethnic content and emphasis when people with unique problems live under similar conditions and associate primarily with one another for generations. The best accounts of Afro-American life reveal how street society, the behavior of youth gangs, and family relations are richly endowed with a peculiarly black style.[37] The cultivation of a black style is emphasized in speech, movement, dress, and of course music and dance.[38] And as Powdermaker observed in the 1930s, a Negro church service is a totally different happening from a poor white one, despite the fact that the two share some common religious origins and institutional forms.[39]

Berger correctly observes that lower-class traits do not become institutionalized or legitimated.* But when class traits are modified and given ethnic content by a national group, they may become institutionalized, that is, conscious, expected, and infused with value (which can be positive or negative). Afro-Americans have long infused value into their music; today Southern food, modes of walking and talking, and even an alleged "supersexuality" have become symbols of group identity and cohesiveness. (The development of

* As many have pointed out, the organization of lower-class people into Christian, Marxist, or trade union associations leads toward middle-class socialization as much as the institutionalization of working-class values.

ethnic cultural values does not, of course, preclude ambivalence; the fact that many people may feel ambivalent toward these phenomena is no argument against their cultural reality. Just the contrary!)

The controversy about the "matriarchy" best illustrates my thesis. Although in recent years social scientists like Moynihan have exaggerated and distorted the subject, the special and different role that the woman and mother have played in the black family and community is a perennial theme in Afro-American life and literature. The black woman (and the cognate issue of male-female relations) is a continuous topic of discussion in black circles, in informal sessions as well as public debates. The emphasis in some parts of the Afro-American movement on black manhood is a reaction to the role of the woman as much as to a racist society's denial of dignity and opportunity.[40] Unlike the lower-class situation where a matrifocal theme operates amid a patriarchal value system that obscures a consciousness of this trend, blacks have directly confronted the issue. In the past few years the so-called matriarchy has been talked about, joked about, defended against, debated pro and con, and more and more actively acted upon—for example, in selecting leadership in community groups. The assessment of the historic position of the woman and the relative roles of male and female in the family, community, and liberation movement is undergoing a spirited reexamination today. This kind of cultural ferment is not characteristic of lower classes or even working classes in America. It points to a dynamic of self-definition through which an ethnic group is shaping its character.

The class and ethnic factors in Afro-American culture are intimately intermingled and thus difficult to distinguish. The effort must be made, however, because the intellectual and social consequences of this apparently innocent distinction are considerable—as I suggest in my conclusion.

Racism

The paradox of black culture is its ambiguous debt to racial oppression. Whereas racism attacks culture at its very roots, and white supremacy in American life and thought has worked tooth and nail to negate the past and present cultural realities of Afro-America, the centrality of racial subjugation in the black experience has been the single most important source of the developing ethnic peoplehood. Racism has been such an omnipresent reality that the direct and indirect struggle against it makes up the core of black history in America, just as the way in which each individual confronted it can be seen as the distinguishing mark of her or his personal biography.* It is through this continuing struggle to surmount and change a racist social system—a struggle which began at least with Emancipation, and has stepped up to new levels each generation, after periods of decline, to the zenith of the present day—that black Americans have created a *political history.* This political history is the core of the distinctive ethnic culture and the clue to the contemporary revitalization movement which celebrates blackness.

Despite the Kerner Report, it is still difficult for most whites to accept the unpleasant fact that America remains a racist society. Such an awareness is further obscured by the fact that more sophisticated, subtle, and indirect forms, which might better be termed neoracism, tend to replace the traditional, open forms that were most highly elaborated in the old South. The centrality of racism is manifest in two key characteristics of our social structure. First, the division based upon color is the single most important split within the society, the body politic, and the national psyche.** Second, various processes and practices of exclusion, rejection, and subjection based on color are built into the major public institutions (labor market, education, politics, and law enforcement), with the effect of maintaining special privileges, power, and values for the benefit of the white majority.

Historians and other analysts of American life are today discovering the prominence of racism and the implicit assumptions of white superiority in the national experience.[42] Specific racist practices and systems of thought have had a profound impact on the career of

---

* The persistence of racial oppression from slavery to the present has solidified the continuity of the Afro-American experience and its traditions. Only this can explain the remarkable fact that the major types of orientations of slaves to the white man's system that Kenneth Stampp identified in his historical study—the cooperative or "white folks Negro," the rebel or "bad nigger," and the clever, crafty "smart nigger"—were the same dominant social types discovered by Samuel Strong in the Chicago ghetto a generation ago.[41]

** If race is a more important division in present-day American society than class, serious questions arise about the tendency to reduce Afro-American culture to lower-class culture. For a lengthier discussion of racism, see Chapter 1.

black ethnicity in America. The alienation of slaves from their African cultural heritages has already been discussed. A subsequent expression of this destructive and exploitative dynamic was the practice of appropriating the cultural creations of Africans in the New World for the purpose of profit. Jazz and other musical forms are the classic example, but it persists widely in many variations such as the present-day absorption of ghetto language by the mass media and white youth cultures.* A third variation of the racist dialectic is the tendency to deny the legitimacy, or even existence, of distinctive ethnic orientations and creations, a common premise in contemporary "liberal" ideology.

Yet it was the same racist society that willy-nilly encouraged the development of Afro-American culture. Blocking the participation of black people in the dominant culture meant that the human need for symbols, meaning, and value had to be met elsewhere. There must have always been many who found these meanings in "separatist" ethnic forms; there were others who sought them in the attempt to enter fully into the larger culture. Whereas many blacks have always known that racism was no aberration but an institution built into the fabric of American life, the dominant tendency may have been a more optimistic attachment to the nation's ideals of equality and democracy, combined always with a sharp awareness of the opposing reality. But even the acceptance of American premises necessitated group struggles against racism that would translate such ideals into practice. Expressed both in collective and in individual efforts to transcend its crippling effects on life, liberty, and the pursuit of opportunity, this century-long battle against racism has created a legacy—the political history of black people within the United States. This political history is the solid core, the hard-rock nonmystical aspect of Afro-American culture.

* In the words of Ralph Ellison: "that idiom, that style, that expressiveness for which we've suffered and struggled and which is a product of our effort to make meaning of our experience—is taken over by those who would distort it and reduce it to banality. This happened with jazz . . . the naive and implicitly arrogant assumption that a characteristic cultural expression can, because it is Negro (It's American too, but that's a very complex matter), simply be picked up, appropriated, without bothering to learn its subtleties, its inner complexity, or its human cost, its source in tradition, its idiomatic allusiveness, its rooting in the density of lived life."[43]

A unique political history plays an essential role in the development and consolidation of ethnic groups as well as nations.* For the Irish-American community in the late nineteenth and early twentieth century, Ireland's struggle against England and the heroes of that national movement were central concerns. As many have noted, the Jews may be the purest example of a people that has institutionalized its political history into culture, ritual, and sacred values. The Old Testament depicts the political vicissitudes of the Jewish nation, and the religious holidays memorialize this millennial struggle for liberation. Perhaps then the attempt of many black nationalist groups to memorialize the date of Malcolm X's birth or assassination as an official holiday—which in some communities has been successful—can be understood as a similar recognition of the relation between political history and national culture.

The content of black political history is beyond the scope of this essay. It is clear, however, that in the past two decades there has been a significant change in its intensity and nature, a change that lies behind the present-day ferment and interest in black culture. In the past the Negro masses—like the lower orders of all colors and nations in most eras—were primarily passive politically, acted upon more than acting. Since the 1954 Supreme Court decision (that last major turning point in American race relations that was intitiated by a decision of a "white" institution), blacks have become the most important social force acting to change the nation's social structure. Beginning in the mid-fifties they have been creating the big news in domestic American history.**

Despite the fateful reciprocity of black and white in America (a theme that has been stressed in the essays of James Baldwin and the fiction of William Faulkner and W. M. Kelley),[45] Afro-Americans share a consciousness of a common past (and a concomitant national

---

* Howard Brotz has noted that sects like the Black Jews and the Black Muslims attempt to attach themselves to a long and respectable political history as well as to unique religions because they understand how important for culture both these elements are.[44]

** Berger noted that modern civil rights groups like the NAACP do not accept the notion of a distinctive Negro culture. By restricting black culture to the Soul complex and ignoring political history, he missed the point that they have unwittingly played a part, and an important one, in developing this culture.

or ethnic identification) to which other Americans are not privy. How could whites perceive, react, and relate to slavery, emancipation, to the South and its history of jim crow and lynching, to early twentieth-century race riots, and even to Montgomery and Watts in the same way as blacks? No matter how democratic our ideals and how sensitive our human capacities, we were *on the other side* sociologically and existentially.

The point I am belaboring has been made succinctly by a reflective blues singer, Al Hibbler. When Charles Keil asked him what it takes to make a Soul singer, Hibbler listed three ingredients, "having been hurt by a woman," "being brought up in that old-time religion," and "knowing what that slavery shit is all about."[46] In a nutshell, this is the essence of the distinctive political history that lies behind the reality of black ethnicity—since no white American can really know "what that slavery shit is all about." Hibbler, of course, was referring not only to the past.

The black man's unique sociopolitical experience also lies behind other elements of Afro-American culture that have been stressed recently. The Soul orientation can be thought of in Dionysian terms and thus be linked to poverty and lower-class status. But it can also be looked at as a philosophy of life or world view that places tragedy, suffering, and forbearance in a more central position than does the dominant American ethos. The construction of an orientation toward inner experience that clashes with the more external instrumental orientation of our industrial culture reflects as much the racism that has excluded black people from American life as it does lower-class status per se.

Another corollary of racism is the prominence of *survival* as a focal concern in the Afro-American culture. The preoccupation with survival is worth examining because of its remarkable salience and because it may appear to be only a reflection of poverty and lower-class status. It is common for black people to argue that the white race would not have survived had it been subject to the conditions, past and present, that their group has been subject to. Indeed, the biological survival and numerical increase of Afro-Americans, along with the continual renewal of their cultural energy, is a remarkable historical achievement. This sense of tough resilience is one of the central themes in the blues and in the mystique of Soul. In the ghetto there is consensus that the problem of every individual is "making it." "How you makin' it, man," is a common form of greeting. This idea of survival now dominates much of the rhetoric of black American leaders. Because white power is threatened by the numerical increase of the black population, particularly in the cities, such measures as birth control campaigns aimed at welfare clients, the draft policies of the Vietnam war, and the plans to put down ghetto riots with heavy military equipment have been interpreted as potentially genocidal strategies.

Poverty and lower-class existence per se make survival an inevitable and insistent preoccupation. But the Afro-American's self-conscious concern with survival and "making it" only reflects in part alimentary and economic subsistence needs. When black people talk about surviving, they are even more pointedly referring to the problem of maintaining life, sanity, and dignity in a racist society. The backdrop of the "making it" imagery is the presence of the Klan, lynch mobs, ghetto police, and the closed, restricted white power and economic structures. "Making it" appears to be a response to poverty and blocked economic opportunities, but "making it with dignity" is the response of a suppressed national group with distinctive ethnic values to defend. Here I refer to the more subtle pressures of white institutions to remake Afro-Americans in those middle-class ways that acceptance and success seem to require. Constraints against the expression of black ethnicity and style are interpreted as racist, and a major factor behind the increasing ambivalence toward integration is the fear that it will lead to assimilation and thereby threaten cultural survival.*

Racist social relations have different cultural consequences from class relations, and therefore black culture cannot be forced into the Procrustean bed of lower-class culture in the way that Marxists at one time and some liberal social scientists today have wanted to reduce race relations to class relations. For several centuries blacks in America

* This suggests another reason why Afro-American culture has been relatively "invisible." Blacks have learned to respond to racist depreciation and opportunistic cultural appropriation by concealing many of their deeply held patterns from the white world.[47] White America therefore has not been prepared to respond to any affirmation of black culture beyond the conventional and usually racist stereotypes. Today this old adaptation is dying out as a new mood of pride motivates black people to celebrate rather than to deny ethnic values.

have lived together in ways that are markedly different from those of the lower and working classes. The manner in which they have been compelled to relate to individual whites and to the larger society has been markedly divergent from the typical relations of the lower classes to the middle classes or from that of the proletariat to a capitalist social order. Racism excludes a category of people from participation in society in a different way than does class hegemony and exploitation. The thrust of racism is to dehumanize, to violate dignity and degrade personalities in a much more pervasive and all-inclusive way than class exploitation—which in the United States, at any rate, has typically not been generalized beyond the "point of production." Racist oppression attacks selfhood more directly and thoroughly than does class oppression. For these reasons, racial and class oppression— while intimately interacting—have diverse consequences for group formation, for the salience of identities based upon them, and for individual and group modes of adaptation and resistance. Class exploitation does not per se stimulate ethnic and national cultures and liberation movements; colonialism and domestic racism do.

Oscar Lewis has recently noted a complementary and conflicting relation between the culture of poverty and ethnic group cultures. The classical lower-class culture characterized by apathy, social disorganization, aggression, sexuality, and other themes lacks strong ethnic as well as organized political traditions. When an ethnic culture is viable or when political working-class consciousness is cultivated (as Lewis believes has taken place among the Cuban poor), the culture of poverty with all its negative and problematic effects declines.[48] If Lewis is correct—and he makes sense to me—the black culture movement among Afro-Americans may represent the revival of ethnic consciousness—the strengthening of the ethnic cultural component, at the expense of the lower-class component.

Culture Building and Its Present-Day Role
The existence of an Afro-American culture does not make black people less American, though it conditions their relation to American life in distinctive ways. The society's ways of doing things have been a major if not an overwhelming influence on black community standards. Because blacks were stripped of their original religion, language, and institutions, they were particularly vulnerable to American values. Prevented from equal participation in their pursuit, however, blacks

assimilated them from a unique perspective, that of the outsider. Thus
a deep skepticism about the big myths of America has been a recurring mood of the black experience, along with a yearning for their
realization. Of course black culture accepts the American emphasis on
money, the material accoutrements of affluence, and many other goals
—probably including even the suburban life style. In its racist dimension America excludes people of color and maintains the ghettoized
communities that provide fertile ground for ethnicity, while in its
inclusive, mass homogenizing dimension America beckons blacks and
all others to identify with its material and ideal symbols and to participate in at least the middle levels of consumption and life styles.
Out of these contradictions have emerged a distinctive ethnic consciousness of the social costs of American values and a sensitivity to
the hypocrisy in public and private life and to the gap between the
ideal and reality. This long-term awareness appears today to be changing into a more outspoken and outright rejection of American middle-
class values by a substantial number of young Afro-Americans.*

  * Recent public opinion data present some documentation for these
generalities. The black population tends to be less enthusiastic than the
white about technological extravaganzas such as the space programs; its
view of national priorities emphasizes the social and economic problems of
the poor (Gallup, August 7, 1969, and May 9, 1965). The most distinguishing thread that runs through the polls is the special *humanistic*
orientation of Afro-Americans. The blacks surveyed express a much stronger
commitment than the whites to such general beliefs as "brotherhood and
love of mankind," hope for the elimination of hate, inhumanity and war
(Harris poll, December 25, 1967), as well as support of such specific measures as ending capital punishment and guaranteeing a minimum income.
(Thus in two consecutive years, 1968 and 1969, Gallup found that nonwhites were overwhelmingly in favor of a minimum family income of
$3200 a year while whites were overwhelmingly opposed. Differences by
respondent's income class were much smaller.) Blacks are more likely to
oppose violent, punitive measures against people involved in social protest.
Two polls showed that whereas whites either favored shooting looters by a
2½ to 1 margin or were evenly split on the matter, the blacks opposed
such reprisals 2½ to 1 and 6 to 1 (Harris, August 9, 1967, and Gallup,
May 29, 1968); and while whites predominantly approved of the 1968
Chicago police action against the Yippie-Radicals at the Democratic con-
vention, blacks overwhelmingly disapproved (Gallup, September 18, 1968).
Another clear trend is the greater religiosity among black Americans. At
the same time, the polls reveal considerable acceptance of such mainstream values as individualism and hard work, and for a large variety of

The fact that black Americans are more actively rejecting the society and its values at a time when that social order has begun to open its doors to their participation appears paradoxical. To some degree and in some cases this may be a defense mechanism, a protection against the anxieties of openness, competition, and new possibilities. But from another point of view, the paradox is resolved if we understand the special career of Afro-American ethnicity discussed earlier. In contrast with the European immigrants, the period of integration and potential assimilation for blacks is coinciding with the upsurge of the group's sense of peoplehood and with the institutionalization of its culture, rather than with the decline of these phenomena. Because Afro-American culture is a homegrown product, it continues to develop within the matrix of American society. The result is that blacks are becoming more and more bicultural, able to shift back and forth between two social worlds.*

Furthermore, blacks are an extremely large and highly differentiated minority, particularly in comparison to the immigrant groups who inspired the sociologists' model of ethnic group assimilation. Most of the latter were small, their members concentrated physically in a few cities and socially in the lower classes. During the long periods of black cultural development the Afro-American minority has become more and more differentiated. The middle classes grow; new political and religious movements proliferate; the black population spreads out

---

attitudes there is little or no racial difference. I suggest taking all these figures with a grain of salt, because public opinion data do not permit easy generalizations about the mood and orientations of ethnic and racial groups.

* The biculturality of Afro-America is not the same as the "marginal man" phenomenon, which tore up many sensitive second-generation immigrants. For the ethnic groups, psychic conflict was inevitable because the more one was ethnic the less one was American, the more American, the less ethnic. This is not true for Afro-Americans because its ethnic culture is profoundly American and because the present-day institutionalization and celebration of blackness legitimates biculturality. The recognition of biculturality makes the idea of cultural deprivation absurd, as black Americans are actually or potentially richer in the complexity of their cultural heritage than most other Americans. I include the qualifier "potentially" because family situation, economic position, and the type of education received do affect how much of one's culture a person incorporates.

more evenly across the country—though it is now predominantly in the urban centers. The diverse "subcultures" within Afro-America —regional, religious, class, and age-based—complicate the overall ethnic development, which moves at an uneven pace, intensifying the ambiguities and paradoxes in the relation between the racial order and the larger society. It is precisely this ambiguous or paradoxical character of black culture that makes it especially critical for group formation and personal identity. The immigrant ethnics had a clear-cut and holistic "traditional culture"; this gave them implicit strength and bargaining power in the game of assimilation and acculturation. They had something deep inside the group and the individual to fall back upon in the event the American staircase became blocked or its climb too perilous. The black man has faced the American colossus with his original culture shattered. But most important, racism is more profound in its destructive impact on personal identity than the prejudice and discrimination that was leveled against the nonblack outlanders.*

The present cultural ferment in the Negro community is not totally new, of course. Well known is the Harlem renaissance of the 1920s, which saw the emergence of a group of self-conscious black intellectuals and artists, along with a somewhat parallel nationalist political development, the Garvey movement.[49] This earlier cultural renaissance came after the post–World War I setbacks to racial democratization, just as today's cultural movement gained its power from the limited successes and possibilities of the civil rights movement— specifically the failure of integration to become a socioeconomic reality. But if culture building feeds on "backlash," this does not mean it is a temporary will-of-the-wisp that will die out when integration finally hits its stride. The totality of the racial experience of the last twenty years is beginning to teach some white people what most blacks have probably always known—that racism is not a dying phenomenon in American life, confined largely to decadent Southern elites and their "redneck" allies. Unfortunately it is on the way out only in these more blatant forms. In various and subtle ways, racism and neoracism permeate the social institutions of society, North, South, West, and East. Thus the black culture movement is a reason-

---

* Even the other third world groups that experienced systematic and vicious racial oppression in this country were spared the unique cultural uprooting effected by slavery.

able response to the realities of a society that in its present socioeconomic and psychic organization is not going to accept people of
African descent without imposing ceilings on their human possibilities.
The stronger that Afro-American ethnicity becomes, the greater the
possibility for black people to utilize both group power and individual
mobility to take what they can from, and give what will be accepted
to, this basically racist society—a process that in time will contribute
to its transformation. For in American life, ethnic culture is identity,
and there is no individual or group progress without a clear sense of
who one is, where one came from, and where one is going.

The black consciousness and culture-building movements of today seem much more significant than the earlier Harlem development,
though for a nonhistorian this can be only an impressionistic guess.
Today's movement is more widespread; it is taking place in every
major locale, not just New York. It encompasses large segments of the
black bourgeoisie and working-class masses, rather than primarily
marginal people and intellectuals. The appeal of black culture seems
especially strong today to the occupationally and socially mobile, a
group that in the past tended to resist ethnic identification.*[50]

The young are of course at the forefront of the black culture
and black power movements. Ironically, if Claude Brown is correct,
E. Franklin Frazier may have had much to do with this generational
change in the outlook of the "black bourgeoisie." Brown mentions that
Frazier's lectures and his book *Black Bourgeoisie* had a great impact
on his own thinking and, presumably, that of other college students.
Of course, there is a sense in which these mobile black youths did not
have to be motivated to become different from their parents; in
America all young people are predisposed to reject their elders and
break away from their parents' life patterns. But in so clearly dissecting
the group-denying and self-negating hangups of their parents, Frazier

* Bennett Berger, however, in the review referred to earlier, argues
that the Soul ideology cannot meet the needs of the upwardly mobile integrationist. It is, he asserts, a lower-class mystique. I think that Professor
Berger is dead wrong on this point. Even in America people cannot live by
bread (or television) alone. The mobile young blacks of today seem to be
seizing upon the Soul concept (and the related black power ideal) because
they provide bulwarks of identity and identification in the face of the very
anxieties of mobility and assimilation into the cultural vacuum of contemporary life.

also helped teach the young generation to identify with their own blackness and with the oppressed ghetto masses. Many middle-class college-educated youth have taken on the tasks of attempting to organize politically, as well as to articulate self-consciously, the less conscious cultural values of the lower-class black community.*

Conclusion

Many liberal intellectuals assume that talk of black culture is mainly rhetorical. They arrogantly demand that its spokesmen clearly define its content and function. Bennett Berger expressed this position well when he asserted that "once the radicals invoke the perspective and rhetoric of Black culture, they place themselves under the intellectual obligation to concern themselves with clarifying precisely *what* patterns of Negro culture they are affirming, *what* sources of institutional support for these patterns they see in Negro social organization, and *how* these patterns may be expected to provide the bases of 'racial pride' and 'ethnic identity' sufficient to motivate the Black masses to claim both their full rights as Americans *and* the nation's respect for their ethnicity."[51] The fallacy here is that the black intelligentsia is expected to provide a clear statement of what its culture is—something that American social scientists have not adequately accomplished for the society as a whole.

The concept of culture—as well-taught undergraduates should know—is very sticky and troubling. Much scholarly controversy and uncertainty surround its essential features. American culture is a most vague and amorphous reality; it simply cannot be pinned down as neatly and conveyed to us as graphically as the ethnographer can capture the culture of a tribal people. This may be partly because we are all caught up in it; more probably it reflects the diversity, the contradictions, and even the weakness of meaning systems and of

---

* The cultural movement also has a tendency to become an end in itself, detached from the overall political and economic problems of the black community. Thus a tension between cultural nationalism and a so-called political or revolutionary nationalism has been apparent for several years in black circles: its roots could probably be traced back much further. Some critics see individual and group culture building as a device for facilitating personal mobility and making peace with the society. A presumed compatibility with black capitalism is a theme of the Panther Party's attack on cultural nationalism.

central patterns in American life. As Harold Cruse has emphasized, it is the lack of ethnic unity, distinctiveness, and indigenous creativity in the white American heritage that has made our society so receptive to and needful of the cultural contributions of black people.[52] It is indeed an irony that the cultural stream within American life whose reality and legitimacy are most systematically denied is its single most vigorous ethnic tradition.[53]

Despite the variety of meanings attached to black power, a common theme is that of self-definition. Self-definition implies that whites no longer can demand that blacks do this or that; Afro-Americans now select the time, place, and manner in which to reveal their plans and strategies outside the group. As a matter of fact, the project of cultural clarification that Berger calls for has been a constant preoccupation in the black experience; what is new today is that many whites are interested in the problem, and consequently a decision has been made to exclude them from the settings in which these complex issues are hammered out. In addition to all-black conferences and informal meetings, the major forums for the discussion of Afro-American ethnicity include Black Studies departments in universities and colleges and an increasing number of new magazines and journals.[54]

That whites are no longer calling the shots on these matters is the great and historic gain of two decades of black protest.* The white intellectual and social science communities are no longer the primary interpreters of black people and their culture. Yet while our academic theorizing is no longer as central as it once was, the black political and cultural movement still operates within those American conditions that we affect. For this reason, white social scientists have a responsibility to probe deeply into the assumptions and consequences of our characterizations of racial realities.

The demand that black spokesmen give us the lowdown once and for all on black culture so that we can define our attitude toward it overlooks a reality that is more profound than new "nationalist" rules for intergroup relations. It reflects a static approach to social and cultural reality. It assumes that Afro-American culture is "all there," or all-

---

* The black power mood, seen from this point of view, is not as total a departure from the previous civil rights activity as most people assume.

determined, needing only to be fully detected so that the chaff can be separated from the wheat. On the contrary, this culture, like all cultures, but today even more so, is *in process*. It is a dynamic, open-ended phenomenon, and that is why it is becoming such a central concern of the protest movement. On the basis of the culture that has already been built out of the experience of the (until recently relatively quiet) masses, a more self-conscious and explicit national culture is in the process of development. This requires the synthesis of the orientations of the predominantly lower-class ghetto dwellers with the articulations of the intellectual and political leaders, the middle classes, and the marginal people, who play a crucial part as cultural enunciators and systematizers.*

The opinion that black culture is only a lower-class life style and that Afro-Americans have no ethnic traditions to value and defend falls within a general concept that I call neoracism. Superficially the argument seems to be that blacks are as American as whites and therefore their cultural orientations reflect their social class position. But, as I have maintained in this essay, such an approach ignores the group-forming and culture-producing effects of racism; therefore, as an analytical position, it leads to the minimization of the reality of racial oppression. This position leads further to an overconcern with

---

* Thus the tendency of white scholars, such as Berger in the Keil review, to dismiss the activities of people like LeRoi Jones who celebrate blackness is misguided. Whether or not their every statement has been judicious and wise, these spokesmen have had an historic hand in the development of black culture. They know "where it's at"; they are there where the action is; and they influence this cultural action process because Afro-American culture is not a finished, determined, or static thing.

The same is true for the notion of Soul, which Berger felt was becoming a stereotype. This does not tell us anything about its present or future significance. The cultural reality of an affirmed trait is not in its statistical or scientific reality but in what it does and accomplishes as a rallying point and symbol. As we have come to know unhappily in less ambiguous race relations situations, stereotypes have living effects whatever the scientist may do to deflate them. The fate, function, and thus reality of Soul (like black power) remains to be revealed in the practical course of events. What Soul is and becomes is therefore a product, in part, of the conscious decisions and political-educational activities of the cultural leadership of the black community and, even more, of the response of its less articulate masses. Its fate will not be determined by white social analysts.

the pathological features of the black community at the expense of its unique strengths and contributions, since the culture of poverty is generally (and correctly) seen in terms of the predominance of suffering and the destruction of choice and of human possibilities. If Afro-American culture is only lower-class culture, then the questionable assumption that *all* black people want integration, mobility, and assimilation seems justifiable as a basis for institutional policy; it is therefore not necessary to consult, to offer alternative choices, or to respect individual diversity. Furthermore, this position is historically tied to past patterns of negating or appropriating the cultural possessions and productions of black people. The racist pattern was to destroy culture, to steal it for profit, or to view it contemptuously or with amusement. The neoracist equivalents today are to deny that culture exists or to envy and desire the values that blacks create and defend as their own. (Witness the pathetic need on the part of many young and not-so-young liberal and radical admirers of the Negro movement to feel that they, too, have Soul.)

The denial of Afro-American ethnicity is the more serious form that white appropriation takes today. Through abstract and intellectual analysis, the full implications of which are not always clearly perceived, the social scientist has attempted to undermine the claims of black Americans to a distinctive ethos and value system. The very existence of our possibility to so influence the cultural process is based on the original alienation of black people from their African traditions. Because colored Americans could use only the English language to carry on their business, their politics, and their intellectual life, their physical and moral communities became vulnerable to the penetration of white Americans, a penetration that other ethnic groups—insulated by exotic languages, religions, and other institutions—could escape. Thus, the original stripping and the subsequent appropriation of indigenous black culture opened up the Negro community to economic and political colonialism, to the contamination of group ideology by alien, pride-destroying perspectives, and to the participation of paternalistic whites in racial movements.

It is time for social scientists to insist that there are no exceptions to the anthropological law that every group has a culture: if black Americans are an ethnic group then they possess an ethnic culture; and just as the Jews explain to the world what Jewish culture is about and Italians define Italian-American culture, we will learn

what Afro-American culture is from American blacks—when they are
ready to tell us—rather than from our own dogmas and fantasies.

NOTES

1. On the concept of cultural revitalization, see Anthony F. C.
   Wallace, "Revitalization Movements," *American Anthropologist,*
   58, no. 2 (April 1956), 264–281.
2. Gunnar Myrdal, *An American Dilemma* (New York: Harper &
   Row, 1944).
3. *Ibid.,* pp. 927–930.
4. Nathan Glazer and Daniel P. Moynihan, *Beyond the Melting Pot*
   (Cambridge: M.I.T. and Harvard University Press, 1963), p. 53.
   Glazer, it is true, views Negroes as an ethnic group rather than
   simply a racial category. But for him the contents of black
   ethnicity are only common interests and social problems. His
   account of black New York ignores the existence of a collective
   ethos, community social structure, and group institutions.
5. M. Herskovits, *The Myth of the Negro Past* (New York: Harper & Row, 1941).
6. E. Franklin Frazier, *The Negro in the United States,* rev. ed.
   (New York: Macmillan, 1957), pp. 680–681. For a later statement, see Frazier, *The Negro Church in America* (New York:
   Schocken, 1964), chap. 1.
7. For example, Charles S. Johnson, *Shadow of the Plantation* (Chicago: University of Chicago Press, 1934); St. Clair Drake and
   Horace Cayton, *Black Metropolis* (New York: Harcourt Brace
   Jovanovich, 1945); and Hylan Lewis, *Blackways of Kent* (Chapel
   Hill: University of North Carolina Press, 1955). The distinctive
   culture of Harlem is emphasized in the writings of James Baldwin,
   and in Claude Brown, *Manchild in the Promised Land* (New
   York: Macmillan, 1956), though not in the scholarly study of
   Kenneth Clark, *Dark Ghetto* (New York: Harper & Row, 1965).
8. Charles Keil, *Urban Blues* (Chicago: University of Chicago Press,
   1966), p. 170.
9. Bennett M. Berger, "Soul Searching," *Trans-Action* (June 1967),
   54–57. This review also appears under the title of "Black Culture
   or Lower-Class Culture" in Lee Rainwater, ed., *Soul* (Chicago:

Trans-Action Books, Aldine, 1970), along with an earlier version of the present essay.

10. Kenneth Stampp, *The Peculiar Institution* (New York: Random House, 1956), p. vii.

11. Janheinz Jahn, *Muntu* (New York: Grove, n.d.), p. 225.

12. Howard Brotz, *The Black Jews of Harlem* (New York: The Free Press, 1964), pp. 129–130.

13. One of the most comprehensive studies of the Eastern European heritage of American Jews was written explicitly in terms of the anthropologist's view of culture. See Mark Zborowski and Elizabeth Herzog, *Life Is with People* (New York: International Universities, 1952), with an introduction by Margaret Mead.

14. Will Herberg, *Protestant-Catholic-Jew* (Garden City, N.Y.: Doubleday, 1956).

15. L. Singer, "Ethno-genesis and Negro Americans Today," *Social Research*, 29, no. 4 (Winter 1962), 419–432.

16. It appears likely that new social forms first emerged on the slave ships. At least in Jamaica scholars have noted that shipmates of the same voyage developed a particular bond and social status that was recognized on the plantations. M. G. Smith, *The Plural Society in the British West Indies* (Berkeley and Los Angeles: University of California Press, 1965), p. 107; and Orlando Patterson, *The Sociology of Slavery* (London: MacGibbon & Kee, 1967), p. 150.

17. Jahn, *op. cit.*, pp. 18–19.

18. Melvin B. Tolson, *Harlem Gallery* (New York: Twayne, 1965), pp. 75 and 94.

19. On African philosophy and aesthetics, see Placide Tempels, *Bantu Philosophy* (Paris: Présence Africaine, 1959); and Jahn, *op. cit.*, as well as the considerable literature on *négritude*. These findings can be compared with the discussions of Soul and Afro-American aesthetics in LeRoi Jones, *Blues People* (New York: Morrow, 1963); Keil, *op. cit.*, and Vernon J. Dixon and Badi Foster, eds., *Beyond Black or White* (Boston: Little, Brown, 1970), esp. chaps. 2 and 4. For another approach to African culture, see W. E. Abraham, *The Mind of Africa* (Chicago: Phoenix, 1966).

20. Arnold J. Toynbee, *A Study of History*, vol. 1 (London: Oxford University Press, 1934), pp. 429–430. His discussion converges with Herskovits' observation that "Africanisms" in religious be-

liefs were stronger than those in the sphere of economics and politics; it also suggests a new light on the Black Panther slogan, attributed to Huey Newton, that "the spirit of the people is greater than the man's technology."

21. On the African bases of Afro-American culture, the most comprehensive scholarship has taken place in the area of music. See LeRoi Jones, *op. cit.*; Paul Oliver, *Savannah Syncopators: African Retentions in the Blues* (New York: Stein & Day, 1970); Gunther Schuller, *Early Jazz: Its Roots and Musical Development* (New York: Oxford University Press, 1968), chap. 1; Richard A. Waterman, "African Influence on the Music of the Americas," in Sol Tax, ed., *Acculturation in the Americas* (Chicago: University of Chicago Press, 1952); Ralph H. Metcalfe, Jr., "The Western African Roots of Afro-American Music," *Black Scholar,* 1 (June 1970), 16–25; Lawrence W. Levine, "Slave Songs and Slave Consciousness: An Exploration in Neglected Sources," in Tamara Hareven, ed., *Anonymous Americans* (Englewood Cliffs, N.J.: Prentice-Hall, 1971), pp. 99–130; Alan Lomax, "The Homogeneity of African-Afro-American Musical Style," in Norman E. Whitten, Jr. and John F. Szwed, eds., *Afro-American Anthropology* (New York: The Free Press, 1970), pp. 181–201; and John F. Szwed, "Afro-American Musical Adaptation," in Whitten and Szwed, *Ibid.,* pp. 219–228.

On language and folklore, see J. L. Dillard, "Non-standard Negro Dialects: Convergence or Divergence," in Whitten and Szwed, *Ibid.,* pp. 119–127; Raven I. McDavid, Jr. and Virginia Glenn McDavid, "The Relationship of the Speech of American Negroes to the Speech of Whites," *American Speech, 26* (February 1951), 3–17; William A. Stewart, *Non-Standard Speech and the Teaching of English* (Washington: Center for Applied Linguistics, 1964); Richard A. Waterman and William R. Bascom, "African and New World Negro Folklore," Maria Leach, ed., *Standard Dictionary of Folklore, Mythology and Legend,* vol. 1 (New York: Funk & Wagnalls, 1949), pp. 18–24; and Daniel J. Crowley, "Negro Folklore: An Africanist's View," *Texas Quarterly, 5* (Autumn 1962), 65–71. Aside from the question of African roots, the literature on black English is enormous. An exemplary case of research and interpretation is William Labov's "The Logic of Non-Standard English," in Alfred C. Aarons, Barbara Y.

Gordon, and William A. Stewart, eds., "Linguistic-Cultural Differences and American Education," in the *Florida FL Reporter*, 7 (Spring, Summer 1969), 60–74, 169.

22. Toynbee, *op. cit.*
23. William H. McNeill, *The Rise of the West: A History of the Human Community* (Chicago: University of Chicago Press, 1963).
24. Thomas Hodgkin, *Nationalism in Colonial Africa* (London: Frederick Muller, 1956), esp. pp. 172–177. The author notes that until recently the view prevailed "that any remarkable work of art or architecture discovered in Africa south of the Sahara must have been produced by non-Africans—Arabs, perhaps, probably Portuguese—since Africans were by definition incapable of this level of achievement. This was the only way in which Europeans could account for the sculptures of Ife and Benin, the castles of Gondar, the fortifications of Zimbabwe, without disturbing their preconceptions."
25. Gilberto Freyre, *The Masters and the Slaves* (New York: Knopf, 1968).
26. See Harold Isaacs, *The New World of Negro Americans* (New York: Viking, 1964), pt. 3, pp. 105–322, for an excellent treatment of attitudes toward Africa.
27. Leslie W. Dunbar, "The Changing Mind of the South," in Avery Leiserson, ed., *The American South in the 1960's* (New York: Praeger, 1966), p. 4. "Only Lillian Smith had the greatness to wrestle with what the others saw, but passed by, and that was the centrality of race to the southern self-consciousness."
28. Interview with Ralph Ellison, in Robert Penn Warren, *Who Speaks for the Negro?* (New York: Random House, 1965), pp. 334–336. See also the stimulating and surprisingly neglected collection of essays by Calvin Hernton, *White Papers for White Americans* (Garden City, N.Y.: Doubleday, 1965). In his *Manchild in the Promised Land*, Claude Brown emphasizes the cultural conflict between the traditional "down home" (Southern) older generation and their more modern urban-oriented Harlem offspring. As a youth, Brown was sent South for a year to live with relatives; this is a fairly common pattern among American blacks. For another instance, see Henry Williamson, *Hustler!* R. L. Keiser, ed. (Garden City, N.Y.: Doubleday, 1965).

29. Ellison, *op. cit.*

30. See Stampp, *op. cit.*, for historical evidence on this point.

31. Norman Podhoretz, "My Negro Problem—And Ours," in Bernard E. Segal, ed., *Racial and Ethnic Relations* (New York: Crowell, 1966), p. 250.

32. Ernest Gaines's recent novel, *The Autobiography of Miss Jane Pittman* (New York: Dial, 1971), gives an excellent sense of this movement.

33. On the long-term function of the immigrant ghetto, see Oscar Handlin, *The Uprooted* (Boston: Little, Brown, 1951). For the vibrancy of cultural development in the Jewish ghetto, see Hutchins Hapgood, *The Spirit of the Ghetto* (New York: Funk & Wagnalls, 1902).

34. For historical accounts of the development of ethnic institutions and associations in the two largest Northern black communities, see Gilbert Osofsky, *Harlem: The Making of a Ghetto* (New York: Harper & Row, 1965), and Allan H. Spear, *Black Chicago* (Chicago: University of Chicago Press, 1967). A more detailed analysis of cultural developments in Harlem in the twentieth century is found in Harold Cruse, *The Crisis of the Negro Intellectual* (New York: Morrow, 1967).

35. The most recent and influential statement (actually a perversion) of this position is Edward Banfield's *The Unheavenly City* (Boston: Little, Brown, 1970), which defines social class in terms of values related to achievement and planning, rather than seeing subcultural orientations as a consequence of objective economic and social circumstances. The latter, more usual treatment is argued by Elliot Liebow in his valuable study of streetcorner men in Washington, D.C., *Tally's Corner* (Boston: Little, Brown, 1967). Liebow argues explicitly that cultural traditions have little relevance in this community. For a criticism of his book on this score see Douglas Davidson, "Black Culture and Liberal Sociology," *Berkeley Journal of Sociology, 14* (1969), 164–183.

36. Berger, *op. cit.*, p. 56.

37. Among the many examples that might be cited are Claude Brown, *op. cit.*; *The Autobiography of Malcolm X* (New York: Grove, 1965); Iceberg Slim, *Pimp, The Story of My Life* (Los Angeles: Holloway, 1969); and Leonard H. Robinson, "Negro Street So-

ciety: A Study of Racial Adjustment in Two Southern Urban Communities," Doctoral dissertation, Department of Sociology, Ohio State University (1950).

38. Johnneta B. Cole identifies style and soul as the most consistent and important themes in black American life. "Culture: Negro, Black and Nigger," *Black Scholar,* 1 (June 1970), 40–44.

39. Hortense Powdermaker, *After Freedom* (New York: Viking, 1939), pp. 259–260.

40. Fortunately a new generation of black social analysts has begun to address these issues, combining firsthand research and the black experiential perspective that is missing in the studies of white scholars. Joyce A. Ladner's *Tomorrow's Tomorrow* (Garden City, N. Y.: Doubleday, 1971) is a thorough and sensitive account of a group of adolescents involved in the process of becoming women; in addition, she provides a new framework for understanding the position of black women in a racist society and corrects many distorted ideas about Afro-American family dynamics. Two further studies of black women by Robert Staples and Lois Benjamin, respectively, still unpublished as this book goes to press, promise to be important contributions. See also the issues of *Black Scholar* devoted to the black male, 2 (June 1971), and the black woman, 3 (December 1971).

41. Stampp, *op. cit.,* esp. chaps. 3, 4, and 8; and Samuel Strong, "Social Types in the Negro Community of Chicago: An Example of Social Type Method," Doctoral dissertation, Department of Sociology, University of Chicago (1940).

42. Robert S. Starobin, "Racism and the American Experience," *Radical America,* 5 (March–April 1971), 93–110.

43. Ellison, *op. cit.,* p. 338. See also his *Shadow and Act* (New York: Random House, 1964). A brilliant analysis of this process of cultural imperialism informs Cruse, *op. cit.*

44. See his perceptive book, *The Black Jews of Harlem, op. cit.,* esp. chap. 4.

45. James Baldwin, *Notes of a Native Son* (Boston: Beacon, 1955); William M. Kelley, *A Different Drummer* (Garden City, N.Y.: Doubleday, 1962).

46. Keil, *op. cit.,* p. 152.

47. The historian Lawrence Levine has found many examples of this in his studies of black songs. See "The Concept of the New

Negro and the Realities of Black Culture," in N. Huggins, M. Kilson, and D. Fox, eds., *Key Issues in the Afro-American Experience* (New York: Harcourt Brace Jovanovich, 1971), pp. 125–147.

48. Oscar Lewis, *La Vida* (New York: Random House, 1967), pp. xlvii–xlviii.

49. For an historical interpretation of the Harlem renaissance and an evaluation of its artistic achievements, as well as some reflections on the relation of black culture and writing to the American context, see Nathan I. Huggins, *Harlem Renaissance* (New York: Oxford University Press, 1971).

50. On the middle-class rejection of black ethnicity, see LeRoi Jones, *op. cit.*; E. F. Frazier, *Black Bourgeoisie* (New York: The Free Press, 1957); and Nathan Hare, *The Black Anglo-Saxons* (New York: Marzani, 1965).

51. Berger, *op. cit.*, p. 54.

52. Cruse, *op. cit.*

53. There is a broad consensus on the assessment of Paul Oliver: ". . . the whole field of Afro-American music may well be considered the one indigenous gift of the modern Americas to the world's art." *The Meaning of the Blues* (New York: Collier, 1963), p. 332.

54. For example: *Black Scholar*, *Black Review* (formerly *Negro Digest*); *Amistad*; *Journal of Black Studies*; *Black Academy Review*; to mention only a few.

chapter 5
chicano
writing*

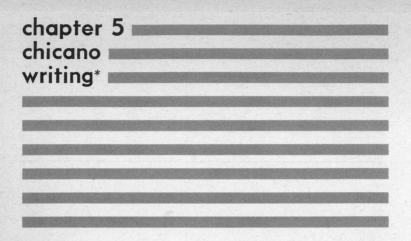

White America seems to have discovered the Mexican-American people in the last few years. On the rebound after a bad experience with the black movement, rejected liberals have needed new causes to espouse, other oppressed peoples to relate to. The great strike of California farm workers provided one such opportunity, and along with Tijerina's land-grant campaign in New Mexico, the Chavez-led struggle has inspired a raft of journalistic interpretations. Publishers are also bringing out more general books on Mexican themes: sociological analyses, documentary histories, readers and anthologies. In California and the Southwest higher education has acknowledged the Chicano presence in ethnic studies programs and admissions policies. Even the Nixon administration is moving in this direction. In a transparent maneuver to further divide the nation's racial minorities, it has announced a decision to deemphasize black problems and to focus on Mexican-Americans, along with Indians and Puerto Ricans. Does this mean we are about to see a new ethnic literature emerge as the brown power and Chicano movements gain prominence in America?

The Psychic Economy of Supply and Demand
There is a common belief—to a great extent misleading—that Chicanos have been following in the footsteps of the black movement, though

* An earlier version of this essay appeared as "The Chicano Sensibility," in *Trans-Action*, 8, no. 4 (February 1971), 51–58. Copyright © February 1971 by Transaction, Inc., New Brunswick, N.J.

perhaps ten years behind. By this logic we would expect an outpouring of Mexican-American essayists, novelists, memoirists, and political commentators to hit the bookstores and interpret for us their group experience much as Baldwin, Ellison, Brown, Bennett, Malcolm, and a host of others have done for the Afro-Americans. A brief consideration of the market for brown writers as compared to blacks, from the point of view of both supply and demand, raises some doubts about this analogy.

Diversified as is the Mexican-American population, the generalization may be advanced that Chicanos tend to relate differently from blacks to the larger white society and to Anglo culture. A prevailing attitude toward Anglo society and its cultural domination has been indifference. This may be why few Chicano intellectuals and writers have been interested in interpreting their ethnic experience to us white Americans. For several centuries there have been blacks who were inspired to plead their case before the forum of public opinion, somehow maintaining a kernel of optimism and residual belief in the fundamental good will of at least a minority of whites. This optimism and hope for racial justice may be on its way out among the Afro-American cultural elite and the younger generation. Yet it still retains a strong hold on many people. It appears that Mexicans in the United States have rarely held such illusions about our vaunted democratic system.* Of course, many individual Mexican-Americans have struggled to make it economically, even disappearing socially and culturally into the Anglo middle-class mainstream. Yet Chicano intellectuals and working people had been living their version of cultural nationalism long before black militants brought the term to public attention a few years ago. Therefore we must be skeptical about the idea that the brown political dynamic is re-creating the black's—the similarity of Brown Beret dress and rhetoric to the Black Panthers' notwithstanding. For the historical and sociocultural context of Mexican-American life has been unique—it cannot be fitted into the pattern of black-white relations, nor to the model of European ethnic group immigration, for that matter.

The shortage of Chicano spokesmen and interpreters is not a

---

* The immigrants interviewed by Manuel Gamio during the 1920s were striking in their loyalty to Mexico and in their critical attitude toward U.S. cultural values and treatment of Mexicans. An aversion to the idea of U.S. citizenship was almost universal.[1]

matter of paucity of talent or absence of literary and political consciousness. Certainly discrimination and racism, particularly in the
schools, have reduced the size of La Raza's cultural and intellectual
elites. But Mexican-American writers (and ordinary folk) express
themselves either in Spanish or a distinctive ethnic amalgam of English
and Spanish. For good reasons that will be discussed later, they do not
embrace English as willingly and totally as European ethnics—and
Asian-Americans—appear to have done. With a strong aversion to the
cultural values of Anglo-American society, Mexican-American writers
have looked in the direction of Mexico for their audiences and their
careers. Would they have done so anyway even if there had been a
domestic market for brown writers? There may be no way to know.*

  Certain mundane facts explain in part the demand side of the
equation, that is, the greater potential readership for black writers that
I infer. The Afro-American population may be between two and three
times as large as the combined Mexican- and Latin-American groups.
Thus there is a larger audience within the minority sector itself. Geographical distribution may be another factor. Chicanos are concentrated in the West and Southwest; blacks are in all parts of the
country. So one might argue that blacks and black power are issues
of national concern and national significance, while browns and
brown power are only regional matters. Plausible enough, especially
when one adds an additional point, the difference in style of protest.
Blacks have been dramatic, confronting the power structure head on,
calling names, serving ultimata, seizing buildings, burning ghettos.
Chicanos appear to have mounted their protests more quietly; the
Delano strike persisted for years. Chavez can maintain his commitment to nonviolence and still remain a hero for brown youth. Yet
there is Tijerina and the many Chicano student groups who have had

  * Another explanation for the short supply of writers has been
offered by Edward Simmen in introducing an interesting collection of short
stories about Mexican-Americans.[2] Simmen presents an oversimplified class
argument: the masses of the poor were illiterate and thus not equipped to
write; the small educated upper classes were inclined in other directions;
and the assimilation-oriented middle classes tended to give up the ethnic
heritage that would-be writers might have built upon. The problem here is
that the same statements could be made about every ethnic or racial
minority; Simmen doesn't seem to realize that literature is written by
talented individuals and not by classes. The question remains, why did not
a small déclassé group of writers emerge?

confrontations as militant as any—styles of protest are created as much by the media, who have chosen to focus their lenses on the black presence, proportionately deemphasizing the brown, the red, the yellow, and the poor white.

There is something here for the still little-understood psychology of racism. We buy black writers, not only because they can write and have something to say, but because the white racial mind is obsessed with blackness. Ellison's phrase "invisible men" can be somewhat misleading. In the American racist dynamic the black man has been unseen as a person, his individuality lost in the distorted, fantasied conceptions we hold of the group as a whole. But blacks as a collective presence have never been invisible nor inconsequential to American institutions and white psyches. Mexican-Americans, on the other hand, have been unseen as individuals and as a group. How else would you explain the fact that in California and other Western states where Mexican-Americans have long outnumbered Afro-Americans, the racially conscious white has been much more attuned to black than to brown people? This is as true for those committed to ending racial injustice as it is for those who strive to keep people of color "in their place," probably even more true.*

James Baldwin has pointed to the deep mutual involvement of black and white in America. The profound ambivalence, the love–hate relationship, which Baldwin's own work expresses and dissects, does not exist in the racism that comes down on La Raza, nor in the Chicano stance toward the Anglo and his society. Even the racial stereotypes that plague Mexican-Americans tend to lack those positive

* This tendency may be weaker in Texas, where anti-Mexican prejudice has been particularly vicious, and in New Mexico where Mexican-Americans retained a numerical majority until well into the twentieth century. Yet recent students at the University of New Mexico inform me that they have observed this phenomenon in the white movement there. It is no accident that the two major studies of Mexican-Americans written by Chicanos up to 1970 bear the title and subtitle, respectively: *Forgotten People* and *Forgotten Americans.*[3]

Joan Moore remarks, "Of the half-dozen texts on minorities on my shelf only one contains more than a paragraph on Mexican-Americans."[4] In an otherwise first-rate introduction to a valuable collection of articles, *White Racism,* the authors characteristically focus on black oppression. Indian policy is discussed for several pages, the internment of Japanese-Americans is mentioned, but the Mexican War and the Chicano people are simply omitted.[5]

attributes that mark antiblack fantasies—supersexuality, inborn athletic and musical power, natural rhythm. Mexicans are dirty, lazy, treacherous, thieving bandits—and revolutionaries. Perhaps only the relaxed mañana—siesta image veils a protest against the harried pace of North American life.

It has been less than a century and a quarter since the United States conquered Mexico, incorporating half its territory, and colonizing the Spanish-speaking, brown-skinned inhabitants who were accorded a nominal citizenship status. In this time, so relatively short compared with our historical encounters with Native Americans and blacks, Anglo and Chicano have lived apart—physically, linguistically, socially, and morally. The two peoples inhabit social and cultural worlds that in some ways are further apart than the distance between ghetto and suburb.[6] Even informed Anglos know almost nothing about La Raza, its historical experience, its present situation, its collective moods. And the average citizen doesn't have the foggiest notion that Chicanos have been lynched in the Southwest and continue to be abused by the police, that an entire population has been exploited economically, dominated politically, and raped culturally. In spite of the racism that attempts to wipe out or, failing that, distort and trivialize the history and culture of the colonized, both expert and man in the street are far more aware of the past and present oppression suffered by blacks.

Mexican-Americans have responded to racist depreciation by calling on the reserve and privacy that appear to be central to the ethos of La Raza. Thus sociologists doing research, like myself, have found that it is much more difficult to get "good interviews" in the barrios than in the black communities—even with Chicano interviewers.* Chicano writers—and would-be writers—have apparently responded in the same way, so that it has been extremely difficult for Anglos to get a sense of the brown experience as lived, felt, and interpreted by Mexican-Americans. All this suggests why we need Chicano writing desperately, why we are unlikely to get as much as

* This reluctance to cooperate with Anglo investigators is at least a hundred years old. The pioneer historian of California and the West, H. H. Bancroft, reported that he and his research assistants were plagued by the "feeble memories," "lack of time," "evasion and lies," and outright refusal to be interviewed on the part of many of the leading Californios they sought as informants.[7]

we could profitably learn from, and why the publications I discuss in this essay are so important.

El Espejo and El Grito

If you are interested in the best contemporary writing by Chicano authors, I suggest you order *El Espejo—The Mirror*, an anthology of selected Mexican-American literature edited by Octavio I. Romano-V, and subscribe to *El Grito*, the quarterly magazine in which a number of the anthologized pieces originally appeared.[8] Both are firsts of their kind: when originally published there were no other journals of Mexican-American culture and thought, nor any other collections of Chicano literature.[9]

The complexity and diversity of the Mexican-American experience is better revealed in *El Espejo* than in any other volume that I know. The poetry, short stories, and essays of its eleven contributors touch on the many facets of past and present history that have created the Chicano—the Indian heritage, the landscape of Mexico and the Southwest, the revolutions and their betrayals, and the flight northwards to migrant camps, urban barrios, and the racist institutions of Anglo society.* Yet *El Espejo* is not proletarian, nor even sociological, literature. Its writers are modern, often avant-garde; the sensibility of the imagination is rarely subordinated to political polemic or sociological point making. *El Espejo* is a collection of first-order talents, which should be read to discover the richness of literature that Chicano writers are creating; the insights into Mexican-American culture are additional, fringe benefits for the citizen and social scientist.

In addition to poetry and prose, *El Grito* publishes journalistic and academic treatments of political and sociological issues, as well as portfolios of Mexican-American artists.[11] The journal is distinguished in design and format, and is inspired by a boldness often approaching sardonic bitterness in defense of the interests of La Raza. The Fall 1969 number, for example, recorded in full the excerpts from the court of San Jose Judge Gerald Chargin. The transcript of four pages—which includes such honorable remarks as "Mexican people, after 13 years of age, it's perfectly alright to go out, and act like an

---

* Only one other work I know of similarly captures the multifaceted dimensionality of the Chicano experience: the powerful poem *I am Joaquín* by Rodolfo (Corky) Gonzales.[10]

animal," "We ought to send you out of the country—send you back to Mexico. . . . You are lower than animals and haven't the right to live in organized society—just miserable, lousy, rotten people"—is begun on page 4, then continued on page 32. Sandwiched in between are 26 pages listing Vietnam War Dead with Spanish Surnames.

Both publications are bilingual: some material appears in Spanish, some in English; sometimes the same story is printed twice, once in translation. Much of the poetry and prose is written in that mix of English and Spanish that is the mode of thought and discourse for many contemporary Chicanos.[12] Here is a sample excerpt from Alurista's *tarde sobria*:

> the man
>> he doesn't know my raza is old
> on the streets he frisks me
>> on the job he kills al jefe
>> en la tienda no atiende a mi mamá
> the man
>> he says he wanna marry mi carnala
> hell no!
>> ella es mujer, no juguete
> the man
>> he likes to play
>> he got a lot o' toys
> and he doesn't know
>> que las tardes que me alumbran
> y las nubes que me visten
>> pertenecen a mi raza
>> a mi barrio*

A story by Nick Vaca, "The Week of the Life of Manuel Hernandez," may be read as a parable of anglicization and alienation. The narrator sketches his life course through the vehicle of diary entries over a period of years. In the opening segment he thinks and writes in Spanish (or Chicano) as much as, or more than, English; from the final entries the mother tongue has disappeared; what remains is a professor caught up in the professional rat race,

* Reprinted by permission of Octavio Romano-V, editor, *El Espejo*, Quinto Sol, Publications.

yet overwhelmed with feelings of nausea for the whole enterprise. (The cultural conflict between Anglo and Mexican values is a theme that runs through *El Espejo*, the poems of Ponce and Montoya are especially effective in their poignant evocation of the technological, commercial, plastic quality of our human arrangements.) Vaca is at his best in "The Visit," a short story that illustrates the never-ending possibilities of the father and son theme. Ralph's father, Don Pedro, was a Man of the Revolution, living in a rusted trailer near Tracy, more or less abandoned by all of his children except the protagonist. The precise part that Don Pedro had played in the Revolution had always mystified his son. The visit to the old man shatters some of Ralph's paternal idealizations and betrays the fragility of his own self-righteous filial sentiments. Like most successful works, this story can be read on several levels. It is a sensitively drawn account of father and son searching for an intimacy they cannot reach; something is being said also about the meaning of the revolutionary past for a whole generation of Chicano youth, a something too subtle for this reviewer to penetrate.

The Revolution is another dominant theme in *El Espejo*, appearing explicitly in the contributions of Villavicencio, Romano, and Velez. As editor Romano points out in "Goodby Revolution— Hello Slum," the Revolution stamped the character of modern Mexico:

> As in all warfare, the Mexican Revolution taught individual Mexicans to fear themselves, especially peasants who for too long had known only how to fear others unlike themselves. As the historical event unfolds around them they personally experience what they can do to others as well as to each other. Such is the human condition, especially the human revolutionary condition. As each individual protagonist comes to realize, or feel, that he fears himself, then at that moment in red time, he knows that he must fear others who are also like him. Inevitably, as the revolution progressed, the day came when everyone in the land feared everyone else. On that day, Mexico was born.

It may indeed be that the Revolution as a group-creating event had an even greater impact on the Mexican-American, for the upheavals, political, social, and economic, of the two decades after 1910 brought about the largest wave of northward migration. Today's

young and middle-aged Chicanos are the grandchildren and children
of revolutionaries, counterrevolutionaries, pretended or would-be
revolutionaries, or those simply uprooted by war and devastation.[13]
In a seminal article that does not appear in *El Espejo*, Romano elab-
orates the centrality of 1910 for Mexican-American culture. He
identifies Indianism, historical confrontation, and Mestizo-based cultural nationalism, as the three dominant legacies of the Revolution that
have molded the heterogeneous Chicano population.[14] For the Anglo,
Romano's article is probably the best guide to an understanding of the
bewildering multilayered character of the Mexican-American experience—and to an intelligent reading of *El Espejo*, from whose pages
these many currents rush forth.

    El Espejo takes its title from the opening short story. Yet the
image of the mirror appears throughout the book. As I interpret it,
the symbolism suggests that Chicanos have been unable to view themselves and their culture directly. In their search for group realities,
Mexican-Americans are caught between the images of the past and
their present reflections in the distorted lens of Anglo culture and
racial oppression. Besides revolution, the past includes the Indian
heritage—the invocation of Aztec and other Indian gods and chieftains
appears in the work of each of *El Espejo*'s poets, Ponce, Alurista,
Montoya, and Estupinián. In "Tata Casehua" by Miguel Méndez an
historic Yaqui king is brought to life in a parable of the Sonora desert
and its landscape—Méndez's fable struck me as the most brilliant confrontation with Indianism in the volume. (Another theme uniting the
writers is a feeling, almost a reverence, for the land and sky of the
Mexican Southwest;* they virtually slap on gobs of color to create
stark and intense painted images. The national colors of Mexico take
on new shades of meaning. Green invokes the forests and the brush;
red is for the desert terrain, and also for the blood spilled in the Revolution; but for the white that should fill out the banner, black is substituted to convey night, storm clouds, and the despotism that has
dashed a people's hopes.) But to return to the mirror—the image is
also a concrete one: the looking glass, in reflecting back the Chicano's

---

    * Elizabeth Martinez remarks that this feeling for the land is the
most difficult idea "for the urban middle-class white liberal intellectual to
grasp." "The land is our mother. It cannot be bought or sold. Without it,
we perish!" "This idea is believed, felt and lived by thousands of Raza
people."[15]

countenance, reveals or reminds him of the historic creation of his race. In this sense the mirror symbolizes a project for the present and future: that of awakening a consciousness of history and culture. One thinks of Stephen Daedalus. As the editor explains in a preface of only three sentences: "To know themselves and who they are, there are those who need no reflection other than their own. Thus . . . *EL ESPEJO—THE MIRROR.*"

The new Chicano writes with a powerful impact, even more so since directness of feeling is circumscribed by all the forms of modernism. It is difficult to summarize the overall emotional tone—were I forced to settle on one feeling tone, I would say that the beauty of the literature is suffused with a *profound grief.* In Alurista's *grietas paredes* (cracked walls) La Raza grieves for the past that is lost, the homeland forsaken, the ancestors betrayed, the promises of the Revolution. Unlike Afro-American forms such as the blues, there is little blending of optimism in this pervasive sense of bereavement; the reader is left depressed. Instead the contrapuntal emotion appears to be bitterness. For many of us the Chicano's bitterness may be uncomfortably brittle; in *El Espejo* it is unalloyed and only highlighted by the discipline of the writing. There is also much contempt, expressed and intimated, for the Anglo and our ways: our ignorance and insensitivity, the shallowness of our culture. But whereas the white man's impact is not denied, he is generally seen as not sufficiently central to be worthy of the basic grief.

Although *El Espejo* and *El Grito* are the collective products of a cultural movement, in another sense they are the personal projects of Octavio Romano. Holding a Ph.D. degree in anthropology and on the faculty of Berkeley's School of Public Health, Romano is very much a man of letters, a writer of considerable talent. This combination, so unlikely among Anglo social scientists, appears also in short-story writer Nick Vaca and the poet Miguel Ponce, who are graduate students in sociology and criminology, respectively.* For *El Espejo,* Romano has provided magnificent English translations of Villavicencio and Méndez, as well as a literary gem of his own, "A Rosary." One of the most remarkable pieces in the book is his "Mosaico Mexicano," which captures the ethos of a South Texas village through fragments of conversation, popular sayings, ballads, and the writer's own poetry.

* Vaca has recently joined the faculty of the University of California, Santa Cruz.

The result is a sense of the people, their community and their concerns, not unlike *Spoon River* or *Under Milkwood*. One difference is that Romano's literary building blocks are the data of social science investigation: the fieldwork notes from his own observations and interviews as an anthropologist doing dissertation research! The fidelity to the dignity and spirit of the culture of this form over the arid, abstract generalizing of the sociologist is an unstated moral of "Mosaico Mexicano."

Cultural Imperialism in Social Research

The quarterly journal *El Grito*, which began publishing in 1967, emerged from the work of a circle of Chicano intellectuals based in Berkeley. The first products of the group were a number of position pieces called the *Quinto Sol Liberation Papers*. The general situation that impelled Quinto Sol to act was the virtual Anglo monopoly of social science studies and characterizations of Mexican-Americans, and the consequent distortion—sometimes subtle, sometimes not so subtle—that accompanies this academic colonialism. *El Grito*'s maiden issue contained Romano's initial exposure of the traditional stereotypes lurking behind the social scientists' conceptions of the Mexican-American personality: "fatalistic, resigned, apathetic, tradition-oriented, tradition bound, emotional, impetuous, volatile, affective, non-goal oriented, uncivilized, unacculturated, non-rational, primitive, irrational, unorganized, uncompetitive, retarded, slow learners, underachieving, underdeveloped, or just plain lazy. In using words as these to describe other people, they thereby place the reasons or causes of 'inferior' status *somewhere in their minds, within the personalities, or within the culture* of those who are economically, politically, or educationally out of power."[16] A year later Romano continued his attack, subjecting most influential monographs in this field to detailed criticism.[17]

To a considerable extent, the black power and black culture movements also are directed against this kind of cultural imperialism. The legitimacy of white "experts" to interpret the historical experience and current realities of Afro-American life is in question, a tendency most dramatically expressed in reactions to Moynihan's report and Styron's novel.[18] In the social sciences, Chicanos have been subject even more systematically to interpretation in terms of white middle-class standards and ideologies; furthermore, they have lacked ethnic novelists and essayists who might counter the sociological wisdom. The tendency to exclude Mexican-Americans from the analysis of their own group problems boggles the imagination. Thus the Society for the Study of Social Problems had two panels on rural manpower at their 1969 meetings in San Francisco at which the Delano farm labor strike was a major focus. There was not one Mexican among the eight people who presented and discussed the papers.*

Aside from that of Indians, the study of the Mexican-American appears to be our most extreme expression of academic colonialism. The proportion of works written by Spanish-surnamed authors (who were not Mexican "nationals") was 18, 14, and 14 percent in three of the most recent and comprehensive bibliographies in this field. The three lists encompassed 235, 1541, and 1408 items by noninstitutional authors, and included published books and articles as well as government reports, hearings, and university dissertations.[20] Thus only *one publication in seven* about Mexican-American issues is written by a member of the group.**

Academic and research colonization of Afro-Americans has not been as total, perhaps due in part to the Negro colleges, which have trained a black intellectual elite, and in part to such movements as the Harlem renaissance, which have produced scores of ethnic writers. Thus Afro-Americans have authored many of the major studies of their own communities as well as studies of race relations in general. Approximately 35 percent of the books on racial themes listed in Myrdal's bibliography (1944) were authored by blacks. The white advantage was greatest for books published before 1930, when the black proportion was only 27 percent; for those published after 1930

---

* Commenting on the political and ethical problems faced by a large-scale study of Mexican-Americans, one of the principle investigators stated: "Like the Negroes, Mexican-Americans—and particularly their leaders—have been studied, surveyed, interviewed, and analyzed to their very considerable boredom and suspicion. The end result seems to be an inclination to deliver something of a set piece. . . . But experience has taught the Mexican-American leader that he may never see the results of his responses: there will probably be no books, magazine articles, noticeable reaction from governmental agencies or local projects having any real meaning."[19]

** Some indication of a possible change is suggested by an analysis of the books that have appeared since 1969, when the three bibliographies were assembled. Ten of the 23 new books I have located are authored by Mexican-Americans.

the percentages were essentially equal.[21] A count of Frazier's (1957) bibliography reveals that blacks authored almost as many books as whites (46 percent).[22] In a more recent and especially comprehensive bibliography (1966) black writers produced 33 percent of the studies where racial identification was possible. Interestingly enough, black-authored works outnumbered or equalled white-authored ones from 1930 to 1949 (confirming the findings from Myrdal); after 1950 white researchers overwhelmed blacks in the published literature.[23]*

The Chicano experience is full of paradoxes. Facing an awesome array of colonial service anthropologists masked as objective scholars, La Raza itself has not been colonized culturally to the extent that blacks and Native Americans have. Among the racial minorities represented on west coast campuses, Chicanos appear to have retained more of their original culture and community integrity than the others.[24] In the Third World Strike at Berkeley in 1969 it was frequently noted that Chicanos exhibited more solidarity than blacks and Asians (Indian students were too few to permit any comparison); in the classrooms also Chicano students seem especially "together." Perhaps it is obvious why Mexican-Americans have experienced less forced transformation of their social organization and group life than African-Americans and Native Americans have. In the first place, Mexican-Americans were conquered and colonized in their own territory, and they have remained physically and culturally attached to the Southwest despite new migration from Mexico and internal movement

* Once again, as with Mexican-American research, it is possible that this may be changing as a result of the third world movement's struggle against cultural imperialism and the new interest of academia and publishing in minority scholars. However, it illustrates the general tendency of whites to crowd out peoples of color from occupations and industries undergoing expansion and prosperity—as did the field of behavioral sciences research in the post-World War II period.

I have made no systematic analyses of the literature on other ethnic groups. It is obvious that research on Indians has been thoroughly dominated by whites—It is reported that only 50 Native Americans hold Ph.D. degrees, in all fields. It is my impression that Chinese- and Japanese-Americans have produced a significant proportion, perhaps half, of the rather scanty literature on Asians in the United States. Jews are the major example of the opposite tendency, for they have virtually monopolized the study of their own history and culture within the United States. It would be interesting to analyze this phenomenon for other European ethnic groups.

in the search for work and better living conditions.[25] They were not uprooted from their homeland and transported across the seas like the blacks, nor pushed across the continent in a 400-year drama of war and removal as were the Indians. And in the second place, because Chicanos are not really immigrants to this country, they do not cheerfully give up their native tongue as did the European ethnic groups and as Anglo schoolmasters expect them to do. Spanish preceded English as the language of the West and Southwest.* To Mexican-Americans forced anglicization in language is the final stage in the U.S. conquest of Mexico and its culture. Spanish is thus not only a medium of communication and expression: it is a central aspect of selfhood and group integrity. The lyricism and grace of the language in contrast with the more harsh and blunt qualities of English come to epitomize the overall cultural conflict between colonizer and colonized.

The encounter between Mexican-Americans and the United States is *sui generis*; it cannot be forced into the ethnic model of immigration-assimilation nor into the category of black-white relations. That is why Chicanos, painfully aware of their unique history, resent and resist being classified, interpreted, or "understood" through analogs with the Afro-American.** It is extremely difficult not to do this, because we do not know enough about Mexican-American society to discuss it on its own terms; in this essay I have several times approached the Chicano experience in the context of my own and the Anglo reader's greater familiarity with black realities. Of course, institutional racism, including the license to kill without sanction, has been the lot of all peoples of color in America. Our understanding and conception of racism, even expanding as it has been in recent years, has been built up almost exclusively from the materials of black oppression. The distinctive features of racism directed against yellow, red, brown, and Spanish-speaking have not been explored in a so-

* In *El Espejo*, a high school counselor tells the hero of a short story by Carlos Velez-I: "I just don't understand why you people are so insistent about speaking Spanish. You people should realize that it's not the American tongue."[26]

** "Many Mexican-Americans regard themselves as a unique group. Virtually any comparison, even rhetorical, with other ethnic groups, tended to threaten their self-esteem and security." Moore goes on to note that the leaders she worked with didn't like being linked with blacks.[27] Vine Deloria discusses a parallel sensitivity among Indians to being understood in terms of the black analog.[28]

ciety many of whose unconscious cultural assumptions and patterns of
thought polarize around the white-black axis.

Thus liberals and radicals alike in America tune in on the black
thing; the intermediary colors strike a weak chord. University departments and administrations make considerably greater efforts to hire
blacks than browns. Certainly the latter are in shorter supply, but
more important may be the psychic energy available for projects of
black inclusion, and the greater emotional payoff. A five-year campaign to increase the numbers of "low income minority" students at
the University of California's Berkeley campus has resulted in a
black-brown ratio of more than three to one (approximately one
thousand to three hundred).* The concentration on black problems is
a constant tendency of white-initiated conferences on minority groups;
in many cases it has led to boycotts, protests, or separate caucuses
among Chicano participants. The poverty program tells a related story.
In many cities Afro-Americans gained control early in the game, at
least on the community level. Spanish-speaking groups, excluded in
the action, were put in the position of fighting blacks in order to make
a dent in the dynamic of neglect and unconcern that is central to anti-
brown racism. Even the white left and the student movement in the
Bay Area have failed to embrace the campaigns of La Raza militants
as wholeheartedly as they took up the Black Panther cause.[30]

"Divide and rule" is, of course, an old trick, a technique made
to order for colonialism, which has not only exploited ethnic antagonisms but has actually "created" many of the races and peoples that
make up the plural society. There are many obstacles to an authentic
cultural pluralism, as well as to third world unity, within the United
States. But the furthering of group consciousness on the basis of historical and cultural uniqueness, so well formulated in *El Espejo* and

* This relative underrepresentation of Mexican-Americans is true
of other institutions committed to integration in recent years. An ethnic
survey of San Francisco's public schools in October 1970 revealed that only
3 percent of teachers and administrators were Spanish speaking—compared
with almost 14 percent of the students. Blacks were seriously underrepresented also but the 1 to 3 ratio between 28 percent of the pupils and
9 percent of the teachers and 8 percent of the administrators was smaller
than the corresponding Chicano-Latino ratio. Chinese underrepresentation
was about the same as for blacks, that of Filipinos (1 to 4) closer to the
Spanish-speaking. The total picture: 35 percent of the pupils were white
compared with 80 percent of the teachers and administrators.[29]

El Grito, can only serve to clarify the terms on which such developments in the future may emerge.

NOTES

1. Manuel Gamio, *The Mexican Immigrant: His Life Story* (Chicago: University of Chicago Press, 1931).
2. Edward Simmen, ed., *The Chicano: From Caricature to Self-Portrait* (New York: New American Library, 1971), pp. 24–25.
3. George I. Sanchez, *Forgotten People* (Albuquerque: University of New Mexico Press, 1940), and Julian Samora, ed., *La Raza: Forgotten Americans* (Notre Dame, Ind.: University of Notre Dame Press, 1966).
4. Joan W. Moore, "Political and Ethical Problems in a Large-Scale Study of a Minority Population," in Gideon Sjoberg, ed., *Ethics, Politics, and Social Research* (Cambridge: Schenkman, 1967), p. 227.
5. Barry N. Schwartz and Robert Disch, eds., *White Racism* (New York: Dell, 1970), pp. 1–66. The Chinese are also omitted, but unlike Mexican-Americans, this might be defensible on the grounds of numbers.
6. This point is emphasized by Elizabeth Martinez in her important rejoinder to Edgar Friedenberg. See "An Exchange on La Raza," *New York Review of Books* (February 12, 1970), 37. The original Friedenberg essay review of two books on the Chicano movement appeared in the December 18, 1969 issue of the same publication.
7. Leonard Pitt, *The Decline of the Californios* (Berkeley and Los Angeles: University of California Press, 1966 and 1970), pp. 280–281.
8. *El Espejo—The Mirror: Selected Mexican-American Literature,* ed. Octavio I. Romano-V (Berkeley: Quinto Sol Publications, 1969); *El Grito: A Journal of Contemporary Mexican-American Thought,* vols. 1–4 (1967–1971). An anthology of the best social science articles from this journal has recently appeared: *Voices: Selected Readings from El Grito,* ed. Octavio I. Romano-V (Berkeley: Quinto Sol Publications, 1971).
9. Since this chapter was originally written, a second cultural

journal has appeared: *Aztlán*, published at UCLA. Simmen's anthology of short stories, *The Chicano, op. cit.*, contains primarily Anglo writers.

10. R. Gonzales, *I Am Joaquin* (Denver: Crusade for Justice, 1964). The poem serves as the text for an impressive film, narrated and directed by Luis Valdez of the Teatro Campesino. It is available for showing in college classrooms.

11. The journal *El Grito* should not be confused with *El Grito del Norte*, the newspaper published in Santa Fe and an important voice of the Chicano movement in New Mexico.

12. See "Pochismos" by Estelle Chacon, *El Grito*, 3 (Fall 1969), 34–35.

13. The interviews of Mexican immigrants in the 1920s confirm the central impact of the Revolution. In many, if not most, instances the original migration of the family or individual is traced to the social dislocations brought about by the larger political upheaval. M. Gamio, *op. cit.*

14. O. Romano, "The Historical and Intellectual Presence of Mexican-Americans," *El Grito*, 2 (Winter 1969), 32–46.

15. E. Martinez, *op. cit.*

16. O. Romano, "Minorities, History, and the Cultural Mystique," *El Grito*, 1 (Fall 1967), 7.

17. O. Romano, "The Anthropology and Sociology of the Mexican-Americans," *El Grito*, 2 (Fall 1968), 13–26. See also Nick Vaca, "The Mexican-American in the Social Sciences: 1920–1970," pt. 1, *El Grito*, 3 (Spring 1970), 3–24; pt. 2, *El Grito*, 4 (Fall 1970), 17–51.

18. For critiques of the Department of Labor Report: *The Negro Family in America* by D. P. Moynihan, see Lee Rainwater and William Yancey, *The Moynihan Report and the Politics of Controversy* (Cambridge: M.I.T. University Press, 1967). For reactions to *The Confessions of Nat Turner* by William Styron, see John H. Clarke, ed., *William Styron's Nat Turner: Ten Black Writers Respond* (Boston: Beacon, 1969).

19. Moore, *op. cit.*, p. 231.

20. The bibliographies consulted were *The Mexican American—A Selected and Annotated Bibliography* (Palo Alto: Stanford University Press, 1969); *The Mexican American—A New Focus on*

Opportunity (The Inter-Agency Committee on Mexican-American Affairs, March, 1969), and Leo Grebler, Joan Moore, and Ralph Guzman, *The Mexican American People* (New York; The Free Press, 1970), pp. 677–741. For purposes of calculating percentages, works authored by institutions rather than individuals were discounted; materials prepared by a mixed team of Anglo and Spanish-surnamed authors were figured as one-half Chicano. There were no appreciable differences among the categories into which the bibliographies were subdivided, that is, among books, journal articles, and dissertations.

21. Gunnar Myrdal, *An American Dilemma* (New York: Harper & Row, 1944), pp. 1144–1180. Omitted for the purpose of calculation were foreign and institutional authors, books about race relations outside the United States, general books about the South, studies of ethnic groups other than blacks, fiction, and autobiography. When the books were coauthored, the race of the first author was used. The result was a sample of 130 books where I was reasonably certain of the author's race; 21 titles could not be classified, because of uncertainty.

22. E. Franklin Frazier, *The Negro in the United States,* rev. ed. (New York: Macmillan, 1957), pp. 715–748. The method employed was similar to that described for Myrdal. See note 21. Frazier's bibliography is divided into five categories. I did not analyze the first, "The Negro Under the Slave Regime," because the historians listed were overwhelmingly white. After the elimination of duplication, the result was 46 black authors, 53 white, four racially mixed, and 26 unknown or unidentifiable.

23. Elizabeth W. Miller, *The Negro in America: A Bibliography* (Cambridge: Harvard University Press, 1966), pp. 1–68. Calculating books only, in Miller's first five most general sections, the result was 108 white authors, 53 black, one other nonwhite, and 20 unidentifiable.

24. "Starting with a language difference and moving on to cultural values of all types, La Raza is even less 'American' than black people in the United States. The villages of Northern New Mexico . . . seem more than any black ghetto to be of another country. . . . The weight and intricacy of family and other relationships, with roots that are centuries old, create a Raza so-

ciety in which layer after layer of truth can be peeled away—
still leaving an outside observer with the feeling that the fundamental has yet to be grasped." Martinez, *op. cit.*
25. As Carey McWilliams puts it:

   Mexicans are a "conquered" people in the Southwest, a people whose
   culture has been under incessant attack for many years and whose
   character and achievements, as a people, have been consistently dis-
   paraged. Apart from physical violence, conquered and conqueror
   have continued to be competitors for land and jobs and power,
   parties to a constant economic conflict which has found expression
   in litigation, dispossessions, hotly contested elections, and the mutual disparagement which inevitably accompanies a situation of this
   kind. Throughout this struggle, the Anglo-Americans have possessed
   every advantage: in numbers and wealth, arms and machines. Having
   been subjected, first to a brutal physical attack, and then to a long
   process of economic attrition, it is not surprising that so many
   Mexicans should show evidences of the spiritual defeatism which
   so often arises when a cultural minority is annexed to an alien culture and way of life. More is involved, in situations of this kind,
   than the defeat of individual ambitions, for the victims also suffer
   from the defeat of their culture and of the society of which they are
   a part. *North From Mexico* (Philadelphia: Lippincott, 1949), p. 132.

   The "situations of this kind" that McWilliams refers to are
those of colonialism and imperialism. *North From Mexico* also
stresses the internal diversity of the Mexican-American group,
particularly the differences in political history and cultural development among the major regional centers of the Mexican
population in the United States. On regional differences in colonial
relationships, see Joan Moore, "Colonialism: The Case of the
Mexican-American," *Social Problems,* 17 (Spring 1970), 463–472.
26. Carlos Velez-I, "So Farewell Hope, and With Hope, Farewell
   Fear," *El Espejo—The Mirror, op. cit.,* p. 131.
27. Moore, "Political and Ethical Problems . . ." *op. cit.,* pp. 228,
   231.
28. Vine Deloria, *Custer Died For Your Sins* (New York: Macmillan,
   1969), especially chap. 8.
29. *San Francisco Chronicle* (May 8, 1971), 2.
30. Nick Vaca has discussed some of these issues in a pair of *El Grito*
   articles "The Black Phase," 2 (Fall 1968) and "The Negro Movement as an Anti-Revolution," 2 (Winter 1969). He polemicizes

against a tendency of some militant Chicano groups to adopt the style and rhetoric of the black movement. In my view, Vaca goes too far in equating black nationalism with racism, and he underplays the positive role of black militancy as a stimulant of the contemporary Chicano movement. But Vaca's essays point to some very basic and sensitive issues that few people have had the courage to discuss openly. This kind of frankness is characteristic of *El Grito* and helps explain why its readership is mounting in Anglo circles as well as within the Chicano communities.

part III
case studies
in institutional
racism

In Parts I and II of this volume I have relied on critical scholarship and interpretive analysis in an attempt to develop a theoretical perspective on race in American life. The essays in Part III are based on a different method, that of participant observation. They were written as a result of my personal experiences with the McCone Riot Commission, the trial of Huey Newton, and university racism. As case studies they are useful for illustrating in a concrete manner some of the dynamics of racism that I have discussed in the more general chapters. This introduction provides background on my involvement in each of these examples of action research and uses the case materials to clarify the concept of *institutional racism* and illustrate several of its distinctive meanings.

The McCone Commission and the Los Angeles Riots

"Whitewash over Watts" was written in December, 1965, a few days after the publication of the official report of the Governor's Commission on the Los Angeles Riots (the McCone Report). In a somewhat tentative manner, it analyses the August events as an "anticolonial uprising." Since this was my first use of the colonial interpretation of domestic racial conflict, the paper represents the initial stage in the development of the framework of the present book.

In September, 1965, I accepted an invitation to become a consultant to the commission. Lacking experience with such governmental agencies, I naively assumed that liberal social scientists like myself could influence the commission and its staff in a positive direction and contribute to a serious, hard-hitting analysis of the social forces underlying the Los Angeles outbreak. During one of our first meetings, the coordinator of research asked me whether a commission report would have credibility if it were based on the testimony of expert informants and community leaders without including the opinions and attitudes of the ordinary citizens of Watts. I said I would laugh at such a report. He seemed to agree and assigned me the task of organizing a survey of community opinion to investigate how the black people of Los Angeles saw the riots. By the time I had prepared a comprehensive questionnaire and trained an interviewing staff of local residents and college students with community ties, the commission began to throw roadblocks in our way: the interview schedule would take weeks to type; there was no cash on hand to pay the indigenous interviewers. Staff meetings I attended suggested that the body was moving toward a law and order approach, freezing out the research arm and its sociological perspective. It was clear that they did not want the kind of survey I was working on, and so I terminated my efforts. A few days before the report appeared I received a call asking whether I wanted to be listed as one of the 26 official consultants. About to say no, I had a premonition. I might want to write a critique of the "whitewash" I was expecting; its legitimacy would be enhanced if my involvement with the commission could be easily verified.

With its predominantly white, middle-class, legal-profession makeup, the McCone Commission, including staff, was itself a manifestation of the institutional racism it purported to understand. Its operations illustrated the most elementary definition of institutional racism: the exclusion of people of color from equal participation in the society's institutions. Even more significant than its racial composition, however, was the fact that it developed its analysis of the 1965 rebellion and the Watts community without even bothering to consult the main actors involved. For the commission, the place of the masses of the black population was to be invisible and unheard.

Bad as the report was,[1] its findings pointed to a second meaning of institutional racism as the interaction of the various spheres of social life to maintain an overall pattern of oppression. Thus low income—the result of discrimination on jobs and of low skill levels, themselves the result of blocked educational opportunities—meant that blacks were concentrated in ghetto areas of south-central Los Angeles, areas that lacked adequate public services such as transportation, which made the search for work extremely difficult. Relegation to such neighborhoods, where the schools do not stimulate achievement, leads a younger generation to begin the same cycle over again. The police patrol ghettos to the point of harassment, which means that black youth have a disproportionately high incidence of arrest; employers use such arrest records to deny people jobs; the hiring decision appears to be made without reference to color. Examples of this type could be multiplied. The important point has been underscored by Harold Baron in "The Web of Urban Racism": this dynamic of interaction among institutions makes it possible for any individual organization or agency to deny responsibility for the racial status quo—neither the employer, the local government, the school, the real estate interests, nor the agencies

of law and justice produced the present situation. Each only
inherited the problems created by other institutions and the social
forces of the past.[2]

The Black Panthers and a Racist Legal System

Approximately one year after the Los Angeles rebellion, the Black
Panther Party was organized in Oakland, California, by Huey P.
Newton and Bobby Seale. The Panthers identified with the ghetto
revolts that were erupting during the early period of their existence,
but they criticized the unfocused and undisciplined character of
spontaneous violence and advocated instead the organization of Afro-
American communities around a revolutionary program. The passage
from Chapters 6 to 7 of this book parallels the transition from
rioting to organizing, from an implicit, incipient anticolonial
consciousness to an emerging revolutionary one.

It was an announced commitment to self-defense and a policy
of carrying weapons that aroused the dramatic response to the
Panthers—in black as well as in white communities. Though armed
self-defense is an old American tradition, when affirmed by people
of African descent it provokes images of blacks running amuck,
gunning down helpless white populations. Negroes are supposed to
submit to oppression, to show trust in white people and their
institutions, or in the least to address their grievances nonviolently.
Brandishing weapons in "a threatening and aggressive manner" is
definitely "out of place" for black people, and as might have been
expected the Panthers evoked terror and retaliation. They were
the latest expression of an historic type with a long tradition in
American race relations, the "bad nigger" who does not accept his
place in the order of things. They were even more dangerous than
the bad niggers of Watts, Newark, Detroit, and countless other
insurrections: their targets were the police rather than television sets;
they were careful to operate within the letter of the law; and they
could be counted upon to sustain their actions much longer than
the essentially leaderless crowds of the ghetto streets.

The incident that led to Newton's arrest and trial illustrates
the mechanisms of racial control discussed in my opening chapter. In
the age of the automobile and equality before the law, Huey Newton
was hardly more free to move about Oakland than the Ibo slave
was to leave his Jamaican plantation. Two black men in a
Volkswagen in the very early morning hours was suspicious in itself,

and when Officer John Frey's radio query revealed that it was "a known Black Panther vehicle," it had to be stopped. What happened after that remains still confused, after three trials.

My involvement with the (first) trial began with the preparation of an *amicus* brief on racism. The defense attorneys were trying to quash the jury venire on the grounds that the defendant's real peers, blacks from the ghetto, were systematically excluded and that white middle-class persons could not fairly judge such a case. Because Judge Friedman would not accept written briefs, I gave my testimony in court. Impressed with my ideas about selecting jurors with a minimum of racial bias, Charles Garry asked me to help the defense by observing their questioning in order to contribute a sociologist's perspective to the more intuitive judgments of the lawyers. Although unsure whether I had anything to offer, I was delighted at the opportunity to witness the trial, the big event at this time in Northern California. By the time the jury had been selected, the bailiffs were used to my presence, and I was able to continue my association with the defense all the way to the end. Initially I hoped to write a book on the case as a whole, but its human drama, legal complexities, and massive social implications proved to be too much for my literary talents. Chapter 7 of this volume analyzes the pre-trial phase in which the jury was selected.

The trial essay—like the others but even more so—departs from the social science tenet that research is best carried out by neutral observers and dispassionate analysts. Of course, many would justify an exception in this particular case on the grounds that only an active participant could have gotten access to the data in the first place. I would go further, however, and argue that, as I hope Chapter 7 demonstrates, social scientists can participate as partisans in those matters of social justice that demand our involvement, and can at the same time gather data that can be reported without sacrificing that component of objectivity that is the scholar's hallmark: namely, an analysis faithful to the complexity of social realities. As an aside to the professional sociologist, I would add that the experience impressed me with the richness of social data that emerge in the conflicts of institutional life and the particular advantage of the legal setting for observing the play of social forces.

The selection of the jury illustrated another aspect of institutional racism. It arises out of indirect processes and from actions that are usually nonintentional, in contrast to "individual" racism, which tends to be more direct and volitional. Thus black people (and other nonwhites also) are underrepresented on most jury panels, even though the selective process is supposedly color blind. In Oakland, California, and most other metropolitan areas, the names of those called to serve are drawn from the list of registered voters. The voter's roll typically contains fewer black people than their actual population proportion. This is not the result of direct racist policies prohibiting Afro-Americans from registering to vote; it is because they are more likely to be, first, poor (and the poor are always less likely to register and to vote); second, geographically mobile and thereby made ineligible by residency rules; or, third, disenchanted with the political process. And those black people who are called up are more likely than whites to be excused from this duty on the basis of financial hardships involved in missing work, greater-than-average family responsibilities, and, in some localities, tests of "literacy" and civic "knowledge" that discriminate against the ethnic and the low-income person, again in a "color-blind" way. The fact that institutional racism is the result of such chains of "unwitting" actions and circumstances has made its existence relatively easy to overlook or deny; this is why it is such an important idea today.

The trial provided a concrete example of one further meaning of the concept of institutional racism: that the contingencies of social position or institutional role are more significant than individual attitude or personality in determining those actions and decisions that make a difference with respect to racial realities.[3] Newton's prosecutor, Lowell Jensen, had a reputation for being fair and unprejudiced on racial matters, the truth of which I have no reason to question. He was reported to be especially close to the few black peers of his law school days and to number Negroes among his current friends. During the trial he did not appeal to bigotry as some of his colleagues in the Alameda County D.A.'s office have done. On a scale of individual racism he would therefore rank quite low, particularly in comparison with other whites in his circles. But he did his job well; that job was to exclude every black person from the jury except one "token" member;* to defend the actions of the

---

* As it turned out, David Harper was anything but a token jury-man.

most racist police officers, who were his main witnesses; and, of course, to fight for a death-sentence conviction of the Black Panther leader and thereby help bring about the aim of Oakland's power structure—weakening the party and its efforts to organize the ghetto. In the last analysis the objective role he played was the significant factor, not his personal attitudes, and indeed before a year had passed he was "rewarded" with a promotion from assistant to chief district attorney.

My emphasis on institutional racism should not blind us to the persistence of the old-fashioned personal variety. There are key points in the cycle of oppression where overt discrimination remains strategic. The most important example is employment; in many occupations and industries people of color are excluded simply on racial grounds. While many of the workings of the judicial apparatus may be color blind, white policemen rarely are—certainly not the Oakland officer who stopped Huey Newton on October 28, 1967, and died to regret it. This kind of racism—which boils down to hostility, fear, and intense dislike of people who are not white—exists in even the most "enlightened" groups, among college professors, for example.

Confronting Racism Close to Home: Higher Education
Violent upheavals in the ghettos and the emergence of militant organizations such as the Panthers shook up a complacent white America in the latter half of the 1960s. Among the institutions that responded with new programs to include the previously excluded, the colleges and universities stand out in importance. Third world students entered in large numbers, and for a period of years the campuses became a major arena of racial conflict. The case of higher education illustrates some of the processes we have seen at work in judicial institutions.

The exclusion of people of color from the nation's universities has not been due primarily to a conscious all-white policy. Formal discrimination was abolished on most campuses probably well before it had begun to recede in other institutions. Indians, Chicanos, Puerto Ricans, and Afro-Americans were rarely in a position even to apply for college entrance. High dropout rates in high school, concentration in nonacademically oriented secondary schools and vocational tracks, low family income and a consequent, heavy

economic responsibility in young adulthood, all contributed to this
situation—along with other factors. Before the recent special programs
were inaugurated, those minority youth who did aspire and apply
to colleges and universities were likely to be denied admittance on
the basis of universalistic criteria, like grades, test scores, and the
quality of their high schools.

Even more profound has been the rooting in the Western
European tradition of the "taken-for-granted" assumptions of the
educational process—assumptions about the goals of learning, the
forms and procedures of instruction, and the very definition of
knowledge. Although these implicit models are not necessarily racist
in themselves or otherwise evil, the lack of a consciousness of their
historical and cultural relativity has led to a racist exclusion of
ways of knowing and ordering experience that are the products of
various non-Western experiences. This example points up again how
an overconcern with conscious feelings of prejudice and overt acts
of discrimination misses many of the most significant dimensions
of racism that are being challenged today.

Yet I do not give such "pure and simple" racism the attention
it deserves in the final essay, "Race and the White Professor."[4]
In part this is because I wanted to stress institutional dynamics. It
may also reflect the possibility that my associates tended to mask
such feelings in my presence; I hope this has not seriously affected the
general validity of the analysis. In meeting after meeting and in
informal conversations over a period of years, I have had ample
opportunity to observe how my own colleagues, those in other
departments and administrators as well, were reacting to each
successive racial crisis. Even more important, similar reactions were
going on in my own head. Although I have concentrated my attention
on the liberal professor because I see him as the modal type and his
social philosophy as particularly strategic, the attitudes and responses
of white radical faculty members have very often been essentially the
same. Radical professors share the privileges of academic status
(except for those who have suffered political recriminations), and
in objective terms we also are racial colonizers.*

My own actions, or lack of them, again are to the point. Since

* Ira Katznelson called attention to my neglect of this point in
Chapter 8. Albert Memmi has written the most pointed analysis of the
"left colonizer."[5]

I first read *An American Dilemma* as a college freshman twenty-five years ago, I have probably been more sensitive than most whites to racial oppression. Yet I was able to live quite comfortably for many years in an all-white university without taking any meaningful action. The Free Speech Movement erupted in my first year of teaching at Berkeley, and it prodded me to reconsider my intellectual interests. I shifted from a rather morbid investigation of the sociology of death to teaching and research about where it was happening to the living—race relations. I can recall that from 1965 to 1967 I criticized white student radicals who in their rhetoric regularly attacked racism (or whatever it was called in those days) · but never thought of threatening their own privileges by acting politically to force integration of their departments. But I wasn't doing anything, either, until an accidental opportunity presented itself. Since I was in debt to "the system" for a recent promotion to tenure, my department chairman was able to cajole me into taking charge of graduate admissions—from which vantage point it became possible to effect a change in the racial composition of the student body.

This particular example, as well as the other case studies, suggests the variety of roles available to the white liberal or radical scholar (if these political labels still mean anything) in a period when direct involvement in the movements of the oppressed is no longer possible. One such role is that of critic of official reports or influential studies that absolve powerful interests of responsibility for racial and other injustice. A second is the role of expert to provide information and support to groups and movements working to transform the society in more equalitarian directions. This would include appearing before public hearings on proposed laws and other measures, and cooperating with lawyers like Charles Garry who defend the interests of oppressed peoples and their leaders. A third role is that of a gadfly to change the racial arrangements and atmosphere within one's own field and home institution. These are all obvious avenues for antiracist whites who would participate in the decolonization of American life. I am sure that with a little imagination the reader will be able to think of others.

Some Cracks in the Wall

In a racially divided society there is an enormous wall between the oppressors and the oppressed. As a result of this wall the white majority knows almost nothing about the history, culture, and social realities of people of color. Because of such ignorance, the colonizer tends to look at racial matters in terms of simplistic formulas; therefore, on many issues the contrast in perspective and approach between third world and white is striking. These walls of race and class and the interests that support them prevented McCone's commissioners as well as ordinary white citizens from understanding the black community and the meaning of the Watts uprising. The opinion surveys revealed that the black population attributed the rioting to long-term social and economic conditions as well as to police provocation; whites were more likely to see the violence in terms of prior revolutionary organization, outside conspiracies, and sheer criminality.

The same walls kept the majority on the Newton jury panel from understanding what the Black Panthers were all about. The questioning demonstrated that most whites knew nothing about Afro-American history and culture and, indeed, had few ideas at all about contemporary racial movements. Such ignorance about the victims of oppression and indifference to their circumstances is not confined to people of modest means and education. The problems college professors have met in relating to a new type of student have made it clear that they too have been living behind the walls produced by racist institutions. Their situation and outlook blocked comprehension of third world experience and perspectives. Consider the Kerner Report. The candidates for the trial jury had not even heard of it. The better informed faculty were familiar with it, though they disagreed with its conclusions. Or consider the idea of white racism. The middle Americans Charles Garry interrogated did not know its meaning. The educated members of the professional elite can provide a definition, but they do not believe it applies to their college or university. Is the difference so great?

Yet the walls of racism are not impermeable. In each setting a combined process of education and political action took place that resulted in a narrowing of the breach. In the case of the governor's Commission on the Los Angeles Riots, this took place only after their report was published, in the form of angry denunciations by the black community and published criticisms of the McCone Report. These reactions had an effect, for the next major official analysis of ghetto rebellion, the Kerner Report, was able to confront American racism in a more serious and complex—though still inadequate—fashion. In the Oakland, California, courtroom where Huey Newton was tried, the long period devoted to questioning the jury's racial attitudes and injecting social issues into the legalistically oriented trial procedures also paid off. Whatever one makes of the "compromise" verdict in the first trial, the jurors who left the county courthouse were different people from when they were first seated seven weeks earlier. They had a new understanding of racism, Afro-American culture, and black militancy as a result of Garry's work, the defendant's own testimony, and the testimony of other black witnesses. Finally, as I emphasize in the last chapter, many college professors have been educated by third world students and their social movements; student perspectives on institutional racism and ethnic self-determination are beginning to gain a greater acceptance in the academic milieu. Perhaps this is the one encouraging feature of these case studies.

NOTES

1. In addition to Chapter 6 of the present volume, other critiques include Bayard Rustin, "The Watts 'Manifesto' and the McCone Report," *Commentary*, 41 (March 1966), 29–35; Anthony Oberschall, "The Los Angeles Riot of August, 1965," in James Geschwender, ed., *The Black Revolt* (Englewood Cliffs, N.J.: Prentice-Hall, 1971), pp. 264–284; and Robert M. Fogelson, "White on Black," *Political Science Quarterly*, 82 (September 1967), 337–367.

2. Harold Baron, "The Web of Urban Racism," in Louis Knowles and Kenneth Prewitt, eds., *Institutional Racism in America* (Englewood Cliffs, N.J.: Prentice-Hall, 1969), pp. 134–176.

3. This is the major thrust of the idea as defined by Stokely Carmichael and Charles Hamilton, who were among the first to conceptualize institutional racism. *Black Power* (New York: Vintage, 1967), esp. chap. 1.

4. For a discussion of institutional racism in graduate schools, which includes material on old-fashioned racism, see Douglas Davidson, "The Furious Passage of the Black Graduate Student," *Berkeley Journal of Sociology*, 15 (1970), 192–211.

5. Albert Memmi, *The Colonizer and the Colonized* (Boston: Beacon, 1967), pp. 19–44.

chapter 6
whitewash
over watts*

On July 27, 1919, a clash of whites and blacks at a Chicago beach resulted in the drowning of a Negro boy and served as the spark to what was to remain the most violent racial outbreak in American history until 1965. For four days black and white mobs were virtually uncontained and it was almost another week before the state militia was able to withdraw, on August 8. The final toll read 38 dead (23 black, 15 white), 537 injured (of whom two-thirds were black), and 1000 people homeless (primarily whites). Less than two weeks after the end of the rioting Governor Frank Lowden of Illinois appointed a twelve-member Commission on Race Relations "to study and report upon the broad questions of the relations between the two races." The hearings and research, which the commission began three months later, occupied them for an entire year; the greater part of 1921 was spent in writing the 672-page report, which appeared in 1922 as *The Negro in Chicago: A Study of Race Relations and a Race Riot.*[1] The commission was most fortunate in selecting for its major investigator Charles S. Johnson, a young graduate student at the University of Chicago, who decades later was to produce a number of classic studies of the American Negro.[2] Thus the 1919 Chicago riots resulted in a significant analysis of the events themselves, as well as of the sociological structure of race relations and of a Northern black community, which served for decades as a model of social science.

* An earlier version of this article appeared in *Trans-Action*, 3, No. 3 (March–April 1966), 3–9, 54. Copyright © March/April 1966 by Transaction, Inc., New Brunswick, N.J.

On August 24, 1965, just one week after public order had been restored in the south-central area of Los Angeles known as Watts, Governor Pat Brown of California announced the appointment of an eight-man commission of leading citizens. In his charge to the group (which came to be known as the McCone Commission, after its chairman, John A. McCone, former head of the CIA), Brown asked it to "prepare an accurate chronology and description of the riots"; "to probe deeply the immediate and underlying causes of the riots"; and finally to "develop recommendations for action designed to prevent a recurrence of these tragic disorders."

For what appears to have been political considerations connected with possible repercussions of the Watts affair on the 1966 gubernatorial campaign, the commission was given December 1, 1965, as the deadline for the completion of its report. Thus only 100 days were available for a "deep and probing" analysis of one of the most destructive incidents of racial violence in American history.

In an atmosphere of speedup that made work on an automobile assembly line appear leisurely by comparison, the commission held a series of sixty formal hearings before which eighty sworn witnesses, including city and police officials, leaders and citizens of the white and black communities, eventually appeared. It also selected a fulltime staff of thirty, primarily lawyers and legal-oriented investigators, to carry out the day-to-day work of assembling data and preparing the report. The staff called upon the services of twenty-six consultants (chiefly university professors in the social sciences) for advice and the subcontracting of research, interviewed ninety persons among the 4000 arrested, and opened an office in the riot area to take testimony from local citizens. After a total expenditure of $250,000, Commissioner McCone presented the report to Governor Brown with the fanfare of television on December 6.

In view of the conditions under which it was hurried into existence, it should be no surprise that *Violence in the City—An End or a Beginning?* is a slim volume with only eighty-six pages of blown-up type.[3] But the report of the McCone Commission is not only brief, it is sketchy and superficial. Its tone and style are disturbing. There is much glib writing, and the approach as well as the format is slick in the manner of illustrated news weeklies. The depth analysis of this fateful outbreak can be read by an average reader in less than an hour—allowing ample time for contemplating the many photographs, both color and black-and-white.

My comparison with the careful and considered report of the Illinois Governor's commission of 1919 that required three years of planning, research, and writing may well be unfair. But with the sizable budget and all the academic expertise available, more was to be expected than the public relations statement of the California commission.

Not only the size and style of the McCone document are disturbing. Its content is disappointing both in its omissions and in its underlying political and philosophical perspectives. There is almost nothing in the report that is new or that gives consideration to the unique conditions of Los Angeles life and politics. As Los Angeles councilman Billy Mills commented, most of the material in the report documented conditions in the ghetto that have been common knowledge to sociologists and the informed public for a generation.[4] The events of the rioting were covered in greater breadth and depth in the daily reporting in the *Los Angeles Times*, a sense of their larger meaning conveyed more perceptively in any of a number of hour-long television documentaries.

More appalling are the report's deeper failures. With a narrow legalistic perspective that approached the riots in terms of the sanctity of law and order, the commissioners were unable (or unwilling) to read any social or political meaning into the August terror. There was no attempt to look at the outbreak from the point of view of the black poor. The commissioners also played a dangerous game with the problem of responsibility. The Negro community as a whole is absolved from responsibility for the rioting while local and national leaders (civil rights moderates and extremists alike) are taken to task for inflaming mass discontent and undermining commitments to law and authority.*

In a crude attempt at "horse trading" in the responsibility market, the positions of the Los Angeles police department and city administrators are consistently protected. By discounting the relevance of police provocation and city policies without presenting any facts or evidence, the commission not only protects powerful interests, it abdicates its mandate to seek out facts and establish as best it could the objective reality. My most general and most serious criticism of the

---

* In a two-page dissenting comment appended to the main report the Reverend James E. Jones, a black commissioner, criticized the report for attempting "to put a lid on protest."[5]

report is this violation of the responsibility to seek truth and the frequent hiding behind opinion and hearsay.

Causes of the Watts "Revolt"

Lurking behind the Watts violence are three basic problems, according to the McCone Commission.

1. the widespread unemployment and "idleness" in the ghetto
2. the cultural and educational backwardness of black children, which prevents the schools from preparing them for the labor market and integrating them into society
3. the troubled state of police–community relations in the Negro neighborhoods

The Crisis in Employment

The chapter on employment is forthright in its emphasis on jobs as a central problem and correct in its understanding that male dignity and family responsibility can hardly be expected when men are unable to find steady work. For example: "The most serious immediate problem that faces the Negro in our community is employment—securing and holding a job that provides him an opportunity for livelihood, a chance to earn the means to support himself, and his family, a dignity, and a reason to feel that he is a member of our community in a true and very real sense."[6] The commission calls upon federal, state, and city government to create jobs for the black and Mexican-American poor. Corporations and labor unions are asked to end discrimination once and for all and to police their progress by keeping careful records on minority employment. Because the commissioners are convinced that the majority of jobless Los Angeles Negroes are presently unemployable, they call for an expanded and better-coordinated program of job training; they wisely recommend that control of this effort be within the black community.

These proposals on employment are worthwhile and necessary, but they encourage a deceptive complacency. The report does not probe sufficiently into the depth and seriousness of the problem. There is no consideration of the impact of population trends and technological developments on the availability of jobs, especially for the unskilled, and no willingness to face the escalating employment needs in the rapid expansion of the minority population of Los

Angeles. The report is irresponsible, because its style and tone convey the impression that its relatively mild and moderate recommendations provide real solutions.

Educational Inequality

The treatment of education is the one section of the McCone Report that is based on a careful and firsthand study. Kenneth A. Martyn, professor of education at Los Angeles State College, investigated five areas within the Los Angeles City Unified School District as a commission consultant. Student achievement was compared for four "disadvantaged areas" (of which two were primarily black and close to the riot centers) and one "advantaged" area (predominantly white upper middle class). Average student reading performances in the fifth, eighth, and eleventh grades reveal a consistent backwardness in the lower-class black and Mexican districts. The gap is most dramatic at the eighth grade, since by the eleventh many of the poorest "achievers" are already dropouts. The average student in the white middle-class area is in the 79th percentile in reading vocabulary based on national norms; the average students in "Negro" Watts and Avalon are in the 13th and 14th percentiles; the average percentiles in the primarily Mexican areas of Boyle Heights and East Los Angeles are 16th and 17th.

Martyn investigated the possibility of discrimination in educational facilities. Some inequalities were found, but hardly enough to explain the systematic backwardness of minority students.* The commission therefore ascribed the problem of school performance to what today is fashionably called a *culturally impoverished environment*. Parents have little education and their own background does not foster an orientation toward achievement and learning; crowded housing conditions are not favorable for disciplined study; and the precariousness of employment and the lack of models of achievement may

---

* Ghetto schools were more likely to be on "double sessions" as a result of greater overcrowding, and some schools lacked adequate libraries, the full complement of academic courses, and especially—given the poverty of their areas—free lunch programs. On the other hand, there seemed to be as many new schools and equal maintenance of physical facilities in the disadvantaged areas, and there was only a slight tendency for teachers to be less experienced. Roughly similar results were found nationwide in the Coleman Report.[7]

further dull incentive. In order to break this pattern and "raise the scholastic achievement of the average Negro child up to or perhaps above the present average achievement level in the city," the commission calls for an intensive infusion of educational resources into the black community, focusing on three programs: preschool learning on the model of Headstart, the reduction of class size, and the improvement of academic and behavioral counseling.

The McCone Report accepts the conventional position that it is the "vicious circular" connection between education and employment that is the crux of the dilemma of the Negro poor. It places its main bet on education and the future, rather than on creating jobs to solve the problems of the present. If the achievement levels of present and future generations of black children can be sufficiently raised, they will be motivated to remain in the school system and assimilate the skills and training that will begin reversing this cyclical process. Unfortunately, the middle-class ethos underlying the commission's emphasis on future orientation and achievement is irrelevant to the needs and outlook of the lower-class adult group whose problems of work and training are likely to intensify.

But even with a crash program in education, can the average ghetto youth be motivated toward achievement and excellence when the condition of his people and community place him in a position of alienation and powerlessness vis-à-vis the larger society? What is missing in the report's analysis is a total picture of the Watts community as consistently deprived and disadvantaged in relation to Los Angeles as a whole. Fragmented hints of this picture abound in the report, particularly in the excellent discussion of the woefully inadequate transportation system, but the fragments are never pieced together. If they were, municipal officials would then have to bear some responsibility for permitting this systematic deprivation to persist. By singling out education as the strategic sphere for ameliorative efforts, the commission aims its biggest guns on the target area in which the city's hands are relatively "clean" and in which it is relatively easy to suggest that the cultural backgrounds and individual performances of black people themselves account for a good part of the problem.

The Police Issue

If we don't get no good out of this, it will happen again. By good I mean an end to police harassment, and we

need jobs. I got eight kids, and I've only worked 10 days
this year. I ain't ever been a crook, but if they don't do
something, I'm gonna have to take something. I don't
know how they expect us to live.[8]

When an oppressed group breaks out in a violent attack on society and its representatives, the underlying causes are those long-term
elements in its situation that have produced its alienation and despair.
Immediate causes are the short-run irritants and grievances that have
intensified feelings of anger and hatred and focused them on specific
targets. The immediate grievances and conditions that spark illegal
violence must have the effect of weakening the oppressed's normal
disposition to accept, at least overtly, the authority structure and legal
norms of the society—otherwise mass violence could not erupt. The
young Watts man quoted above seems to be saying that from his
standpoint "jobs" are the underlying cause, "police harassment" the
immediate issue. The governor's commission disagrees with his analysis
and has its own explanation for the ghetto's sudden loss of commitment to the legal order.

It answers its own question "Why Los Angeles?" in a way that
almost totally relieves the city and county of implication. The rapid
migration of Southern blacks to the city's ghetto serves as their starting point, for these migrants are unrealistic in expecting that California
living will solve all their problems. In the context of this "crisis of
expectations" black frustration and despair were fanned by three
"aggravating events in the twelve months prior to the riots":

Publicity given to the glowing promise of the federal
poverty program was paralleled by reports of controversy
and bickering over the mechanism to handle the program
here in Los Angeles, and when the projects did arrive,
they did not live up to expectation.

Throughout the nation, unpunished violence and disobe-
dience to law were widely reported, and almost daily
there were exhortations, here and elsewhere, to take the
most extreme and even illegal remedies to right a wide
variety of wrongs, real and supposed.

In addition, many Negroes here felt and were encouraged
to feel that they had been affronted by the passage of
Proposition 14—an initiative measure passed by two-thirds

of the voters in November 1964 which repealed the
Rumford Fair Housing Act and unless modified by the
voters or invalidated by the courts will bar any attempt
by state or local governments to enact similar laws.

To locate the argument it is necessary to pass over the invidious
and insidious tone of this passage—the back-of-hand slap at the national civil rights movement, the implication that our country's injustices to people of color are as much "supposed" as "real," and the
incredible insinuation that Afro-Americans required political spokesmen to tell them they were being affronted by the passage of an initiative in which 70 percent of their white fellow Californians said, "We
don't want you moving into our neighborhoods." But the point is
clear. Aside from some blunderings over the antipoverty war, it was
Negro leadership that undermined the commitment of law-abiding
black citizens to authority and legal methods of redressing their grievances. What is important is the assumption that the black poor's
acceptance of political authority was not weakened by its own experience with police and other official representatives of society, but was
instead subverted by an extremist and opportunist leadership.

Such an analysis gives the commission a free field to discount
the role of the Los Angeles police and their presence in the ghetto as
immediate precipitants of the violence. In short, the commission has
"bought" the line of the Chief of Police William Parker who has consistently argued that the riot was a revolt of the criminal and lawless
element, prodded on by a black leadership that inflamed the Los
Angeles black community with the "bugaboo" of "police brutality."

The report devotes a chapter to law enforcement and police–
community relations. It takes note of the severe criticism of the police
department by many black witnesses and frankly admits "the deep
and longstanding schism between a substantial portion of the Negro
community and the police department." Considering the virtual una-
nimity in the black community concerning police practices as the
foremost immediate cause of the outbreak, why did not the commission seriously investigate the role of law enforcement in the ghetto?
The commission acknowledges that *feelings* of oppressive police action
were significant conditions of the rioting. It violates its responsibility
to truth and impartiality by refusing to examine the factual basis of
black opinion while stating the beliefs and hearsay of white officers in
an aura of established truth:

. . . the police have explained to us the extent to which
the conduct of some Negroes when apprehended has required the use of force in making arrests. Example after
example has been recited of arrestees, both men and
women, becoming violent, struggling to resist arrest, and
thus requiring removal by physical force. Other actions,
each provocative to the police and each requiring more
than normal action by the police in order to make an
arrest or to perform other duties, have been described
to us.

Precisely the same line is taken with respect to Chief Parker.
The commission duly notes that the outspoken chief is a focal point of
criticism and is distrusted by most blacks. They feel he hates them.
Yet the report conveniently omits all rational and objective bases for
such "beliefs," including a whole series of public statements made long
before the riots.[9] The inference is that "Negro belief" rests on mis-
interpretation of fact and paranoid reactions.

However, not only embittered black attitudes, but facts exist
about the police presence in the ghetto—if the commission had only
looked for them. For example, a study by a Youth Opportunities
Board was available to the commission. It was based on intensive interviews with 220 people in the Watts, Willowbrook, and Avalon districts, undertaken only two years before the outbreak in this very area.
The sample included 70 delinquent and nondelinquent children, 26
parents, and 124 high administrators and lesser personnel of the major
agencies in the community (schools, welfare and probation, recreation
and youth groups). Attitudes toward the critical agencies of the community were probed, and it was found that of all the "serving institutions" of the larger society, the object of the greatest hostility was
the police department. A majority of adults as well as children felt
that the behavior of the police aggravated the problems of growing up
in the black community rather than contributing to their solution; this
was in direct contrast to their attitudes toward the schools, the parks,
the health services, and the probation officers.[10]

The real issue has perhaps been muddied by the outcry against
"police brutality," the term that blacks use to sum up their sense of
grievance against law-enforcement agents. The police liberalization
policy of recent years may well have reduced the number of cases of
"classic" brutality, like beatings and cruel methods of questioning.

What the black community is presently complaining about when it cries "police brutality" is the more subtle attack on personal dignity that manifests itself in unexplainable questionings and searches, in hostile and insolent attitudes toward groups of young Negroes on the street or in cars, and in the use of disrespectful and sometimes racist language—in short, what the Watts man quoted above called "police harassment." There is no evidence that this assault on individual self-esteem and dignity has ceased.[11]

Another facet of police brutality is the use of excessive force to control criminal and illegal behavior. Characteristically the commission neglected its opportunity (and obligation) to assess the use of force by the various law enforcement agencies that put down the August violence, despite its considerable attention to their logistical and coordination problems and the concern of blacks and liberal groups like the ACLU with what appeared to be unnecessary shootings of looters, including young children.

The police chapter is primarily devoted to the adequacy of procedures presently available for processing complaints against officer misconduct and to recommendations for improving both them and relations in general between law enforcement and the black community. Yet, the demand of Negro leaders and white liberals for an independent civilian review board is described as "clamor"; the proposal is rejected because this device would "endanger the effectiveness of law enforcement." Experience with its use in two cities "has not demonstrated" its "advantages," but characteristically no evidence is given and the cities are not even named. Instead the report advocates strengthening the authority of the present Board of Police Commissioners, the civilian heads of the department, and establishing the new position of Inspector General under the authority of the Chief of Police. The latter "would be responsible for making investigations and recommendations on all citizen complaints." In addition, the police should improve its community relations programs in the ghetto areas and strive to attract more blacks and Mexicans to careers in law enforcement. That there might be a connection between the way in which white police operate in the ghetto and the remarkable lack of interest of black youth in such careers never enters the heads of the Commissioners.*

---

* A *New York Times* survey in 1971 entitled "Recruiting of Negro Police Is a Failure in Most Cities" concluded that "the major recruitment

The report correctly notes that all seven riots in the North in
1964 (as well as the one in Watts) began with a police incident and
in every case "police brutality" was an issue. But in a monument to
twisted logic it concludes from these observations:

> The fact that this charge is repeatedly made must not go
> unnoticed, for there is a real danger that persistent criti-
> cism will reduce and perhaps destroy the effectiveness of
> law enforcement.

Instead of asking why poor blacks come to believe that law and authority are not their law and their authority, the report goes on to
preach sanctimoniously:

> Our society is held together by respect for law. A group
> of officers who represent a tiny fraction of one percent of
> the population is the thin thread that enforces observance
> of law by those few who would do otherwise. If police
> authority is destroyed, if their effectiveness is impaired,
> and if their determination to use the authority vested in
> them to preserve a law abiding community is frustrated,
> all of society will suffer because groups would feel free
> to disobey the law and inevitably their number would in-
> crease. Chaos might easily result.

Character of the Watts Outbreak

There is very little explicit consideration of the character and meaning
of the outburst in the McCone Report, in spite of its great concern
with causes. The commission missed an important point of departure
by not viewing the Watts violence as a problematic phenomenon, the
essence of which needed to be determined through a careful weighing
of evidence and through social and political analysis. For this reason
the report's assumptions must be inferred because they are introduced
in passing and never clearly spelled out.

The perspective of the analysis is overwhelmingly riot control
rather than collective or crowd behavior. The attempt of "responsible"

---

problem among blacks appears to be the negative image of the police in the
black community, compounded by discrimination on the forces."[12] As of
May, 1971, the proportion of black policemen in Los Angeles was 5.2
percent, in contrast with 17.9 percent of the city's population.[13]

leaders to cool off the mobs is discussed, but the major emphasis is on
the tactics used by the various law enforcement agencies. After a
fairly thorough discussion of the arrest that set off the events, the
black people who participated in violence are almost excluded from
the story. The very language of the report suggests that it has pre-
judged "the meaning of Watts."* On its opening page, it calls the outbreak a "spasm" and "an insensate rage of destruction." Later it calls
it "an explosion—a formless, quite senseless, all but hopeless violent
protest." Only in the discussion of the business targets that were
looted and burned does the commission attempt to find a meaning or
pattern in what the rioters did, and here they conclude—unlike most
informed observers—that there was no "significant correlation between alleged consumer exploitation and the destruction."

The legalistic perspective of the commission and its staff seems
to have blocked their sensitivity to the sociological meaning of the
riots. When they view them simply as an uprising of the criminal
element against law and order (aggravated of course by the social,
economic, and political causes of frustration already discussed), the
commissioners need not look seriously at the human meaning of the
turmoil, nor need they understand what messages may have been communicated by the rocks, gunfire, and Molotov cocktails. Let us not
romanticize the Watts violence. I don't claim that everyone involved
and everything done had rational motives. But it is a more humble and
scientific attitude to leave the question open and to examine the limited
evidence that is available. For the assumption of meaninglessness, the
emptying out of content and communication from any set of human
actions—even nonrational violence—reduces the dignity of the actors
involved. In the present context it is a subtle insult to the Los Angeles
black community. The report ostensibly avoids such an insulting
stance by minimizing participation and exculpating the bulk of the
community from responsibility for the antisocial outbreak—but not
its leaders, of course, who aggravated the underlying tension.

* That the character of the outbreak is a difficult and real question
is suggested by the debate within the black community as to the appropriate
term of reference. Many people felt that the automatic reflex use by the
media of *riots* as the label of designation missed the essence of what had
happened and thus subtly distorted the issues. A preference for the word
revolt and other similar terms was often expressed, though unfortunately
we do not know how widespread these usages became.

In the ugliest interval which lasted from Thursday through
Saturday, perhaps as many as 10,000 Negroes took to the
streets in marauding bands. . . . The entire Negro population of Los Angeles County, about two thirds of
whom live in this area (that of the riots), numbers more
than 650,000. Observers estimate that only about two
percent were involved in the disorder. Nevertheless, this
violent fraction, however minor, has given the face of
community relations in Los Angeles a sinister cast.

No evidence is presented for the two percent estimate, nor for
the total of 10,000 participants on which it is based. We are not told
how the commission defines being "involved in the disorder." A number of distortions are apparently obvious, however. Even if 10,000
was the upper limit, this figure would indicate participation by far
more than two percent of the blacks in Watts. The curfew area, with
some 50,000 residents, contains many neighborhoods of comfortable
middle-class people who were far from the riot center; they should
be eliminated from a calculation of the extent of participation in an
outbreak of the poor and dispossessed. Second, the total population
figures include women, children, and the aged. A more appropriate
(and still difficult) question would concern the extent of participation of young and mature black men in the low-income districts that
were the centers of the action.

Unfortunately, I cannot answer this question precisely, but in
view of the commission's unscientific methodology and dubious de-
ductions there is no reason to accept their view of the participation
issue. Consider on this matter the opinion of Bayard Rustin, who
visited Watts with Martin Luther King a few days after the outbreak:

I could not count heads but reports I have received and
my experiences with the people leads me to believe that
a large percentage of the people living in the Watts area
participated. Most of them did not themselves loot
and burn but they were on the streets at one time or
other.[14]

As Rustin suggests, the question is not simply how many engaged in lawless acts. Essential to the meaning of the revolt is the
attitude of the "nonparticipants" toward those who erupted in hate

and violence. In the most popular revolutions it is only a small minority that storms the Bastille or dumps tea in Boston Harbor. Only through considering the attitudes of the "silent mass" is it possible to know whether the Watts riots represented an action by a large segment of the Negro poor of Los Angeles rather than a cutting loose of a small "violent fraction." Had the McCone Commission done its job, it would have conducted a systematic survey of community opinion to determine the distribution of sentiment in black Los Angeles.

My informants reported widespread support within the ghetto for the violent outbreak. Moral approval (as well as active participation) was stronger among youth and among the poor and working class. Old people and middle-class Negroes were more likely to feel ambivalent and to hold back. But there seems to have been at least some participation from all segments of the black community. In the countless interviews and feature stories that appeared in the press and on television, Watts citizens were more likely to explain and justify the riots rather than to condemn them; certainly the mass media would have little interest in censoring accounts of black disapproval. In a statewide public opinion survey conducted in November, 1965, only 16 percent of the blacks interviewed attributed the riots to "lack of respect for law and order" in contrast with 36 percent of the whites; "outside agitators" were seen as a most important cause by a scant 7 percent of the blacks compared with 28 percent of the whites. Seventy-nine percent of the black respondents fixed upon "widespread unemployment" and "bad living conditions" as prime causes, compared with only 37 percent of the whites. And months after the rioting a poll conducted by ABC Television found that the proportion of Watts residents who felt that the summer's events had helped their cause was twice as large as of those who felt it had hurt them.

If the Los Angeles revolt was not simply a "spasm" of lawlessness reflecting the violent inclinations of a minor criminal group, but represented instead the mood and spirit of the low-income black community, then we must look more closely at what the crowds were attempting to communicate.

As the Governor's report correctly notes, the uprising was not organized in advance. Yet it was neither formless nor meaningless. The people on the street were expressing more than the blind rage and the antiwhite hate epitomized in the "Burn, baby, burn" slogan. They seem to have been announcing an unwillingness to accept indignity and frustration without fighting back. In particular, they were communicating their hatred of policemen, firemen, and other representatives of white society who operate in the black community "like an army of occupation." They were asserting a claim to territoriality, making an unorganized and rather inchoate attempt to gain control over their community, their "turf." Most of the actions of the rioters appear to have been informed by the desire to clear out an alien presence, white men, rather than to kill them. (People have remarked how few whites were shot, considering the amount of sniping and the degree of marksmanship evidenced in accurate hits on automobile lights and other targets.) It was primarily an attack on property, particularly white-owned businesses, and not persons. Why not listen to what people in the crowds were saying as Charles Hillinger of the *Los Angeles Times* did on the night of August 13.

> "White devils, what are you doing in here?"
> "It's too late, white man. You had your chance. Now
> it's our turn."
> "You created this monster and it's going to consume you.
> White man, you got a tiger by the tail. You can't hold
> it. You can't let it go."
> "White man, you started all this the day you brought
> the first slave to this country."
> "That's the hate that hate produced, white man. This
> ain't hurting us now. We have nothing to lose. Negroes
> don't own the buildings. You never did a decent thing in
> your life for us, white man."[15]

A "Native" Uprising

Any appraisal of the Watts uprising must be tentative. I suggest, however, that it was not primarily a rising of the lawless, despite the high participation of the lumpenproletariat and the clear-cut attack on law and authority. Nor was it a "conventional race riot," for the Los Angeles terror arose from the initiative of the black community and did not fit the simple pattern of whites and blacks engaging in purely racial aggression. It was certainly not a Los

Angeles version of a mass civil rights protest. Its organization was
too loose. More important, the guiding impulse was not integration
with American society but an attempt to stake out a sphere of control by moving against that society.

Instead my interpretation turns on two points. On the collective level the revolt seems to represent the crystallization of community identity through a nationalistic outburst against a society felt
as dominating and oppressive. The spirit of the Watts rioters appears
similar to that of anticolonial crowds demonstrating against foreign
masters, though in America the objective situation and potential power
relations are very different. On the individual level, participation
would seem to have had a special appeal for those young blacks
whose aspirations to be men of dignity are systematically negated
by the unavailability of work and the humiliations experienced in
contacts with whites. For these young men (and reports indicate
that males between the ages of 14 and 30 predominated in the
streets), violence permitted expressing their manhood in the American
way of fighting back and "getting even."

The gulf between Watts and affluent Los Angeles is disturbingly
similar to that between "natives" and their colonial masters. The
Afro-American's alienation from the institutions and values of the
larger society was made clear during the revolt. The sacredness of
private property, that unconsciously accepted bulwark of our social
arrangements, was rejected. Black people who looted, apparently without guilt, generally remarked that they were taking things that "really
belonged" to them anyway. The society's bases of legitimacy and its
loci of authority were attacked. Law and order were viewed as the
white man's law and order. Policemen were the major targets, police
activity the main issue, because uniformed law enforcement officers
represent the most crystallized symbols and the most visible reality
of colonial domination.

Thus Watts was not simply a racial revolt. Negro police and
"responsible" moderate leaders also were the objects of the crowd's
anger. Black businessmen who were seen as close to the community
were spared damage. From the standpoint of the poor, there was
thus an implicit division of the black middle class into those two
segments that are found in the colonial situation: a "national bourgeoisie" on the side of liberation and a "native middle class" that
serves as an agent of the dominant power arrangements.

Fanon has argued that in violating the integrity of indigenous ways of life and in creating the social status of "natives," colonialism reduced the manhood of the peoples it subjected.[16] The condition of slavery in the United States and the subsequent history of economic exploitation and second-class citizenship have constituted a similar attack on black manhood. A new generation of militants created in the civil rights movement a vehicle for the affirmation of their manhood in the political struggle against its systematic negation. But the nonviolent movement that grew up in the South (with its religiously oriented population, cohesive communities, and clear-cut segregation problems) is not well adapted to the social conditions and psychological temper of Northern blacks. Unless new possibilities for the expression of initiative, assertiveness, and control are opened, we can expect violent revolt to become increasingly frequent.

A young boy, who had been involved in a number of situations of arson, told me that he enjoyed it. "You mean you enjoyed seeing buildings going up in fire?" I asked. "I did," he replied, "because it gave me a feeling of being powerful, of being somebody. And if I can't go downtown and be a man, at least up here I can set something on fire." These youths, blocked from asserting their manhood in constructive ways, turn to violence. And this is a society in which violence has come to be related to manhood.

In some families Negro men who had participated in the riots were treated with awe and respect by their wives and children. They were no longer the passive victims of the ghetto, to be pited or hated, often both, by their families. Now they were—if even for a moment— men who had asserted themselves through action. A jobless young man of 18 who already had a number of common law marriages and six children by different women, told me that the first time he felt like a man was when he saw the building he set on fire burn to the ground.[17]

The Watts revolt was also a groping toward community identity. South-central Los Angeles has been a vast ghetto with very amorphous neighborhood and district boundaries—and a glaring lack of leadership and organization. Most of the major civil rights groups were nonexistent in the ghetto; the gap between official Negro spokesmen and the poor was even greater than is typical. The word "Watts" itself as a locational reference for the ambiguously defined district around 103rd and Central Avenue had become a stigmatized term among blacks as well as whites and was rarely used by residents. During the August uprising a reversal in all these tendencies became apparent. The mass action strengthened feeble communal loyalties. The term "Watts" appeared painted on walls and windows as an expression of pride and identity. Youth gangs representing the adjacent neighborhoods of Watts, Willowbrook, and Compton ceased their long-standing wars and united to provide a core of organization during the rioting and the subsequent work of rehabilitation. Many middle-class blacks saw that their interests could not be severed from those of the ghetto's poor, particularly when their streets and residences were included within the curfew boundaries drawn by the militia—thus dramatizing the fact of common fate. Since August 1965, a proliferation of community organizing, political action, and civil rights groups have arisen in the Watts area.[18] All these processes —intensified communal bonds, ethnic identity, the hesitant return of the middle class, and a new sense of pride in place—are graphically summed up in the experience of Stan Saunders, a Watts youth who had moved out of the ghetto to All-American football honors at Whittier College followed by two years abroad as a Rhodes scholar. His return two weeks before the revolt may be prototypical.

> At the height of the violence, he found himself joyously
> speaking the nitty-gritty Negro argot he hadn't used
> since junior high school, and despite the horrors of the
> night, this morning he felt a strange pride in Watts. As a
> riot, he told me, "It was a masterful performance. I sense
> a change there now, a buzz, and it tickles. For the first
> time people in Watts feel a pride in being black. I
> remember, when I first went to Whittier, I worried that if
> I didn't make it there, if I was rejected, I wouldn't have
> any place to go back to. Now I can say 'I'm from
> Watts.' "[19]

The McCone Commission missed the meaning of the Watts revolt because of the limitations inherent in its perspective. The surface radicalism of its language (in calling for "a new and, we believe, revolutionary attitude toward the problems of the city") cannot belie its basic *status quo* orientation. The report advocates "costly and extreme recommendations," and while many of their excellent proposals are indeed costly, they are by no means extreme.

Truly effective proposals would hurt those established institutions and interests that gain from the deprivation of Watts and similar communities—the commission does not fish in troubled waters. Possibly because they do not want black people to control their ethnic neighborhoods, they do not see the relation between community powerlessness and the generalized frustration and alienation that so alarm them.

In their approach to the problems of Watts, the commission was guided by values and assumptions of a white middle-class ethos, which are of dubious relevance to the majority of lower-class blacks. Their chief hope for the future was the instillation of achievement motivation in the ghetto poor so that they might embark upon the educational and occupational careers that exemplify the American success story. I am not against middle-class values—but in the immediate critical period ahead "middle-classification" will be effective with only a minority of today's poor. Needed were a perspective and set of recommendations that spoke to the collective character of the situation, the overall relation between America's black communities and larger structures of power. The legalistically oriented commission—with primary commitments to control, law and order, a white-dominated *status quo,* and a middle-class ethic—was not able even to formulate the problem on this level.

Postscript 1971

In the six years that have elapsed since "Watts," there have been vast amounts of social research on both the Los Angeles events and other ghetto rebellions that followed. These studies have disproved virtually all of the McCone Commission's sociological generalizations and explanations, and have tended to confirm my dissenting analysis. It may be valuable to summarize the most important of these findings.

First, the thesis that the riots were the work of the "criminal, lawless" elements has been put to rest. In a supplementary volume to the 1968 report of the Kerner Commission, the authors identify this commonly-held "riff-raff" theory of ghetto violence, and marshall statistics from a variety of cities to counter it.[20] The UCLA study of the south-central Los Angeles curfew area, undertaken shortly after the 1965 uprising, found that blacks in the lowest income levels were no more likely to riot than others.[21] Indeed riot participation and support tend to be associated with slightly higher-than-average levels of education and political sophistication, as well as with attitudes of racial pride and militancy.[22]

Second, research has found that levels of participation and support were far higher than the McCone estimate. The UCLA investigators calculate that approximately 15 percent of the adult black population were *active* in the events. An additional 35 or 40 percent were active as spectators.[23] All classes of people participated, middle-class as well as poor, employed as well as unemployed, those without arrest records as well as those who had been in conflict with the law. Similar results were found in other cities. The Southern immigration thesis did not hold up, either. Sixty percent of the UCLA sample had lived in the city ten years or longer, and support for the revolt was as great among these long-term residents as it was among the more recent arrivals.[24]

Third, the uprising did not look as irrational to the black population as it did to the commissioners. It is true that the majority of the Los Angeles sample decried the burning, sniping, and looting; at the same time they expressed sympathy for those engaged in these acts. They felt that business and other targets were selected because of specific grievances and not at random. Blacks in the curfew zone were twice as likely to feel that the uprising had a purpose or goal than to deny one; incidentally, a white sample was just as convinced that there was no purpose to the violence. Eighty-five percent of these whites referred to the events either as a *riot* or by some other negative expression such as disaster, tragedy, or mess. Only 54 percent of the blacks chose these terms (primarily the riot one); 38 percent preferred to use a more political definition—revolt, revolution, or insurrection.[25]

At the beginning of this chapter a comparison of the McCone Report with the 1922 *Negro in Chicago* study was suggested. In conclusion it might be appropriate to consider briefly the most important riot study which has since appeared, the *Report of the National Advisory Commission on Civil Disorders* of 1968.[26] The connection is a real one, for the staff of the Kerner Commission was quite conscious of the inadequacies of the California study; my critique which originally appeared in 1966 (as well as others) was studied closely so that similar errors might be avoided.

There is no doubt that the Kerner Report, more than 600 pages long, is a more solid and better balanced work. The amount of time, energy, and social research incorporated is impressive. It is a serious document, filled with countless footnotes, statistical tables, and appendices. It is a good expression of the liberal approach to our racial crisis, whereas the McCone product was a shoddy rendering of the conservative position.

The National Advisory Commission attempted a sociological approach rather than a legalistic, riot-control perspective, though traces of the latter appear in sections. Instead of focusing primarily on law and order, it "introduced" the American public to the idea that white racism was the underlying condition of ghetto violence. The police role in intensifying racial tensions was more frankly dealt with, the opinions of black people were taken more seriously. Thousands of recommendations for change were made. Comprehensive as these were, their goal was limited reform, rather than a basic overhaul of the institutions that make up a racially oppressive society. But even with its own limitations,[27] the report received a cold reception from the administration and, apparently, from the general public also—as I document in the next chapter.

NOTES

1. *The Chicago Commission on Race Relations* (Chicago: University of Chicago Press, 1922).
2. Charles S. Johnson, *Shadow of the Plantation* (Chicago: University of Chicago Press, 1934), and *Growing Up in the Black Belt* (Washington: American Council on Education, 1941).
3. *Violence in the City—An End or a Beginning?* A Report by the Governor's Commission on the Los Angeles Riots (December 2, 1965).
4. For example, a few months before the McCone Report was written, Kenneth Clark's *Dark Ghetto* (New York: Harper & Row, 1965) appeared.
5. *Violence in the City, op. cit.,* pp. 87–88.

6. *Ibid.* Quotations that follow, without a reference citation, are from the McCone Report.

7. J. S. Coleman, *et al., Equality of Educational Opportunity* (Washington: Office of Education, 1966).

8. "A young man in a striped shirt," as quoted by Louise Meriwether, "What the People of Watts Say," *Frontier* (October 1965).

9. During the riots Parker stated to the Watts population, "We're on top, you're on the bottom." He said the rioters were behaving like "monkeys in the zoo." Anthony Oberschall, "The Los Angeles Riot of August 1965," in James Geschwender, ed., *The Black Revolt* (Englewood Cliffs, N.J.: Prentice-Hall, 1971), p. 266.

10. Professional social workers as well as delinquent youth concurred on many points of fact with respect to the police presence. Officers were overconcentrated in the ghetto, children felt themselves under constant police surveillance, youths were frequently stopped for questioning even when there had been no apparent wrongdoing, and many instances in which innocent bystanders or observers of fights and disturbances were arrested along with or instead of the guilty parties were cited. True, the police were aware of their "negative image," a number of officers were undoubtedly trying to do a difficult job in a spirit of justice and fairness, and a minority of the sample felt that they were doing a good job. But unfortunately more typical appraisals were those of the public welfare director and the "well-adjusted" nondelinquent Negro youth in the 12th grade quoted below:

> The attitude of the authorities toward the youth of this area is brutal and oppressive for the most part. The police are afraid, to a certain extent, of the Negro population. There is a tremendous tension between the police and the Negro community.
>
> When you come up in Watts, you can live practically any place because you know that if you're around, whatever happens when the police get there, you know they're going to take you even though you didn't do anything. Say, for instance, if you were coming home from the store, and there was a fight across the street, and you . . . stayed to watch it, the police come by, and they'll grab you.

Youth Opportunities Board of Greater Los Angeles, *First In-*

   terim *Report on the Area Survey in South Central Los Angeles:*
   A Working Document (June 1963).

11. The UCLA survey seems to confirm this point. Forty-five percent of the sample said they had personal experience with nonviolent police malpractice: insulting language, stopping and
   searching cars, unnecessary frisking. The proportions who reported experiencing or witnessing more violent forms were much
   smaller: 13 percent for unnecessary force in arrests, 1 percent
   for beating people in custody, 6 percent for unnecessary home
   searches. However, 65 to 70 percent believed that the latter
   practices occurred; the same proportion felt that the less violent
   behaviors were common. Source: Nathan Cohen, ed., *The Los
   Angeles Riots: A Socio-psychological Study* (New York: Praeger,
   1970), p. 11.

12. Paul Delaney, "Recruiting of Negro Police is a Failure in Most
   Cities," *New York Times* (January 25, 1971), 1 and 14.

13. *San Francisco Sunday Examiner and Chronicle* (May 9, 1971),
   sec. A, 19, summarizing an article "The Dilemma of the Black
   Policeman," *Ebony* (May 1971).

14. Bayard Rustin, "The Watts Manifesto," *New America* (September 17, 1965), 7.

15. *Los Angeles Times* (August 14, 1965), 2.

16. Frantz Fanon, *The Wretched of the Earth* (New York: Grove,
   1968). On this point see also Sartre's preface.

17. Rustin, *op. cit.,* pp. 7, 8.

18. *The New York Times* (November 7, 1965) reported more than
   100 organizations established in the Los Angeles ghetto since
   the riots.

19. Shana Alexander, "My Friend in Watts," *Life* (August 27,
   1965), 18.

20. R. M. Fogelson and R. B. Hill, "Who Riots? A Study of Partici-
   pation in the 1967 Riots," *Supplemental Studies for the National
   Advisory Commission on Civil Disorders* (Washington, 1968).
   See also David O. Sears and T. M. Tomlinson, "Riot Ideology
   in Los Angeles: A Study of Negro Attitudes," in Geschwender,
   ed., *op. cit.,* pp. 375–388; and Nathan Caplan, "Identity in
   Transition," in Roderick Aya and Norman Miller, eds., *The New
   American Revolution* (New York: The Free Press, 1971).

21. Cohen, *op. cit.,* pp. 3, 140–257.

22. Caplan, *op. cit.*

23. Cohen, *op. cit.*, p. 3. Other similar estimates of riot participation appear in the articles collected in Geschwender, *op. cit.*, and in Allen D. Grimshaw, ed., *Racial Violence in the United States* (Chicago: Aldine, 1969).

24. Cohen, *op. cit.*, pp. 2–3.

25. Sears and Tomlinson, *op. cit.*

26. *Report of the National Advisory Commission on Civil Disorders,* with an introduction by Tom Wicker (New York: Bantam Books, 1968).

27. There have been many critiques of the Kerner Report. Symposium on "The Kerner Report, Social Scientists, and the American Public," six essays, *The Social Science Quarterly, 49,* no. 3 (December 1968), 433–473. See also Gary T. Marx, "Two Cheers for the Riot Commission Report," *The Harvard Review, 4* (Summer 1968), 3–14; Amitai Etzioni, "Making Riots Mandatory," *Psychiatry and Social Science Review* (May 1968); and Tom Christoffel, "Black Power and Corporate Capitalism," in Barry N. Schwartz and Robert Disch, eds., *White Racism* (New York: Dell, 1970), pp. 333–340. On the politics of riot commissions, see Robert M. Fogelson, *Violence as Protest* (Garden City, N.Y.: Doubleday, 1971); and Michael Lipsky and David J. Olson, "Riot Commission Politics," *Trans-Action* (July-August 1969), 9–21.

chapter 7
the huey newton
jury voir dire*

During the past few years an increasing number of black militants have been arrested and tried in cases arising out of racial and political struggles. Some arrests, such as that of Ahmed Evans of Cleveland, have taken place in the course of ghetto rebellions; others have occurred during more organized demonstrations, particularly on the campuses; many have resulted from individual confrontations with the police. Police incidents precipitated the trials of Black Panthers in Oakland, Los Angeles, Chicago, and New Orleans; other Panther cases in New York and New Haven followed arrests on conspiracy charges. Most recently, the militancy among black convicts, exploding into actions against prison guards, officials, and the judicial process, forms the general background for such celebrated cases as the two groups of "Soledad Brothers," Angela Davis, and Ruchell Magee. Of all these many trials, perhaps none was more pointed in its social, political, and legal implications than that of *The People of California v. Huey P. Newton,* which unfolded in the Oakland (Alameda County) Superior Court before Judge Monroe Friedman during the summer of 1968. The Newton case was strategic because the defendant was the founder and Minister of Defense of the Black Panther Party, the group that had most aggressively advanced the policy of armed self-defense in the Northern ghettos; because the Panther leader was indicted on a first-degree murder charge for the alleged

* This article appeared originally as "Sociology in the Courtroom," in Ann Fagan Ginger, editor, *Minimizing Racism in Jury Trials.* National Lawyers Guild (Box 673, Berkeley), 1969, pp. 43–71.

shooting of a white policeman; and because this trial dramatized the issues in a way that set precedents for the legal and political climate of many that followed in its wake.

On the morning of October 28, 1967, John Frey, a white Oakland police officer, was shot and killed in a deteriorating section of the West Oakland ghetto. Another white policeman, Herbert Heanes, was shot and wounded. Frey had stopped a car driven by Huey Newton, who received bullet wounds in the stomach and was arrested later that morning at the hospital where he had sought medical attention. Although the prosecutor argued that Newton had pulled a gun and deliberately murdered Frey, the weapon the Panther leader allegedly used was never located. The State's main witness was Henry Grier, a Negro bus driver. Grier stated that he saw Newton fire at Frey, but the credibility of his identification of the defendant was weakened by many contradictions between his grand jury and trial testimonies. Another principal was Del Ross, a black youth, who was expected to testify—in support of the third charge, kidnapping—that Newton had commandeered his car to get to the hospital. Ross's memory went totally blank on the witness stand. Finally, Gene McKinney emerged as the defense's "mystery witness." He had been Newton's companion that morning, and he took the Fifth Amendment when asked about his role in the events. The lack of hard evidence and the confusion that still surrounded the case after all the "facts" had been presented led to what most courtroom observers considered a compromise jury verdict. Newton was cleared of the assault charge against Heanes and convicted of voluntary manslaughter of Frey rather than murder. The third kidnapping charge had already been dropped after Ross would not testify.*

* After almost two years, during which Newton was imprisoned at Vacaville and at the California Men's Colony near San Luis Obispo, the verdict was overturned on appeal by a higher state court. The major ground was judicial error; the appellate review reasoned that Judge Friedman was negligent in not presenting the possibility of a verdict of involuntary manslaughter in his instructions to the jury. In the summer of 1971 the Oakland district attorney began a second Newton trial, this time on the reduced charge of manslaughter. Perhaps due to exhaustion from a series of crucial trials, perhaps because of less political focus on the second trial, Charles Garry, the defense attorney, abandoned most of his elaborate jury challenge and voir dire procedures. Aside from a few changes, the trial proper was a rerun of the first drama, except that the prosecutor,

The full story of the Newton case is beyond the scope of this study.[1] I concentrate instead on that phase of the trial in which I participated as a consultant to the staff of defense attorneys: the selection of the jury and particularly the attempt to detect the existence of, and evaluate the degree of, racism among white jurors through the voir dire (questioning of prospective jurors). From the standpoint of legal precedent and social interest, one of the many innovative aspects of this trial was the introduction of racism and racial prejudice as a legitimate area for extensive probing of the state of mind of the members of the jury panel. In this chapter I shall discuss how the voir dire worked, how we attempted to uncover racial attitudes, and how the defense staff made its decisions related to jury selection. Limiting our interest to the pretrial phase of the case, we omit the significant legal and sociological issues involved in the trial proper.

The opening segment of *The People of California* v. *Huey P. Newton* was unusually lengthy, significant in legal issues, and well organized, even for a murder case. Three days were devoted by the defense to the testimony of expert witnesses and to the introduction of motions challenging the system of jury selection in Alameda County. Charles Garry and his associates argued that the method by which jury lists were drawn from the rolls of registered voters resulted in a nonrepresentative panel, systematically underrepresenting members of the black and low-income populations. Furthermore, the defense challenged the very competence of a jury, conventionally drawn and constituted along prevailing concepts of "representative of the community," to provide a fair trial in the case of a black militant leader accused of murdering and assaulting white police officers. It was argued that "a jury of one's peers" in this context must mean a jury drawn from the ghetto, composed primarily—if not entirely—of Afro-Americans with life conditions and experiences similar to the

---

Lowell Jensen, assigned the case to one of his aides, assistant district attorney, Donald Whyte. The jury, out for six days, was dismissed on August 8, 1971, because it could not come to any agreement. Judge Harold Hove declared a mistrial. A third trial began in October 1971 with an all-white jury. On December 11 it ended in another mistrial with the jury split 6 to 6. After three days of deliberation it was "impossible" to reach a verdict. A few days later District Attorney Jensen decided not to prosecute again, and Huey Newton was free.

defendant's. The Kerner Report, which had appeared four months earlier, was cited to document the prevailing white racism in America, which makes problematic the unbiased deliberations of the conventionally drawn "representative" jury. Seven expert witnesses, including six social scientists—among them Hans Zeisel, Professor of Law at the University of Chicago, Nevitt Sanford, a coauthor of *The Authoritarian Personality*, and Floyd Hunter who had studied the community and power relations in Oakland after his pioneering work *Community Power Structure*—provided research data and expert opinion in support of various aspects of these motions.

The several motions challenging the jury selection system were denied, as was probably expected, but they enhanced the interest and seriousness of the jury selection over the course of the following two and one-half weeks. It took two weeks and the questioning of 99 prospective jurors to constitute the regular jury (defense attorney Garry used all 20 of his peremptory challenges; prosecuting attorney D. Lowell Jensen, now chief district attorney, then an assistant district attorney, of Alameda County, used only 15). Approximately two-and-a-half days and 53 panelists were required to choose the four alternate jurors, none of whom had the chance to substitute for the regulars during the trial proper.

The voir dire, and in fact the entire trial, provided a natural experiment, a test of the validity of the significant charges contained in the defense motions and in the expert testimony. The methods Garry used to question jurors on social and political attitudes were copied or adapted in other racially and politically relevant trials by attorneys defending both black and white militants.[2] The voir dire was fascinating for the glimpse it provided of the racial attitudes and concerns of a natural sample of American citizens a few short months after the murder of Martin Luther King. Though my analysis is based only on this single case study, I find the experience of jury selection in the Newton case profoundly disturbing with respect to certain fundamental tenets of American justice.

The data that follow should be read in terms of their implications for some basic principles of our legal system. Is it possible to take seriously the norm of the "fair and impartial" juror, especially in racially charged cases, or must we view impartiality as an outdated legal fiction? What does it mean to speak of a jury representative of "the community," when the community itself is split into diverse and often conflicting segments based on race, class, style of life, and political attitudes? Does the present system of challenges, by which counsel are free to eliminate a fixed number of jurors, aid or obstruct the goals of impartiality and representativeness? And, finally, if white racism cannot be adequately uncovered by the innovative methods used by an exceptionally able Newton defense, how can racial prejudice be minimized as a factor in trial by jury?

The Voir Dire in Theory and Practice

The reader unfamiliar with trial procedures must first grasp the basic elements of the voir dire. After a master panel of prospective jurors has been selected and sworn in, portions of that panel are selected at random and assigned in blocs of 15 to 50 to the various courtrooms where juries are being chosen. The court clerk spins a wheel, the name of a juror from the list is chosen by lot, and he or she is called to the stand. After the judge has read the charges in the case and furnished other instructions, the two opposing counsel are free to question the prospective juror in order to determine her or his state of mind with respect to the legally salient issues of the case.

Theoretically, the purpose of the voir dire is to guarantee a neutral, objective, and relatively unbiased jury. Thus, if the questioning is thorough it elicits information that will permit the elimination of jurors who have close personal ties with one of the parties of the case. Because this was a capital offense, the views of the prospective juror on capital punishment also were relevant. In the context of California law in 1968 as interpreted by Judge Friedman, it was permissible to oppose the death penalty on principle, but not to be so fixed about it that the juror would not consider death at all should the trial result in a verdict of first degree murder and thus require a second trial to deal with the penalty phase.

The theoretical purpose of the voir dire may be realized in the majority of civil and criminal cases in which political and social issues are at most peripheral. But the norm of impartiality is strained to the limit in cases involving black militants. The Newton case was the most highly charged criminal trial in the Bay Area in a decade, probably the most publicized "political" case since the 1930s. On the one side, the mass media had covered the "facts" of Frey's killing and Newton's arrest in such a way that many—if not most—white citizens automatically assumed that the defendant was guilty. Leading citizens, including the Mayor of Oakland, had made inflammatory statements against Newton and the Panthers just before the trial opened. On the other side, black militants aided by white radicals had organized a "Free Huey" movement, asserting that his arrest represented a frameup for the purpose of crushing the Black Panthers. The Newton case thus served to further polarize the extremes of opinion in what may already have been the most polarized metropolitan area in the United States.

The two major symbols in this case were the black militant and the white policeman. (In the trial proper, the majority of defense witnesses were to be blacks, generally but not exclusively "militant" in tone and style; the majority of the prosecution witnesses were to be white officers.) In the late 1960s it was virtually impossible for Americans of any color not to have had some sort of preconceptions toward aggressive black nationalists; in fact most white Americans are considerably threatened on one level or another by militant Afro-Americans. Several prospective jurors in fact expressed the fear that sitting on the jury would invite physical retaliation from the militants.

Attitude toward police is an issue upon which whites and blacks are markedly divided. The problem of impartiality is further compounded by the fact that a significant proportion of the white citizenry have friendly social ties with individuals in law enforcement, whereas almost none from the majority group have similarly close relations with black people, let alone militants. In the Newton jury selection, 13 of the first 20 persons questioned on this point affirmed that they counted a policeman as a friend or relative. A few of these people admitted that this would bias them as potential jurors; the majority, however, insisted that they could be perfectly neutral. One man, while protesting his impartiality, expressed the opinion that no police officer would ever attack a citizen; others indicated that they would tend to believe the sworn testimony of a law enforcement officer, yet expressed various reservations about crediting a Black Panther witness. In a case whose major actors so epitomized the polar conflicts of our society, the reader can imagine the incredulity of the court audience when one somewhat confused Berkeleyan stated, "I am pro-police but I am also pro-Black Panther so I don't know where I stand."

Despite its theoretical function, the voir dire is actually a contest between the two adversaries with the goal of selecting a jury most favorable to their case. The contestants win a round when they succeed in having the judge accept a challenge "for cause," thus eliminating a prospective juror who appears to be unfavorable to them. In the Newton case, only 48 of the 99 prospective jurors who were examined during the selection of the regular jury actually sat in the box for a period of time. The others were either challenged for cause (sending them to be assigned to another courtroom) or removed by stipulation (agreement of the two attorneys in cases of ill health, financial hardship, impending vacations, and the like).

The two main criteria for a challenge for cause were prejudice and a rigid anti-death-penalty stance. Twenty-three from the regular panel were successfully challenged for a state of mind containing bias; in all cases except two or three these were people prejudiced against Newton; they thought that he was guilty, or revealed some other tendency to favor the state's case. Fourteen persons were eliminated because of a fixed opposition to capital punishment. The principle behind a challenge on account of bias toward the defendant seems perfectly clear. It is less apparent why the present law permits a challenge for cause toward persons strictly opposed to the death penalty, since, as attorney Garry repeatedly pointed out, this position need not interfere with neutrality in judging guilt or innocence. A murder trial jury is less representative when people who feel strongly against capital punishment have no chance to become jurors. Some of the social scientists also presented data to show that people opposed to the death penalty tend to be more liberal, humane, and less prejudiced than those in favor of it.[3]

The role of the judge is crucial here since both prejudice and the precise line where opposition to the death penalty results in an inflexible position are extremely vague. But on this score, the Court gave something to both sides; he questioned jurors and made his rulings with the intent of trying to keep the juror seated whenever possible. Thus Friedman made it very difficult for Garry to establish prejudice; but he was no easier on Jensen in the latter's attempt to establish a rigid anti-capital-punishment position.

When a possible challenge for cause is at stake, the voir dire resembles a see-saw or tug-of-war in which the prospective juror is pulled back and forth between the two adversary counsel. Jensen interrogated the panel member first; sensing a "friendly" individual with a bias toward the prosecution's views, he presented his questions

in such a way as to "coach" the person toward the appropriate responses that make up the front of neutrality. Garry, getting his turn,
tried to trip the man up, getting him to reveal apparent bias. Jensen
objected or intervened, and getting the man back for questioning, tried
to reestablish an impartial position so that the judge would deny the
defense's challenge. Or, finding someone opposed to the death penalty,
the prosecutor tried to box this potential juror into a rigid position
and, if successful, challenged for cause. Then the judge or Garry
would intervene, giving the person every opportunity for a more
flexible position that might "save" him.

The other element in the contest is the peremptory challenge.
Each attorney strove to get an apparently unfavorable juror dismissed
"for cause" in order to save his peremptory challenges. Because the
Newton trial was a capital case, each party was permitted twenty
challenges to be used against people who for some reason did not suit
them. No reason is given for challenging peremptorily; it is sufficient
that the attorney just doesn't like his face. But, in fact, the adversary
counsel tended to base their challenges on information or cues brought
up during the voir dire. Thus, another standard function of the questioning is to get a sense of the prospective juror in order to make an
intelligent decision whether or not to use a challenge on her or him.
But a delicate element is involved here also. If one side questions the
juror thoroughly enough to be absolutely sure that this is a man he
likes, this will give the opposing counsel information to use his peremptory challenges more intelligently.

It is instructive to examine what kinds of people were thrown
out by each side. In keeping with his methodical style, Jensen's challenges could be divided neatly into three main categories: blacks,
Berkeley residents, and anti-death-penalty people. He used 21 challenges in all, 15 in selecting the regular jury and 6 for the alternates.

Eight of the prosecutor's 21 challenges were used against
Negroes (three out of the four who were seated in the regular jury
voir dire; five of the five seated during the alternate voir dire). He
left one black man, David Harper, a loan officer for the Bank of
America, on the regular jury. Although Jensen might have preferred
an all-white jury, he knew that Judge Phillips of the same superior
court had recently granted a mistrial when the prosecutor had thrown
out every black. (The regular Newton jury contained also one Japanese-American man and two Mexican-American women.) But it is

clear that Jensen was doing all that was possible to limit the number of Afro-Americans on the final jury. Of the 50 white people who were "passed for cause," that is, seated, if only temporarily, in the jury box and thus vulnerable to his peremptory challenges, he dismissed 13—or 26 percent. Of the nine blacks passed for cause, he threw out eight—or 89 percent.

In addition, the number of Negroes who might have become jurors was already limited by their underrepresentation in the panel and by the tendency of black people to be against capital punishment (a consistent research finding that was brought out in the pretrial testimony of Dr. Zeisel and Dr. Sanford). In the Newton voir dire, 10 of the 21 blacks called up were challenged for cause because of fixed attitudes against the death penalty; this compares with only 16 of the 122 whites called up. Of course, these data are not a perfectly accurate indication of racial differences on this issue, even for our limited sample. Persons in the voir dire situation do not always present themselves with complete honesty. It is quite possible that some blacks (as well as some whites) who wanted to avoid judging this highly charged political case exaggerated their negative position in order to avoid service. In the same way, a number of whites whose main interest might have been keeping off the jury claimed prejudice and fixed judgments of guilt. Garry took notice of the racial bias in Jensen's use of his challenges and demanded a mistrial because blacks were being kept off the jury systematically. Judge Friedman, whose brand of liberalism combined an ideology of color blindness with an intense personal interest in everybody's ethnicity, replied that Mr. Jensen had allocated his peremptory challenges in a most lawyerlike fashion and implied that the charge of racial bias was ridiculous.[4]

The second group of persons dismissed by Jensen were whites who might be suspected of relations or ties with antiestablishment subcultures. During the regular jury voir dire the prosecutor threw out all but one of the seven citizens who lived in Berkeley. (Six were white, one was black. During the alternate jury selection, Jensen dismissed one black Berkeleyan but permitted two whites to remain.) In only one case did the person appear to belong to the "hippie subculture"; he was a long-haired potter who made ceremonial tea bowls and whose main news source was *The Berkeley Barb*. The others appeared only to have soaked up, in various degrees, some of the liberal-to-radical sentiments that are important in this city. In addition to Berkeleyans, women with college-age children, who expressed some sympathy with the "dissenting generation," also were dismissed.

Once again, the use of peremptory challenges in this manner raises questions about the representativeness of a jury in Alameda County, where the city of Berkeley and various youth-radical-hippie subcultures in and out of Berkeley compose a significant minority of the East Bay populace. In residential terms, Jensen seemed to prefer jurors who lived in such middle-class, virtually all-white suburbs as Fremont, Castro Valley, San Leandro, San Lorenzo, Hayward, Livermore, Alameda, and Albany. He challenged only three persons of the 27 passed from these towns; in contrast he dismissed 18 of 35 from Oakland and Berkeley!

Six of Jensen's challenges were used on persons opposed to the death penalty—very often older white women. In fact, every juror who indicated serious reservations about capital punishment and who was not immediately eliminated "for cause" was subsequently removed by the prosecuting attorney. This does not necessarily mean that the final jury contained only people strongly supportive of the death sanction; certainly, many prospective jurors had learned to give the "right answers," glossing over some of their actual feelings. But it does raise the substantive problem of whether a jury in a capital case can be truly representative if it can be composed only of persons favorable to "death," considering that a sizable minority of the population—indeed, almost half—is opposed or ambivalent to this extreme verdict.*

Garry, of course, tended to favor those whom Jensen disliked. He never challenged any potential juror who appeared to be against the death penalty. And he never peremptorily challenged a person from a racial minority group. Some Afro-Americans who were temporarily seated were not even questioned by the defense; it was sufficient that they were black people from the ghetto for him to

* Three of Jensen's 21 challenges did not fall into the three categories. The residual cases were white working-class people: a retired sheet metal worker, a printer, and a self-described "Okie" with some experience with black people. Thus Jensen seemed to be negative to working-class people also; only two manual workers were on the final jury. The total challenges, now grouped into four categories, add up to more than 21 because a few of the blacks and Berkeleyans were also opposed to capital punishment.

assume that they would be better, more appropriate jurors than the whites. The two Mexican-American women seated, both of whom became final jurors, were asked very few questions, particularly about racial and social matters. The Japanese-American man, also to become a regular juror, was given a similar mild treatment. Garry also tended to distrust people from the white suburban areas; in fact, 20 of his 25 challenges were of people from the primarily white communities mentioned above. In addition to Berkeley residents, there was less suspicion of those whites who lived in some of the "mixed" areas of Oakland—such persons were expected to be more appreciative of the social issues in the case.

Age was another category that the defense found relevant: young people in America are more likely to be sympathetic to the black movement than their elders. Despite the fact that the final jury included five people under 35, the panel as a whole appeared to be stacked against the young. My estimates of age distribution (in some cases age was asked, in others I had to rely on guesswork) show that more than half of the regular panelists (53 of 99) were more than 50 years old. Another 31 appeared to be between 35 and 50, leaving only 15 out of 99 under 35 years old. (During the alternate selection, approximately half were over 50 but there was a higher frequency in the 21–35 group, perhaps one-third).

The principles behind the defense attorney's challenges were not so clear-cut as the prosecutor's. Garry is a less methodical personality, and he often made his decision on the basis of an intuitive hunch about the prospective juror.* Garry's quick intuition was aided by the force of his personality. Unlike Jensen, whose neutral, bland style evoked a response in kind, Garry related to prospective jurors quite personally. He expressed his feelings freely and, with his strong presence, made it difficult for the other to maintain a neutral stance. Thus while many were "won over," the hostility of some became explicit, and this aided the counsel in sizing them up.

But there is another reason, perhaps the most basic, why the Garry team could never be as sure of their decisions as the prosecutor appeared to be. Garry was committed to the position that a fair trial was only possible with a jury from North and West Oakland, the

---

* I had doubts about some of Garry's challenges, since in a few cases my intuition differed, whereas virtually all of Jensen's challenges (except perhaps for one) made sense, given his purposes.

primarily black ghetto where the defendant lived and the death of the policeman occurred. On this count, virtually all the jurors who were seated in the box failed the test. Whereas Jensen usually challenged a particular juror because he was the one person seated at the time whom he wanted off, Garry was often in the situation of really not wanting at least half of the prospective jurors. Another way of saying this is that the jury panel seemed to contain more "good" prosecution people—that is, ones who were propolice, for "law and order," and at least mildly antiblack—than "good" defense people—ones critical of the police, sympathetic to the need for social change, and problack. Such a distribution undoubtedly reflected the realities of political attitudes among whites in Northern California, though the balance may have been further tipped toward the prosecution by the biases introduced along the slow path to jury selection, and feelings were probably intensified by the negative publicity given the Black Panthers and their indicted leader.

Despite all this, there were some patterns in Garry's challenges. A number of young whites with a generally conservative posture, an orientation toward the military and the police, and racial attitudes and general hostility that were only thinly hidden were quickly dismissed. Others who admitted an initial negative attitude toward Newton and the Black Panthers, but somehow survived a challenge for cause, also were thrown out. People who revealed racist attitudes were always challenged, including several whites with more subtle racist tendencies, who expressed rather self-righteous attitudes about their "liberalism." For the most part, however, Garry seemed to rely on his hunches as to whether a particular juror was hostile to him and his client—though he readily sought the advice of other attorneys and consultants like myself before coming to a decision.

How is all this relevant to the larger legal issues raised at the beginning of this chapter? Theoretically, the contest between adversaries during the voir dire should strike a balance, furthering the goal of a jury that is both representative and reasonably impartial. It seems, however, that the dynamics of the peremptory system results in a jury that is more middle-of-the-road than representative of the diversity of a heterogeneous populace. Thus, the prosecutor in this case was able to minimize or virtually eliminate from the final jury Afro-Americans, lower-class people, principled anti-death citizens,

Berkeley residents, and persons from dissenting subcultures. Garry may have been successful in eliminating extreme racial bigots, right-wingers, and militaristic police supporters. Granted that the impartiality of all such persons may have been questionable and that the attorneys were practicing good law in these decisions, the analysis at least suggests an impossible contradiction between the goals of impartiality and representativeness in racial and political cases.

Garry's Use of the Voir Dire: Multiple Functions

The situation was further complicated for the defense because Garry was employing the voir dire for a variety of purposes, which sometimes appeared to conflict. His first goal was to select the best possible jury for his client. Specifically, this meant getting a majority opposed to the death penalty and selecting a group with as little racism as possible, given the situation. But a second purpose, political education, was almost as important. Garry welcomed the long voir dire period, because his questions and what Jensen called his "speeches" gave him the chance to deepen the sensitivity of the final jury on racial matters, to insist upon the constitutional rights of the Black Panthers, and to dispel automatic assumptions of guilt and the natural tendency to assume that law enforcement always acts within the law.

The problem of combining the best possible legal defense and using the trial as an act of radical political education at times resulted in ambiguity and conflict; in some cases the political goal seemed to supersede the strictly legal one. Although this may be unusual in the profession, it was not unlawyerlike. As Charles Garry saw it, the social and economic circumstances of black people in America and the political actions of his client went to the heart of the legal issues in the case. In his aggressive social critique of racism, Garry was also carrying out the desire of his defendant who preferred the most militant political offensive in the courtroom, even though it might adversely affect his own personal fate.*

* An example of apparent conflict occurred during the voir dire. Jensen had passed his last challenge and it was Garry's turn. The potential jury that was seated did not look too bad. Some of the defense attorneys recommended that Garry also pass, because if the process continued, a much worse jury might result, whereas Garry's pass would constitute the present twelve as *the jury*. Garry opposed this, and a lunchtime talk with Newton strongly seconded his view that all his peremptory chal-

Then, too, there was a third function for the voir dire from the point of view of the defense. This was to expose the multiple dimensions of racism existing on the panel: outright bias and prejudice; pure ignorance and unconcern about people of color; insensitivity and lack of involvement. This purpose was relevant to the first, that of selecting the most favorable jury, because information gained was useful in making challenges. But it was also necessary in order to establish the inability of a predominantly white and middle-class jury to deal with the case. Establishing that inability would strengthen both the legal appeal that might be necessary and the political attack against racism. It would link the findings of the voir dire to the motion to quash the jury venire, as well as to the testimony of the social science experts. Yet, at the same time, Garry wanted to see his client acquitted; therefore, he would have welcomed a jury composed of lower-class blacks and antiracist whites. Thus, we detect a contradiction in the purposes of the defense: a need to see its attack on the jury system and white racism confirmed, along with a desire for the kind of jury that would undermine its own social and legal critique. The paradox was expressed in a shift in the public statements of the defendant. Before the pretrial proceedings began he stated that he could receive a fair trial only from a jury drawn from the Oakland ghetto. After the final twelve were selected and at the time they began deliberations, he expressed his confidence to the press that they would come to a fair decision and acquit him.*

Finally, the voir dire served a fourth function for defense attorney Garry. Since some two weeks could elapse between the sitting of persons who might become regular jurors and the opening of the trial proper, he had an opportunity to gain their allegiance through the force of his striking personality—expressed most importantly in a winning charm, a spontaneous wit, and the sincerity of his energetic espousal of his client's case. The courtroom style of Garry and the contrasting manner of the prosecuting attorney are worth examining, since they may have been important to the jurors' ultimate outlook.

----

lenges must be used—on political grounds. Otherwise the argument that the procedures for drawing a jury were biased against the possibility of a fair trial would be considerably weakened.

* This change was not simply a public relations tactic. The defense team as a whole had expected a much tougher jury and was cautiously optimistic as the deliberations began.

In the first place, Garry was more personal and also more aggressive than his counterpart. He exuded warmth and a spontaneous interest in the potential juror, whereas Jensen appeared impersonal, mechanical, even cold. The defense counsel would ask old people about their aches and pains; he always seemed to find a personal inroad to a juror. His style was dramatic because his manner and emotions changed so rapidly, from homey chitchat to hostile frontal attack and back again. It was clear that jurors tended to enjoy their exchanges with Garry (though many were also apprehensive and intimidated); it could be a battle of wits, a testing of mettle, a chance to outsmart a clever antagonist or to gain the approval and friendship of an important man.* In contrast the bloodless quality in Jensen's questioning (toward a hostile juror he came on like a crafty spider rather than like the lion Garry resembled) did not seem to engage the individual deeply.

With middle-aged women Garry was especially effective. A handsome, impeccably dressed man (the journalistic cliché was "dapper"), approaching sixty but looking years younger, only he himself seemed innocent of the seductive, even overtly sexual, nature of his approach. Thus, a standard Garry opener for females was, "Has anything I have asked the other jurors today triggered off something in the crevices of your conscious or unconscious mind that you would like to tell me about?" Finally, we take note of the spontaneity and flexibility of his wit. When it appeared that Garry was making friends through his ready humor, Jensen attempted some jokes of his own, but they always had a forced quality to them. And when the two of them exchanged barbs and jocular comments, it always seemed to be the humor of Garry that won the juror. I shall refrain from documenting these points, since wit depends so much on the situation. The courtroom jokes would probably not impress the reader as funny.

The Search for White Racism
The Newton voir dire was precedent-shattering, because Garry questioned the prospective jurors at some length about their general racial attitudes. The questions were not directly related to the issue of prej-

---

* Friendship may seem an exaggerated term but for those unfamiliar with long trials it is difficult to convey the intense and intimate atmosphere of the daily proceedings.

udice in the sense of preconceived opinions about the guilt or innocence of the defendant. Through the weight of pretrial motions and
testimony, Garry convinced the Court that a juror's state of mind
about black people and current-day racial issues was relevant to his
or her ability to be fair and impartial in judging the case at hand.
Thus, the defense counsel asked the panel members whether they had
heard of white racism, whether they believed it existed in America,
what they understood it to mean, and whether they had within them
white racist feelings. In the same vein, he probed for knowledge of,
definition of, and feelings toward, black power. Prospective jurors
were asked their position on Proposition 14, the referendum that overturned the (Rumford) open housing law in California; whether
Negroes lived in their neighborhoods; and whether they had ever
moved to a new area because "too many black people were moving
in." They were asked about unpleasant experiences with "members of
the black community" and about their general feelings toward people
of color.

The first time a "racial" question was asked, Lowell Jensen
usually objected on the grounds of irrelevance and immateriality.
Throughout the entire trial the prosecuting attorney attempted to restrict the case to the more narrow framework of facts and strictly
legal issues; he constantly asserted that this was not a political case, a
racial trial, or a sociological investigation. The three charges against
the defendant and the facts related to the charges were the matter of
the case from the State's perspective. The presiding judge sustained
many of Jensen's objections, but the court record is more impressive
for the number of social and racial questions that remained in the
voir dire. Perhaps Friedman's most significant restrictive decision was
his ruling out matters of race in the nation as a whole—one could ask,
for example, only whether black people were deprived or discriminated
against in Alameda County. He ruled out of order the question about
how a person had voted on Proposition 14; acts in the electoral booth
were protected by privacy. He was impatient with "vague" questions
related to the juror's perception of social and racial issues; he consistently limited a question to how the particular person felt, thought,
or had acted. The judge seemed to favor a color-blind approach to
racial matters—after a storekeeper had attested to some difficulties
with black customers, he asked gratuitously whether the businessman
had ever had any similar trouble with whites.

Since the county's jury panel is supposed to be representative of the larger community, the aggregate of its responses might reflect how East Bay residents were thinking about race and the racial crisis in July 1968. Limiting our discussion to the whites questioned, the results are certainly not very encouraging. Taking all answers at face value for the moment, the predominant way in which these citizens were relating to the racial crisis of the time was *indifference:* lack of knowledge, lack of interest, and certainly lack of personal involvement. There was also a consistent tendency for prospective jurors to say the "right things" in response to certain questions, but these appropriate, even liberal, statements were almost always on the level of clichés rather than opinions suggesting complexity, sophistication, or the experience of feelings seriously dealt with or positions thought through.

Thus, no one questioned on the point had read the Kerner Report, which had made the headlines five months before and was readily available in paperback; only two persons had seen some excerpts from it in the press; almost no one else had even heard of the report. The majority of the panelists had not heard the term "white racism" before Garry used it in court. Many were familiar with the related idea of white supremacy however, and a scattered few attempted a definition of white racism. When asked whether they had racist or racially-prejudiced feelings, some denied it completely, some others admitted the likelihood—but it did not seem that many in either group were sure what they were talking about. Black power had been in the news for almost two years; certainly the term had saturated the media as "white racism" had not even begun to do. Most people did recognize the term. They had heard of it; but the great majority claimed they had no idea what it meant. And the minority who had never even heard of black power was larger than the infinitesimal proportion who expressed some understanding of its meaning.

The prospective jurors were on the whole favorable, though ambivalent, toward fair housing. Most were in favor of a man's right to live where he could afford to buy a home. But many were not sure that a law to enforce such a right was a good idea, and a sizable number questioned were equally or more solicitous of a person's "right" to sell to whomever he wished.

The answers—with some important exceptions—suggested that the majority of whites had had little meaningful experience with black people during their lives. A few persons had Negro neighbors, coworkers, or tenants—or had had in the past—but most appeared to be living a substantially segregated existence. As a result, the answers to questions about general feelings toward black people tended to lack a concreteness based on generalization from any richness of contact. Thus, there was the unconvincing character of such clichés as "all people are the same" or "they're human beings too."

The following excerpts from the court record illustrate the prevailing themes of indifference, ignorance, and detachment:

1. *July 23, Prospective Juror No. 10, a Southern-born skilled worker living in Fremont:*

MR. GARRY: Have you heard of Black Power?

ANSWER: Yes.

QUESTION: You have any disagreement with the black people's desire for black power?

MR. JENSEN: Object to this as being ambiguous.

THE COURT: Do you know what black power is?

JUROR: I don't know what their aims are, to be honest with you, sir, no.

THE COURT: All right.

MR. GARRY: Do you know anything about black power at all?

ANSWER: I have heard of it, that is all. I don't know what it is about.

QUESTION: How does it strike you when you hear about it? What reaction do you get from it when you hear about it?

ANSWER: Well, I haven't any reaction because I haven't given any thought to it.

QUESTION: Never thought about it at all?

ANSWER: I didn't give it a thought.

2. *July 23, Prospective Juror No. 8, an elderly woman, husband retired, living in Oakland:*

MR. GARRY: Have you ever heard of Black Power?

ANSWER: Yes, I have heard of it.

QUESTION: What do you understand Black Power to mean?

MR. JENSEN: Object to that as incompetent, immaterial, improper voir dire.

JUROR: I don't know what it means.

COURT: She has answered. She doesn't know what it means. Proceed.

MR. GARRY: Do you have any objection to the use of the words, Black Power?

ANSWER: No, no, I haven't.

QUESTION: Have you ever heard of white racism?

ANSWER: Yes.

QUESTION: What does white racism mean to you, the term?

ANSWER: I don't know what that means either, really.

QUESTION: You don't understand what that is either.

ANSWER: No, that is the first time I heard of it is today.

QUESTION: Not until today, you have never heard of white racism?

ANSWER: I never heard of it.

QUESTION: You have heard of white supremacy, have you not?

ANSWER: Yes, I have heard of that.

QUESTION: What does that mean to you?

ANSWER: Well, I don't know.

   3. *July 30, Prospective Alternate Juror No. 2, a middle-aged skilled worker living in Hayward.*

MR. GARRY: Do you know anything—have you ever heard the term called Black Power?

ANSWER: Yes, I have heard of it. I don't know anything——

QUESTION: (Interrupting) And what is your—do you think that's good or bad?

ANSWER: Well, I don't think it's too good.

QUESTION: What's wrong with it?

ANSWER: I don't think—the other term you called, white power, is too good either.

QUESTION: Do you believe that there has been nothing but white power for three or four hundred years in this country?

ANSWER: Well, I couldn't say.

QUESTION: You don't know whether there has been white racism in America for some three or four hundred years?

ANSWER: No, I couldn't say.

QUESTION: Well, do you believe there is white racism in Alameda County?

ANSWER: I don't know.

QUESTION: Do you believe there is white racism right where you are living in Hayward?

ANSWER: Not that I know of.

QUESTION: Do you think there is such a thing called white power?

ANSWER: I have never heard of it until the last couple of days here at Court.

QUESTION: Do you believe that the white people are the ones that control the destiny of the Black people in Alameda County?

ANSWER: I wouldn't know.

QUESTION: Is this because you have never given the matter any thought or you just have never observed it?

ANSWER: Well, I haven't given it thought and I haven't observed it either.

The important thing about these examples is that they were typical of the responses of a substantial proportion of the whites interviewed. Furthermore, *each of these three prospective jurors was passed for cause.* This means that under our present system, such total ignorance and indifference to racial matters is perfectly acceptable as a qualification to judge the case of a black militant leader. Ignorance and indifference, in fact, increased a potential juror's chance of sitting in the box—if only temporarily. In the Newton case, the type of person that is held up as ideal for a democratic polity—the concerned, knowledgeable, and politically active citizen—had the worst chance of all to become a juror!

Another inference can be made from the voir dire excerpts. People may have been hiding some of their real feelings under the cloak of ignorance. There is no way to ascertain how often this took place; though in individual cases the defense team could sense racist attitudes in persons who were careful to make no biased responses. After several days of questioning, the principals and observers in the courtroom anticipated that overt racists would mask their opinions in one way or another. Thus, when one woman freely admitted that she had moved from a neighborhood because it was becoming a black area (and this woman struck me as being more equalitarian than most on racial matters), the question had to be asked and answered three times, because everyone—judge, counsel, audience—was convinced a mistake had been made. All previous jurors had vehemently denied such a possibility.

Of the 150-odd prospective jurors, perhaps 50 were questioned fairly thoroughly on their racial attitudes. Of these, only *one* man openly expressed general anti-Negro feelings. He said he was quite happy that there were no blacks living near him, that he imagined most people felt like that—at least out his way—and, finally, he never really "had anything to do with them people." He, like the more liberal woman whose family was perhaps the last of the whites to leave a black neighborhood, was dismissed because of antiblack attitudes. Yet a great deal of social research agrees on the conclusion that approximately one-third of white Americans are overt and extreme in their racial feelings. (Most of the remaining two-thirds are prejudiced in more subtle ways, though they would not fit the category of "bigot.") It is logical to assume that a considerable number of the prospective jurors actually lied in denying a general antiblack set. These facts suggest the possibility that from the point of view of defense counsel a juror who is open and honest about his or her prejudices may be a better bet than the apparently nonracist juror.

I am suggesting, then, that even Garry's innovative and imaginative questioning failed to plumb the depths of racial attitudes. Why this was so is to a large extent built into the situation. The question and answer format makes it easy for the juror to hide his opinions and protect himself with acceptable answers or feigned ignorance. The adversary situation in the courtroom permits the prosecution counsel to put a stop to sustained questioning in depth. Jensen, for example, objected every time a new question was asked, made interruptions, and otherwise protected the juror against intrusion into his "private" thoughts. And the Judge, although he permitted many social issues to be introduced, also took a protective, even paternalistic, stance. When Garry seemed to be pushing someone rather aggressively, Friedman often stopped a line of questioning. Playing the role of benevolent father, he could not permit a person doing his civic duty to experience too much discomfort—unless he himself had become irritated with that person. Part of the problem is the public character of the voir dire. It does not seem sporting to badger and embarrass a prospective juror, to penetrate into his deep prejudices, in front of a large audience.

As an observer and participant of sorts, I felt that the defense's relative failure in uncovering racism was at times due also to weaknesses in Garry's manner of questioning. To my nonprofessional eyes, Garry conducted a masterful trial, and he was especially brilliant in cross-examining witnesses *and* in interrogating jurors. Yet during the voir dire, it was on racial matters that he most often seemed unproductive. I have already mentioned the inherent difficulties in the task; this was also something new in his 30 years of trial experience. Yet from the point of view of the techniques of interviewing that have been developed in the social sciences and clinical fields, Garry made mistakes and wasted valuable time. He had a prepared list of questions that he intended to ask, and he kept asking those questions even when experience showed they produced no useful information. Thus 15 or 20 persons were asked whether they had read the Kerner Report; one day's work with this question was enough to ascertain that the answer would universally be no. More significantly, the defense counsel often appeared to be asking questions too directly, putting answers in the juror's mouth, rather than querying in the more indirect open-ended manner that elicits fuller and more honest replies. For example, a middle-aged white woman was asked a characteristic Garry question: "Do you have any feelings of white racism?" She answered no. She might have denied prejudice no matter how the question was put, but Garry's wording made it easier to give a negative, essentially uninformative reply. Another question to the same woman was, "Black power, does that create a revulsion in your mind?" Who would answer yes to such a question? The expert interviewer would recommend the open-ended: "Tell me what feelings black power brings to your mind?" To a middle-aged woman from Oklahoma Garry made reference to a previous witness, who had said that the Black Panthers made a mockery of the law, and asked, "You don't feel that the Black Panthers do that, do you?" Of course she said no, but we will never know what she would have said to the simple question, "What do you think about this opinion?"

I made some of these criticisms and suggestions to Garry at the time. Perhaps one reason he did not alter his style—considering how open to advice the man is in general—is that the answers to voir dire items were to a great extent irrelevant in the light of his method of work. With intuitive brilliance, he usually sized up the hostility or friendliness of the prospective juror on the basis of more subtle cues, side comments, and general demeanor. If he disliked a juror, he was only interested in a line of questioning if it would prove the basis of a challenge for cause, and such challenges were almost impossible to win on the grounds of general racial attitudes. Therefore he seemed to ask his questions as much to educate and intimidate other panelists and prospective jurors as to gain information. If he had decided a juror was "good" (always in a relative sense) for his defendant, his questions were asked as much to influence the person to see the case as he saw it as to find out more about that person's state of mind.*

* This might explain what would otherwise be inexplicable omissions in the voir dire. An elderly woman who was to become one of the regular

The strain of the trial was enormous. Garry had his good days and his bad days, and this might explain some of these lapses. Yet it is important for our analysis to note that his difficulties and failures tended to occur while questioning racial attitudes. In searching for the more concrete bias of a fixed opinion in the Newton case, the defense attorney was consistently creative. His flexibility and quickness of intuition here contrasted with the often stumbling mechanical character of the voir dire on race. Unfortunately, there is not space to document this adequately, and the brilliance of the performance comes across only in the courtroom—even the complete rendering of the transcript dulls the shine, since like other dramatic situations, timing and intonation are more central than words. Two examples will show something of his skill.

An elderly retired printer appeared to have great difficulty accepting the premise that a defendant must be considered innocent until proven guilty. Garry submitted a challenge when the gentleman continually refused to accept Newton's innocence: for example, "That's a question (his innocence) I can't answer before I hear the evidence." Jensen argued that it was a matter of semantics, the potential juror being foreign born. The judge concurred, and Jensen was able to drill the man into the "proper" responses. Then Garry resumed the voir dire and the following denouement settled the matter:

MR. GARRY: Mr. ——, again I ask you that same question which you have answered three times to me now—

THE COURT: No. Please ask the question without preface.

MR. GARRY: As Huey Newton sits here next to me now, in your opinion is he absolutely innocent?

———
jurors admitted that she had some subjective feelings of racism. Instead of following this up with the obvious query, "Tell me what some of those feelings are," he continued, "And because of these subjective—some subjective feelings you have, do you make allowances for your own shortcomings in that regard?" She answered yes, and although a graduate student would flunk a test in social research for such an obvious error, Garry's method may have been the successful one for his purposes. The woman turned out to be one of the best jurors from the defense's standpoint. Perhaps the persuasive effect of Garry's "too-direct" question was more valuable in educating this woman than the information a better wording might have gleaned.

ANSWER: Yes.

MR. GARRY: (Raising his voice dramatically) But you don't believe it, do you?

ANSWER: No.

THE COURT: Challenge is allowed.

Garry made another point in the case of a police reserve deputy who insisted he would be impartial. He asked the man whether he was carrying his police badge, and the man had to produce it to the defense attorney. Garry's description of the badge to the courtroom cinched the challenge.

The data I have compiled from courtroom observation and the case transcript reveal that 41 persons were successfully challenged for the cause of prejudice. In all but two or three cases these people admitted or revealed, under intense cross-examination, a tendency to believe in Newton's guilt, an animosity toward the Black Panthers, or a strong inclination to see policemen as several cuts above other mortals. In bringing such attitudes to the surface, Garry eliminated a substantial proportion of the most negative panel members, whereas in probing on racial prejudice, he was able to eliminate only two—including the one woman previously mentioned whose honesty and openness might have made her a more fair and impartial juror than the average.

Although the above point is important, prejudice in the case may often have been based on a deeper racial bias. A preconceived hostility toward Huey Newton and the Black Panthers in many instances reflected a more general hostility and a fear of black people. The inability to award Mr. Newton the presumption of innocence may have been based on unconscious assumptions (and often conscious also) that Negroes are violent and are lawbreakers. Still, it is interesting that people were more honest about case bias than about race bias; the former is still socially acceptable; the latter no longer is.

So far in this essay I have presented a rather dim view of the possibility of deriving a fair and impartial jury for a case such as *The People* v. *Huey P. Newton,* considering the background and social attitudes of those representative citizens who made up the jury panel. I will attempt to support this position even more vigorously in the concluding section. There remains one positive phenomenon, however, that should not be overlooked. Although struck with the dishonesty and simulation of many prospective jurors, I was impressed and pleasantly surprised by the old-fashioned American "fair play" of quite a few others. Many persons, admitting their bias in the case, stated that they did not think their presence on the jury would be fair to the defendant, and they seemed sincere in saying this. Even when attorney Jensen worked hard to "save" them, coaching them in the proper attitudes, a number maintained their self-doubts: they would be less inclined to credit the testimony of a Black Panther than other persons; they could not set aside the assumption of Newton's guilt, which they had gotten from press accounts; their allegiances were with the police and they would not pretend impartiality. In some cases this frankness may have been prompted by a calculated desire to stay off the jury, but there was still a significant group of prejudiced panelists who did not play the game of giving only the right answers.

The prejudiced and honest individuals may be contrasted with another group, those who denied their biases and tried to hide their preconceptions against Newton and the Black Panthers, but were unable to do so. These were generally conservative men who were aggressive and self-righteous about their political ideas, and who had a great need to make their views known. Thus one man attested to his primary allegiance to "law and order," said he held black militants and the Panthers responsible for riots, but argued vehemently that he would be a fair and impartial juror. Garry was usually able to trip up such persons in their own contradictions and win a challenge for cause. There were parallel examples on the other side of the case. Two or three prospective black jurors openly stated that they had doubts about their impartiality because they had long-standing friendships with members of the Newton family. And there were two or three white liberals or radicals who did not choose to play it cool in order to help the defense use up the peremptory challenges of the prosecution. They proclaimed that their commitment to the black movement and their sympathies with the defendant made them inevitably partial.

How the Defense Made Its Decisions

Despite the fact that the sociopolitical milieu and the panel seemed stacked against the possibility of a truly representative and impartial jury, the defense team nevertheless had twenty peremptory challenges to use, and therefore some degree of control over the jury's final makeup. How, then, did Garry and his associates decide which persons should be dismissed from their seats, and which should be left in the jury box?

In addition to relying on the direct statements, Garry seized upon subtle gestures, cues, and especially side comments to form an intuitive assessment of a person. "Freudian slips" were closely attended to. A very self-righteous liberal, who had been proclaiming his fairness, vision, and social compassion, said, "I don't think I would be *impartial,"* when he had intended to say "partial." A prospective alternate protested her lack of bias, despite friendships with police officers, including an Oakland cop who had visited the wounded officer Heanes in the hospital. After claiming to accept the presumption of innocence, which puts the burden of proof on the prosecution, she went on to say that the defendant would have to be "proven innocent."

Apparent lapses or slips were made by "friendly" jurors also, including the pivotal David Harper, the one black man among the final twelve. When Garry asked the bank officer whether he believed Huey Newton killed Officer Frey, Harper answered, with perhaps more emphasis than he intended, "I have *never* been of that opinion." Note how he toned down his very next response: "It is a question of—the opinion that's in my mind is I don't know, and I can subscribe to it." A gratuitous side comment by the same juror was also crucial in contributing to the defense's judgment. When Jensen asked him whether he had ever discussed the case with people at work, Harper replied with a slight trace of bitterness that his colleagues never discuss such matters in his presence—even when Dr. King was shot nobody said anything. It was important for the defense to find evidence of political and racial consciousness in this particular black man since other clues suggested that Jensen wanted him on the jury; in fact, because of such suspicions, Garry questioned Harper at greater length than other blacks.

The defense observed other unintended behavior. The Southernborn skilled worker, whose denial of any thought or opinion on black power has already been quoted, was perspiring freely during this section of the voir dire. Other panelists fidgeted uncomfortably under Garry's probing, while disclaiming any attitudes of racial prejudice. On the other side of the fence, a Mexican-American woman gave a little spontaneous laugh when she said no—that she had no feelings of white racism. We interpreted this gesture to mean that she saw herself as a victim of prejudice, rather than a possible victimizer.

Equally or more important were the words a juror chose, his or her side comments and reactions to Garry's questions. Such cues appeared to be the best basis for judgment in those marginal cases where the person was difficult to size up. It was simple to form a judgment when the individual could not mask his attitude. One ex-marine was overeager to be seated, a tendency the defense deeply distrusted because it seemed to imply a wish to send the defendant to the gas chamber. This man gave himself away with smart-aleck grins in reaction to Garry's statements. There is a sense, then, in which the political heat and polarized sentiment about the case were helpful to the defense, since they made it easier to recognize many of the hostile people.

Realizing that the prosecution would dismiss any juror who was overtly friendly to Newton's case, the defense was trying to maximize the number of open-minded members of the jury. We were looking for people who were basically honest, who appeared to have a capacity to learn and grow in the course of the trial, who had some degree of personal empathy—in short, we were looking for good human beings, if I may use such a nebulous concept. How did we intuit such elusive qualities? In one case an elderly Italian-American woman replied, "We can all make mistakes," in response to whether she would be biased by Newton's previous felony conviction; we took this as a sign of personal compassion. A retired small businessman first referred to black people as "colored," an old-fashioned expression, which often indicates a prejudiced orientation. But because he was old and foreign-born, we attributed the usage to the norms of his generation. Later he spoke of an unfortunate experience with a "colored boy" who turned out to be 25 years old. When Garry pointed out that Negro adults don't particularly appreciate being called boys, the man seemed genuinely surprised. Rather than reacting defensively, he appeared to understand and to have learned something from the exchange. This incident dove-tailed with a general impression that the man was a warm, empathic person. A similar openness and honesty was conveyed by a middle-aged saleslady who, unlike the previous gentleman, was to remain as a juror for the trial phase. Though by no means politically left or even "liberal," she appeared to be a woman who had thought about racial matters, someone who habitually wrestled with her con-

science. She admitted being very upset when a Black Panther spokesman appeared before her church discussion group and accused all
white Christians of being racists. His speech and her anger had made
her think quite a bit.

In some cases, however, significant cues and side comments were
misinterpreted with the result that some unfriendly jurors who could
have been peremptorily challenged became a part of the final twelve.
There is no way to know whether particular individuals consciously
put on a false front, but in one instance the circumstantial evidence
was strong. A middle-aged worker in a meat factory, married to an
Oakland fireman, was conspicuous for her mod dress (Nehru blouse,
medallion, miniskirt) during the first days of the voir dire. When
questioned, she appeared sophisticated, liberal, and "hang-loose." She
knew that the Panthers were a "militant" group—an admittedly
minimal level of political knowledge, but still more than the typical
panelist showed. She implied that she and her husband were on
friendly terms with the two Negro firemen in his station. When asked
whether she had any objection to the Panther terminology of "pig"
for policeman, she replied that it wouldn't prejudice her at all. "People
used to call them fuzz and that didn't bother me either." I think this
comment won Garry over, and he stopped his questioning without
going further into the topic of racism, probably expecting that Jensen
would eventually dismiss this woman. During the course of the trial her
demeanor changed considerably, and the sketchy accounts available
suggest that she was one of the more pro-prosecution jurors.

To an observer in the courtroom, some of the defense's challenges may have seemed surprising. Garry was not trying to get the
most "liberal" jury in strictly political terms. In fact, three men were
seen as potentially dangerous jurors because they took a common
present-day position that might be termed "pseudoliberal." A school
principal in an all-white suburb would not discuss white racism without making the point that there were also black racists, a category into
which he placed the Panthers. He was dismissed by Garry, as was a
bank officer from the same suburb, who was certainly one of the most
knowledgeable panelists interviewed. The latter gave a good definition
of racism, and was the only person who could report the main conclusion of the Kerner Report: "It states there our civil rights problems
are primarily due, I believe, to the fact that we have a racist society."
But this man implied also that some of our civil rights problems must

be due to characteristics of the Negro group. He opposed racial discrimination but was adamant for hiring people on the basis of their qualifications, and it did not bother him that there were no black people in his particular branch bank. He favored open housing, but supported the right of a man to sell property to whomever he wished. It was not just the attitudes of such men that put Garry off. After all, some of the jurors probably had "worse" attitudes. It was a quality of smugness, a cocksureness about the purity of their racial views, that made the pseudoliberal type seem worse than a more open-minded conservative or an apolitical person.

The bases for the decisions discussed may make more sense when placed in the context of how the jury appeared to be shaping up as the two weeks of the voir dire passed. In the first stage, a major concern of the defense was to eliminate or minimize the likelihood of a first degree verdict and the possibility of a death sentence. During this time Garry was as concerned about filling the jury spaces with persons opposed to the death penalty as he was in finding nonracists. If someone looked good on this issue, yet had managed to survive Jensen's challenges, Garry often didn't even question him on racial matters. About half-way through, it began to look to me as if the jury would be at least against capital punishment, and anxieties on this score declined. The jury was shaping up better than had been anticipated; the defense became more optimistic and began to set the higher goal of aspiring toward a jury that would acquit or at least "hang."* In this second stage the main quality looked for was the openness, honesty, and capacity for growth that I have referred to. Then about two-thirds through, it became evident that Jensen was going to dismiss all the blacks except the banker, David Harper. This introduced a new element into the calculation because Harper was a strong personality, and the defense was beginning to infer that he might be, or become, sympathetic to their case. In the informal camaraderie among prospective jurors the black banker was developing into a social leader. Garry and Ed Keating hoped that he might become the strong man of the jury, the leading influence, and, indeed, he was later elected foreman. Thus the desire to enhance Harper's position was another reason why the two pseudoliberals discussed above were dismissed. If these highly educated, high-status, and articulate men were empaneled, they might compete with Harper for

* In the sense of a *hung*, not a hanging, jury.

the role of opinion leader. A final point is that Garry had used up his challenges at a time when Jensen still had five of his, saved by passing his turn. Therefore, toward the end of the selection period, Garry was in a box, and he had to accept the last two or three people seated whether or not they were to his liking.

Though it inevitably involves speculation, one might wonder why the assistant district attorney decided to leave David Harper on the jury, considering that the defense built such considerable hopes around this man. As already mentioned, Jensen threw out every other black person. It is reasonable to infer that he could not challenge every Afro-American without preparing the ground for an appeal that would have met almost certain success. Opting for tokenism, the question is, why Harper? It is my judgment that Jensen liked Harper because he seemed to be a highly assimilated "white" Negro. He was solidly middle class, he lived in a primarily white section of Oakland, and he worked for a conservative institution, the Bank of America. Jensen must have assumed that such an Afro-American would see things from the point of view of established society and would not readily identify with Huey Newton and the ghetto blacks who were to be the defense's witnesses. In conducting his voir dire, Jensen seemed much less comfortable with, and certainly more hostile to, Negroes who were lower- and working-class, from the ghetto, and less acculturated. It was my opinion, even during the voir dire—after all, hindsight is easy—that Jensen was making a serious mistake in choosing Harper for his putative "house nigger" over some other possible candidates for this role. He was evidently unaware that racial nationalism and political militancy are perhaps more likely to be the product of the ambiguous status and identity conflicts of today's middle-class blacks than of the more oppressed condition of lower-class ghetto dwellers.

Aside from the question of Harper, I felt that the district attorney could have worked harder for a jury that would have been tougher and more likely to convict. Had he used all his challenges, some of the people who were mildly congenial to the defense could have been removed and Garry would have been forced to accept two or three quite biased jurors. The constellation would no longer have had that "middle of the road" character, which six weeks later was to result in a compromise verdict.* Jensen may have been overconfident

* As jury foreman, Harper presumably played a leading role in engineering a verdict that must have been a strong disappointment to the prosecution. The verdict was a disappointment to the defense also. Thus it

about the strength of his case. Perhaps, also, he felt more rapport with the conservative but moderate juror than with the extreme bigot. In addition, he may have had enough of the voir dire and have wanted to get on with the trial.

Racism and Fair Trials: Some Concluding Issues

The process by which a trial jury is selected in Alameda County—the voir dire and the challenge system—may be reasonably effective in eliminating those members of the panel who are strongly biased toward a particular side of the case. But the experience of the Newton trial, pioneering as it was in the introduction of racial questions, suggests that this process is ineffective in finding a jury that is the most free of racial bias. In fact, the very procedures by which the twelve final members are selected from the original panel appear to impose obstacles to the seating of a nonracist or antiracist jury.

The remarks I made as an expert witness on racism during the pretrial testimony are relevant here. I began my testimony with the generalization that racism—in the objective sense of control of the society's institutions by white people and systematic subordination of people of color and their relegation to the less powerful, prestigious, and rewarding positions—is a basic reality in America. The subjective aspect of this objective or structural pattern is the white group's sense of its own superiority and the inferiority of blacks and other nonwhites. This sense of superiority is almost inevitable, and it is shared by all white people—on conscious, subconscious, or unconscious levels.

Positive Selection as a Counterbalancing Mechanism

The most effective way to eliminate white racism from the judgment of a racially relevant case would be to form a jury of citizens from the racial minority groups. Although people of color have themselves been influenced by the racist assumptions of American culture, still their experience as victims of discrimination makes them more aware of the totality of circumstances motivating black and other nonwhite defendants.[5] But assuming that the courts are not yet prepared to move this far, we need to devise new tests or criteria for selecting the least racist whites. As yet, such tests do not exist. In response to Judge Friedman's request to propose an improved method, I put forward

---

became widely regarded as a compromise formula, not readily reconcilable to the evidence presented during the trial.

four tentative criteria along which jury panelists might be evaluated. Granted that my criteria make an extremely tough test and that they are the invention of one sociologist rather than of a commission of social scientists and legal experts, it may nevertheless be informative to use them to evaluate the Newton jury experience.

First, I suggested that the least racist person would not deny racial prejudice, but would be aware that he reflected elements of the society's pervasive racism. He would be sensitive to his racist tendencies, would keep them in his consciousness rather than suppress them, and would, of course, strive to reduce their influence. During the Newton voir dire, most people denied that they had any elements of racism or prejudice within them. Often this closed the discussion, and this denial or "affirmation of purity" made it easier for them to be "passed for cause," that is, seated as prospective jurors. A significant minority of citizens admitted some peripheral prejudices; in some cases the defense appraised this cue as a sign of insight, honesty, and good will—though we may have been misled in one or two instances by putting too much stock in this criterion.

The second criterion dealt with knowledge. In order to combat racism effectively, a white person should not see blacks as "invisible" but should be attuned to the social circumstances of the present and the forces in the past that have produced our racial crisis. Therefore, I suggested that the least racist whites would have some substantial knowledge of the history of race relations and a familiarity with the content and character of Afro-American culture. No questions that really tested this criterion were asked during the voir dire. It was clear that almost no one among the 140 white panelists—like American whites in general—knew anything about black history and culture. Ignorance about racial discrimination and the black movement was the typical pattern. Such ignorance or indifference actually made it easier for the panelists to be seated, since there was no possible line of questioning that might lead to a challenge for cause. And because of the system of peremptory challenges, any prospective juror who could have met this knowledge criterion would have been suspect of problack bias and thus dismissed by the prosecuting attorney!

The third point involved contact and experience with members of the minority group. The social and cultural barrier between whites and blacks is a keystone of the racist system; leading a life that is primarily segregated in terms of work, residence, and friendship in itself reflects and maintains white racism. The vast majority of white panelists in the Newton trial led just such segregated lives, though there were exceptions. Again, attorney Jensen was free to dismiss those few persons who were committed to racial integration in action.

Finally, I suggested that a nonracist must be involved in efforts to combat discrimination and prejudice. Personal, subjective racism can be eliminated or diminished only in the process of undermining the objective racism in the society and its institutions. Thus, another criterion would be some personal project directed toward the goal of racial justice: in local communities, in occupations or professions, or in leisure pursuits, as well as in work with organized political groups. Garry employed this standard when he asked persons who said they disapproved of the exclusion of blacks from their fraternal and leisure associations whether they had ever acted to end this state of affairs. From the voir dire testimony, it is apparent that the overwhelming majority of the potential jurors had never been involved in combating racism. If anyone had testified positively, he would certainly have been challenged by Jensen.

Thus, as I have shown, the logic of the voir dire makes it difficult to minimize white racism in the selection of a jury. This is ultimately a product of the overwhelming presence of racism in our society. People who are somewhere along the line of movement to a nonracist position: the aware, the knowledgeable, .the integrated, and those oriented toward change make up only a minuscule proportion of the white population. Such a frequency distribution makes it possible for all such people to be dismissed when they appear. The prosecutor need not worry about using up his peremptory challenges against antiracists, whereas the defense attorney will not have enough to reject all the racists.*

There is another factor in the logic of the voir dire and chal-

---

* An incident in another trial, that of the State of California versus John Cluchette and Fleeta Drumgo (the two "Soledad Brothers" remaining after the murder of George Jackson), suggests that the legal mentality poses further obstacles to the introduction of "positive selection." During the pretrial phase I testified in San Francisco toward the end of 1971 as an expert on racism in jury selection. Immediately after, one of the prosecuting attorneys attempted to dismiss my testimony on the grounds that I had admitted my own bias in coming across clearly—and in the course of a personal exchange, angrily—as *opposed to racism*. From such a perspective which was not challenged by the Court, being racist and antiracist

lenge system. The assumption is that every citizen has the makings of a fair and impartial juror; therefore, the sole object of the questioning is to discover any negative factors, bias, prejudice, unusual opinions or personal ties, that might vitiate a juror's impartiality. But racial bias cannot be dealt with as if it were some negative property that can be detected through the voir dire. It is so omnipresent in American society that the only reasonable means of minimizing it in a predominantly white jury entails a process of positive selection: setting up a series of qualifications or tests to identify that *least-racist* minority who then, along with nonwhites, would constitute the panel from which the final jury could be drawn.

The Myth of Impartiality and the Dilemmas of Representativeness

The foregoing analysis raises some serious and possibly insoluble questions concerning the several philosophical and legal tenets that underlie the juridical ideal of the "fair trial." The data from the Newton case suggest that the kingpins of the trial-by-jury system—the impartial juror, the representative panel, and the challenge method—are filled with ambiguities and at war with one another. It is possible that the legal fiction of the "impartial" juror should be disposed of as a "cultural lag" hopelessly out of tune with reality—at least for politically significant and highly publicized cases. A juror without any significant biases relevant to a case like *The People* v. *Newton* is almost a nonexistent animal.

Further, such a state of mind might not even be desirable. A man or woman without any preconceptions related to a trial growing out of a confrontation between a black militant and a white policeman would have to be a person of apathy, ignorance, even stupidity, or at least someone who is not living in today's social world. The issue of partiality has to be redirected and new questions have to be asked by legal theorists and social scientists. As a start, there may be a need for a separation between the question of being able to act with detachment, an ability that probably requires appreciation of the complexities of race and politics, and the problem of preconceptions with respect to guilt and innocence.* We need to know what kinds of biases make

----

appear to be equally objectionable deviations from a truly "unbiased" position: neutrality on the whole matter!

* I am indebted to Philip Selznick for pointing out this distinction.

a person unfit for fair and deliberate decision making in various kinds of cases; what kinds of conceptions and social attitudes are positive or at least neutral?

Our analysis also reveals a contradiction between the goal of impartiality and that of representativeness. A selection procedure that aims toward maximizing the number of least-partial people (as the present idea of impartiality is conceived) is not likely to achieve the goal of representing well the many cleavages and interest groups that make up a socially heterogeneous population.[6] It will bias the composition toward the middle of the road. As we have seen, the challenge system serves to keep the extremes of political position, cultural style, and racial commitment off the jury. This poses some difficult questions for legal norms. If we see the relevant jurisdiction as the county or the metropolitan area in which a "crime" takes place, then, by this logic, should a representative jury faithfully encompass the depth and pervasiveness of white racism in this "community"? Attorney Jensen, who himself did not play on racial bigotry during the trial, nevertheless seemed to think so. It followed from his concept that the case had "two sides," that the constituency and values of the dead policeman should be taken into account as much as the interests of the defendant. But the case of a criminal defendant is different from that of two adversaries in a case of civil litigation. From the philosophical tenets of our legal system—as I understand them—only the individual Huey P. Newton was entitled to a fair trial. The "justice" accorded the deceased and his family, the wounded officer, the Oakland Police Department, and the white racist community should have been totally irrelevant to the trial that took place. For this reason I cannot subscribe to the argument that a jury representative of the county's actual racial attitudes would serve our ideals of justice and the elusive but still to be pursued goal of a fair trial. This throws the issue back to the perplexing problem that was debated in the defense motions and in the propaganda of the "Free Huey" movement: what is the community that would guarantee a trial by a jury of the defendant's peers?

Internal Colonialism and the Court System

The Kerner Report noted that America was moving toward a society made up of two separate nations: one white and one black. It documents the depth of the racial cleavage and suggests that the experience

of life in the dominant white American culture is fundamentally different from that of the subordinated black ghettos of the land. The
Kerner analysis thus suggests that an overall multiracial *community*,
of values, interests, and life experience, does not at present exist in the
United States and, in fact, has never existed. Sociologically, the white
and black populations must be viewed as distinct communities, though
there is much overlap and interaction between them, as well as
division and heterogeneity within each racial group. If we take this
official federal report (and other sociological studies) seriously, we
must conclude that a black militant from the ghetto is not being tried
by a jury from his community when the panels are selected as they are
in Alameda County, California, and in the nation's other metropolitan
areas.

As I have argued throughout this volume, the black population
is not simply a distinct and largely segregated community; Afro-
Americans are a nationality that has been colonized within the borders
of the United States. The model of "internal colonialism" is gaining
acceptance because it alone points to the systematic way in which
black ghettos are controlled from outside in a striking parallel to the
domination of nonwhite peoples by European overseas powers during
the colonialist era.

Our legal forms reflect this situation of internal colonialism even
more clearly than other institutions do. In fact, in America the
administration of justice for people of color is more directly racial
than it was in many contexts of classic colonialism—where native
courts and "indirect rule" were common. Thus, a black man like Huey
Newton is tried under a system of law developed by white Western
European jurists. He is confronted in the black ghetto by white police
officers, then indicted by an all-white, or predominantly white, grand
jury, prosecuted by a team of all-white district attorneys, tried by a
white judge, convicted by a predominantly white jury, and denied bail
on appeal by white state appellate courts and a white federal judge.
It is not simply the color of the principals that is at issue, but the more
profound point that the various officials and processes in the system
represent institutions that reflect and are responsive to values and
interests of the white majority—a power structure and a community
that benefit from keeping black people in "their place," namely, in the
ghetto and without power.

The ambiguities, dilemmas, and even contradictions within the law that my case study has uncovered reflect only in part the uneven development of judicial decisions. For the most part they derive from the conflicts and tensions within our society, those same oppressive social conditions that produced the trial of Huey Newton. I believe that the issues at the heart of the case and its jury selection can only be resolved through the dynamics of decolonization, which would establish some form of "home rule" in the black communities.

The problems—political, technical, and legal—in developing radically altered systems of law enforcement and administration of justice are indeed enormous. Members of the legal profession as well as social scientists might begin to devise concrete models of such institutional arrangements—working as closely as is possible with organizations in the ghetto. Let us opt for changing the conditions that result in the need for self-defense and police surveillance in the black community, so that groups like the Panthers can devote their energies to the serious work of organizing the ghetto and so that the great talents and possibilities of the future Huey Newtons will not lie wasting in penitentiaries, but will contribute directly to the well-being of their people.

NOTES

1. A number of books have been devoted in full or in part to the Newton trial. For an unusually sensitive personal perspective, see Gilbert Moore, *A Special Rage* (New York: Harper & Row, 1971). For the account by a defense attorney, including the court transcript of significant testimony, see Edward Keating, *Free Huey* (New York: Dell, 1971). Discussion of the trial appears also in Reginald Major, *A Panther is a Black Cat* (New York: Morrow, 1971), pp. 179–181, 215–238; Gene Marine, *The Black Panthers* (New York: New American Library, 1969), chap. 9; and Bobby Seale, *Seize the Time* (New York: Random House, 1970), pp. 201–254. See also Kathy Mulherin, "Stalking the Panthers," in Barry N. Schwartz and Robert Disch, eds., *White Racism* (New York: Dell, 1970), pp. 240–251.

2. *Minimizing Racism in Jury Trials,* ed. Ann Fagan Ginger (Berkeley: P.O. Box 673: National Lawyers Guild, 1969), was prepared as a manual to inform other attorneys about Garry's method of

handling the voir dire. The book contains a list of the questions Garry asked related to race, 120 pages of extracts from the transcript of the voir dire, a preface by the chief attorney, and the appellate brief to the higher courts on jury selection prepared by his chief associate Fay Stender. The present chapter also appeared in a slightly different version in *Minimizing Racism*.

3. Hans Zeisel, *Some Data on Juror Attitudes Towards Capital Punishment* (Chicago: Center for the Study of Criminal Justice, University of Chicago, 1968). With Harry Kalven, Jr., Zeisel coauthored *The American Jury* (Boston: Little, Brown, 1966).

4. This charge of racial bias was discussed at some length in "Appellant's Opening Brief to the Court of Appeal of the State of California" (First Appellate District, Division Four, No. 1, Criminal 7753) prepared by Newton's attorneys.

5. For a defense of this position, see Editorial Board, Yale Law Review, "The Case for Black Juries," *Yale Law Journal*, 79, no. 3 (January 1970), 531–551.

6. Many of these issues are discussed, with abundant citations from case law, in Jennie Rhine, "The Jury: A Reflection of the Prejudices of the Community," *Hastings Law Journal*, 20 (May 1969), 1417–1445.

chapter 8
race and the
white professor

In the late 1960s the hallowed university, long seen as the institution with the most enlightened race relations, became the focus of intense racial conflict. In the year and a half following the assassination of Martin Luther King, the thrust of militant black protest shifted from the streets of the ghetto to the administration building and the tree-lined malls of the college campus. Predominantly liberal in politics, professors experienced their own version of the crisis of racial attitude that white liberals as a group underwent during the decade. Liberals had long been committed to the goals of the civil rights movement: ending discrimination and achieving social and economic equality through the strategy of integration. As long as the battlefield was in the South or in the "inner city" comfortably distant from his suburban residence, the liberal's commitment was free of inner conflict, though perhaps somewhat abstract. But when racial protest moved northward, when a new philosophy of black power came into ascendancy, and when the militants began to adopt more aggressive, even violent, methods, the issues were no longer abstract and distant.[1] As in the case of the Harlem and Bedford-Stuyvesant teachers, the white liberal's material and professional interests were threatened. Individually, and as a group, he was subject to intense attack. He was termed as much the racist as the worst Southern bigot, indeed at times even the more so, since a liberal "facade" in the face of racial privilege added up to personal hypocrisy.

Were race relations on the campus during the premilitant period really so enlightened?* If they were relatively liberal and low key, the

* It may be impossible to generalize about the thousand or more

fundamental reason is that there were so little of them. Though precise
figures are not available, a number of studies indicate that between 3
and 5 percent of all undergraduates in the early 1960s were black.
Since 50 to 60 percent of Afro-American students were then in Negro
colleges, the proportion in predominantly white schools must have been
2 to 3 percent.[3] With these "integrated" students concentrated in state
and city colleges, probably no more than 1 to 2 percent of the enroll-
ments at the better universities and elite colleges were Negro. And as
late as 1969 when the Carnegie Foundation surveyed a random sample
of faculty, black professors made up less than one-half of one percent
of the sample at the universities the study classed as "high and
medium quality," and less than one percent at the "high and medium
quality" four-year colleges.* Thus the exclusion of third world students, faculty, and administrators from the major universities was
virtually total, with the exception of Asian-Americans who were fairly
well represented as students and professors. But when black students
(and to a lesser degree Chicanos and Puerto Ricans) entered the
campuses in somewhat more than token numbers during the late
1960s, "race relations" came to the university with a vengeance,
bringing the racial crisis of the larger society home to roost for the
white professor.

In this chapter I shall examine the situation and the outlook of the
white professor, particularly how he responded in action and in shift
of perspective to the new immediacy of racial issues. Assuming that
the dominant philosophy of the professoriat has been liberalism, and
that liberal values are institutionalized within the structure of the university, I shall argue that the liberal framework of most faculty members was severely tried by the changing conditions, notably new
university commitments to roll back racial exclusion and the educational and political challenges of third world students. Over a period
of time that has now extended about five years, a dialogue from
conflicting perspectives between white faculty and students of color

---

institutions of higher learning, but minority students who have written
about this period are more likely to stress the pervasiveness of racism,
sometimes petty and overt, more often subtle and subconscious, even on
the most cosmopolitan campuses.[2]

* Among the "low quality" universities, blacks were 1.8 percent of
the faculty sample. They made up 10.4 percent at the "low quality" four-
year colleges, yet only 0.3 percent at the junior colleges.[4]

over the nature of the university and the role and relevance of race and racism in the society at large has been taking place. This dialogue has been expressed in specific confrontations, both in the classroom and in the arenas of campus decision making. The concrete issues that have divided the contestants have been many, varying with the unique situations on particular campuses. The two most pressing and frequent ones have been admissions policy and black or ethnic studies departments. These controversies have exposed underlying conflicts of interests and values between the two main protagonists. On one side we find the faculty defending its privileged position in the university, its distinctive academic values, and its generally liberal social philosophy. On the other side stand previously excluded student groups with an interest in establishing a base in higher educational institutions, and newly equipped with perspectives on race and society (black, Chicano and third world consciousness) that in no small degree have grown out of the failure of civil rights liberalism to achieve its ends. Although this conflict has a material basis in the struggle for educational resources and is played out in concrete terms, on the level of ideas it is succinctly crystallized in different "definitions of the situation," particularly with respect to the characterization of "the race problem" and explanations of racial inequality. The liberal faculty began with (and to a degree clings to) the notions of the 1950s, that prejudice and discrimination lie at the heart of racial injustice, whereas third world students conceive of *racism* as an overriding reality, a systematic process structuring the entire society and its institutions. As of 1971 the students appear to have had more educational impact on faculty conceptions of race relations than vice versa. For the general dialogue and specific crises have resulted in an erosion of the liberal position, which previously had appeared to be based on a consistent philosophy that made sense of social issues and indicated policies for their amelioration. The racial perspectives of most white professors are now in a state of flux.

Despite their liberalism and commitment to reform through democratic political participation, white professors were largely passive on racial matters during the past decade or two. Of course, some individuals were activists during the civil rights period, many advised federal and local governments or wrote about urban problems, and there were others who worked quietly behind the scenes to integrate their professions and campuses. But by and large the faculty was content with the university as an institution and its position within it;* it did not act until jolted from this complacency by movements that effectively disrupted the tranquility of teaching, research, and the leisurely walks from classroom to faculty club to library. Thus faculties as collective bodies were not the primary forces that initiated challenges to the institutional racism of their universities. Professors responded to other initiators, usually students, at times the administration; and with few exceptions they took action only when their own college, their department, or their professional association was threatened.**

One could account for the white faculty's role or lack of role, on the grounds of its essential and ingrained racism, and let it go at that. But such a dismissal would be an oversimplification, as well as unjust. This is not to deny that professors, like all white Americans, share many of the racist assumptions of our culture, and partake of certain privilege and advantage because of their color and European background. But if racism is to be a useful concept for understanding oppression and social change in America, it cannot be used as a magical catchphrase to be applied mechanically to every situation without analyzing its specifics. Crucial for an adequate understanding is the context in which university and professorial racism is embedded. The struggle against racism is not primarily a matter of the clash of individual attitudes and preferences, but instead a clash of group values and interests, which vary in different classes, occupations, and institutional settings. Thus, in order to understand the white professor in the face of the recent racial challenge, we must look at his political

---

* This has been most true at the major universities. At less prestigious universities and colleges the faculty is relatively less privileged, and often considerably dissatisfied about salary, teaching load, and lack of autonomy. Studies at Columbia and San Francisco State suggest that the less privileged faculty is more likely to support student protest on the campus.

** It is important to stress that the faculties of some universities responded much more rapidly to third world movements and student aspirations than others. Certain private universities such as Harvard, Yale, Northwestern, and Stanford, moved rather quickly to initiate black studies curricula. These institutions tend to be better protected from political pressures than public ones. On the other hand, some of the first Afro-American studies departments were established in junior or community colleges such as Merritt College in Oakland, California.

outlook, the structure of the university and its academic culture, and, in particular, the dominant philosophy of liberalism—as these factors relate to present-day racial controversies.

There are many reasons why the analysis I put forward must be tentative. My ideas are based primarily on my participation and involvement in campus race relations at one university, and not on systematic research within the thousand or more institutions of higher learning, which differ in regional climate, proportion of minority students, academic level, and private versus public status. No studies yet exist on the subject of the racial attitudes of the faculty, though the Carnegie-sponsored investigation of higher education will contain important material. The many books on major crises that I have drawn upon reveal very little about faculty thinking, and the same is true of detailed journalistic accounts, such as the *New York Times* coverage. To some degree this is an indication of the weak political role of faculty, to which I have alluded; it also reflects the general reluctance of professors to speak out on public issues, especially such sensitive matters as race. Those who have spoken out undoubtedly represent the attitudes of others than themselves, and I have incorporated their perspectives in this paper. But to a considerable degree I generalize on the basis of my experiences at the University of California in Berkeley.

Limited as these are, I think it likely that students and professors on other campuses will recognize themselves in the discussion that follows. For the central issues of controversy have been the same at all major Northern universities; on most campuses students of color, though diverse in many ways, are characteristic of a "new breed," and the faculty is composed of roughly similar distributions of political and social positions. Thus radical professors are a minority at Berkeley just as elsewhere, the dominant consensus is liberal, not conservative, and I therefore assume that the values and conflicts of the liberal colleagues with whom I have worked and argued at the University of California are shared by their counterparts at other institutions. As a fellow professor, I have tried to examine the outlook of this liberal majority in a spirit of appreciation and fairness, but, as a radical often operating with different assumptions and priorities, I have most likely not always succeeded.*

* My study is an attempt to characterize the faculty as a whole and important tendencies within it. Therefore I do not deal with those individ-

Some Observations on Faculty Politics

Many commentators have noted an apparent paradox in faculty politics. On matters affecting their work, profession, and home institution, professors are remarkably conservative. On issues of national and international scope, college teachers tend to be one of the most liberal, even left-wing, occupational groups in our society. University and college professors are probably the most consistent supporters of civil liberties;[5] they are more concerned than the average citizen with issues of social justice; they tend to favor liberal economic reforms; and of course they have been especially active in opposition to the Vietnam War.[6]

The conservatism of the professor on his own turf is in part a matter of the bureaucratic sclerosis that affects every organization and institution. The scientific and professional fields within the academic world are much like traditional guilds. The faculty is jealous of its craft autonomy, its authority over the standards of entrance into its discipline—hence the notion that only graduate training in the major universities provides apprenticeship and socialization into its specialized field of learning and, therefore, the union card for membership in the academic community. The professor is oriented toward molding the student in his own image, and he is likely to feel that the only satisfactory training is the kind of education he himself received in graduate school.

The professor tends to be conservative in his method of work also. The scholar and teacher respect the authority of past knowledge; the research worker is governed by scientific norms that he rarely

---

ual professors who have been heavily involved in race relations through controversial public action or publication. Here I refer to such people as Arthur Jensen, Professor of Education at Berkeley, who has raised the issue of genetic differences in "intelligence" by race; Harvard's D. P. Moynihan, famous for his report *The Negro Family* and advocacy of "benign neglect"; Edward Banfield, author of *The Unheavenly City*, and others.

Some critics of this essay have questioned the prominence given to the liberal professor. For example, one reviewer of this book in manuscript suggests that faculties have experienced a significant infusion of younger and more radically oriented professors, and that these new elements have been actively challenging academic racism. I have not observed this at Berkeley where the lack of expansion has kept new blood at a minimum; if this has been an important trend at other institutions it points up the problems of generalizing from a case study.

questions. The methodology of men of learning is based on the pains-taking accretion of new findings that result in the gradual improve-ment of previous formulations rather than the dramatic and "revolu-tionary" breakthroughs sought by artists, for example.*

The departmental organization of the university is another factor. The professor is primarily a member of a department, a seg-ment of the university, that represents his special discipline. His primary loyalty to his own field prevents him from developing a vision of the university as a whole, particularly of the need for institutional change and responsiveness to new publics. Here administrators have an advantage. We tend to think of college presidents and deans as men of more conservative mettle than their faculties. And yet, with some exceptions, administrators have generally been more innovative than professors on racial issues in the recent period. At the University of California, the significant opposition to the kind of Black Studies Department the students advocated came from influential faculty and not the administration. Many college presidents—Berkeley's Roger Heyns, Cornell's James Perkins, John Summerskill of San Francisco State—were ahead of their faculties on such issues as admissions policy and the hiring of minority faculty.**

It is true that university personnel in general, professors as well as administrators, operate within a social context that limits their political options. The control over budget exercised by state officials and trustees, the priorities that have been put forward long in advance

* I am indebted to Jessie Reichek for this point.
** Probably the most well publicized exception to this rule was Columbia where President Grayson Kirk appeared less sensitive than many professors to the concern of black students with the building of the gym-nasium in Harlem. There were also important universities, such as Harvard and Yale, where the faculty appears to have supported and participated in racial reform. Still, one might speculate as to why administrators often have been more change oriented than their faculties, particularly with respect to the interests of third world communities. One hypothesis is that college presidents are in contact with a wider range of publics and ad-visors than is the typical faculty member. In urban centers they meet with representatives of ethnic communities. And whereas the typical professor in an all-white department rarely or never talks with third world colleagues, some of these few minority professors on the campus will have the ear of the president, and thus his perspective on racial matters is likely to be broader.[7]

by various educational master plans, make up the larger picture in which the faculty response to the demands of new constituencies unfolds. Thus, professors frequently do not have the freedom and power to put their views into practice.

Yet when forced to choose, the faculty has tended to defend its own interests and values. Here I refer to its privileged position in society: a virtual monopoly on intellectual work; tenured employment and freedom from accountability for the consequences of its ideas; relatively high social status and income; the free time, vacations, opportunity to travel, and leisurely routine absent from most work-a-day jobs.[8] The liberal professor is also defending certain values that have been institutionalized in the university and have generally been nonexistent or precarious elsewhere. These make up the "academic freedom" complex: freedom of inquiry; the pursuit of universal questions about the nature of life, art, and society; the commitment to dialogue; the clash of ideas; and the intellectual life. That universities do not always live up to these ideals is beside the point. They are part of the liberal culture of the academy, and the professor will resist change to defend them.[9]

Paradoxically, the strength of this commitment to liberalism may explain, in part, faculty conservatism. Institutionalized within the university format, liberal values tend to take on the rigidity associated with organized structures and procedures. The inflexibility that results threatens to make these same values conservative ones, for liberal principles must adapt to new conditions in order to retain their essence.

With respect to racial matters in the recent period, the predominant liberalism of the faculty has been a mixed blessing. Initially professors were predisposed positively toward minority students, to equal access to higher education, and to integration of the university through reform. But at the same time, and unbeknownst to most faculty, the liberal outlook also contained a number of tenets that were to become obstacles to fundamental change in race relations in the 1960s. These assumptions and values came into serious conflict with the values and assumptions of the new ethnic consciousness that college students from third world backgrounds were developing. We can see this process at work if we examine a number of new issues and situations that posed dilemmas for the faculty: changes in admissions policies, the increasing third world presence in the classroom and in campus politics, and the demand for ethnic studies departments.

Admissions Policy and Liberal Universalism

Professors played, at most, a minor role in the special admissions programs that set the stage for later events in the campus racial drama. Until the 1960s only a handful of Northern colleges, such as Oberlin, had taken any special interest in recruiting Negro students. The programs that existed were small; they concentrated on promising youth with middle-class backgrounds and aspirations, and were often criticized for paternalism. Awakened by the civil rights movement and its growing militancy, a number of universities and colleges began, in the mid-1960s, to set up "educational opportunity programs," particularly at the undergraduate level.* Traditional entrance criteria were expanded to emphasize such qualities as potential and motivation; the rigidity of grade point and test requirements were correspondingly relaxed. These "special students" were typically afforded financial assistance to cover tuition, books, and sometimes other costs, and tutoring programs were introduced to make up academic deficiencies. The result on many campuses was a rapid increase in the visibility of black students, though their numbers remained relatively small, especially in proportion to the student body as a whole. Thus, at the University of California in Berkeley the black student enrollment at the end of the 1960s stood at about 1000 (4 percent) compared with about 100 (0.4 percent) at the beginning of the decade. The freshman class of Dartmouth in 1969 included 90 blacks (10 percent), compared with 30 in 1968, and 8 to 10 during previous years. Similar increases took place at Harvard, Brown, Yale, Northwestern, and many other campuses.[12] Government figures suggest that the most dramatic gains came between 1968 and 1970. In this brief period the proportion of black students virtually doubled at many of the best institutions, and among freshmen the percentage rose from 5.8 to 9.1.[13] Characteristically, the increase in enrollment of other third world groups, Chicanos, Puerto Ricans,. and Native Americans, has not kept up with that of the blacks.

At the outset, those faculty who were aware of the new programs probably approved them, though with a certain ambivalence.

* One of the first, at Hofstra University, began in 1964 and was called NOAH (Negro Opportunity at Hofstra).[10] Other early programs were the E.O.P.'s (Educational Opportunity Programs) at Berkeley and San Francisco State College. Northwestern University began an aggressive effort to recruit black freshmen in the summer of 1965.[11]

The university was doing something about racial exclusion; it was assumed that with adequate tutoring and compensatory study black students would eventually relate to the university much as white students did. Many professors were troubled to see these new students clustering together at defined campus hangouts; this was not the way integration was supposed to look.*

These early programs were usually under the aegis of the president, administered by a special office. Few faculty participated in their operation, nor were they or their departments much affected by the new campus presence. The departments, which typically control the admission of graduate students, were much slower to take notice of and act upon the exclusion of minorities from their programs and their professions. However, stimulated by the undergraduate example, administrative prodding, or the special initiative of a chairman or faculty member, some began to move to change the situation. As of 1969 a survey of graduate department minority programs revealed that special admission or recruitment efforts were in operation in at least 96 specific graduate departments and 111 professional schools in addition to university-wide policies at 42 graduate institutions. Law, medicine, business administration, social work, and theology among the professional schools, and sociology, history, and English among academic fields, were the most frequently represented.[16] By 1971 the proportion of black graduate students was about 5 percent at many of the most prestigious universities. Institutions lesser in repute were, in general, still predominantly segregated at the graduate level.[17] The one event that spurred many universities and departments into action was the assassination of Martin Luther King.**

* Friedland and Edwards report from Cornell, "Blacks moved around the campus in groups and were never found fraternizing with whites. This was upsetting to most faculty and students."[14] And at the University of Connecticut, the editor of the student paper noted that "The Blacks are suddenly visible around the campus. They walk around in groups of fives and sixes to classes, and the whites eye them nervously."[15]

** The failure of departments to act sooner (and many still have not acted) can be attributed as much to faculty inertia and the traditionalism of admissions procedures as to principled objections. When I proposed a plan for vigorous third world student recruiting to the Berkeley Graduate Department of Sociology in 1967, I received the strong support of the chairman, whose political orientation was made up of conservative as well as liberal elements, and a unanimous mandate to proceed from the faculty

As the number of minority students began to increase, many professors became uneasy about admissions developments. The idea of a special recruiting effort could be tolerated, especially since each applicant was to be treated individually and no determinate number was promised. But third world students on many campuses "upped the ante" and demanded that a certain number, or a certain proportion, of each class must be black, Chicano, Puerto Rican, or of other ethnic background. Many professors attacked such formulas as equivalent to the kinds of restrictive quotas the Jews at one time had suffered under. Administrators who accepted or negotiated compromises with the demands were seen as submitting to student pressure or the threat of disruption. On urban campuses, like City College of New York and San Francisco State, students demanded open enrollment for all people of color. In general the faculty has felt that such a policy would be undesirable (if not disastrous) as well as unrealistic; the fear most commonly expressed has been of the probable undermining of academic standards, intellectual eminence, and cultural style of the university.*

Special admissions policies favoring students of color came into conflict with the central value of the liberal philosophy, universalism. The universalistic ethic insists that everyone be viewed and treated in terms of the same criteria. The sociologist Talcott Parsons considers universalism one of the dominant value orientations of modern industrial

---

as a whole, representing a wide range of political persuasions. Some fears of the institutionalization of quotas were expressed, the advisability and ambiguity of special "remedial" seminars were debated, but the general reaction was enthusiastic. In my own department, and on university campuses in general, problems developed later—when third world students came on the scene in large enough numbers to make a difference.

* In an influential paper delivered to a state-wide University of California meeting on urban issues, the Berkeley sociologist Martin Trow attributed the increasing racial conflict at Berkeley to an admissions policy that emphasized recruitment from ghetto high schools and overselection of politicized youth, whose militancy was viewed as evidence of academic potential. Trow suggested that minority admissions be focused on middle-class blacks and that emphasis be shifted from undergraduate to graduate and professional training.[18] At the same time, black student organizations were often demanding that the university reverse policies that had been favoring the "assimilated" Negroes; at Northwestern, for example, in April 1968 they demanded "that at least half of each year's incoming Black students be from the inner city school systems."[19]

societies, and he contrasts it with particularism, the orientation to men and action on the basis of group affiliations, such as family, clan, race, religion, sex, or place of origin. Liberal universalism has been one of the great progressive ideas, affirming the essential humanity of all people; it has also been a wedge against graft and favoritism in public life. For my purposes in this essay, the importance of universalism is its implication that race and ethnicity should not be taken into account in judgments about people and in the arrangement of institutions.

The liberal wants to judge a man in terms of his individual uniqueness and his universal humanity, not in terms of "accidental" features like skin color. Universalism thus goes hand in hand with individualism, and in the area of race the two join in the ideal of "color blindness." Unlike the conservatives, who make up only a minority of college faculty, the liberal is uncomfortable with the consciousness of color. Again, unlike the conservative, particularly the Southern breed, the liberal does not like to think of himself as *white*— why, therefore, should minority people make so much of their blackness or brownness?[20] People are human beings first. Then they are unique individuals. The group identities appropriate to the modern world are the more universalistic ones, like occupation and associational membership. For the professorial generation of the 1950s and 1960s, the period of the Second World War was the crucial political experience; color consciousness brings unpleasant memories of Nazism —and the fact that a considerable proportion of professors at prestige universities are Jewish has been significant in reinforcing such an association.

Related to universalism is the faculty's general commitment to assimilation as the solution for racial and ethnic inequalities. Most liberals accept, at least in theory, the idea that no important differences exist between whites and blacks in America—either biologically or culturally. When distinctive attitudes, values, and life styles are recognized, they are usually explained in terms of social class rather than ethnicity or culture. Assimilation is seen as part of the ineluctable logic of the large-scale social trends that characterize modern, urban, industrial societies.*

The Carnegie survey of university and college faculty documents the prevailing universalistic perspective, indicates a considerable split

* See Introduction to Part I.

among the faculty, and suggests that there may be significant internal conflict within individual minds on this matter. Fifty-nine percent of the sample disagreed with the statement that "more minority group undergraduates should be admitted even if it means relaxing normal academic standards of admission." However, the higher the quality of the university or college, the more likely faculty were to favor special admissions. At the high prestige universities, professors were evenly split between those who agreed with the statement and those who disagreed, though most of those who agreed did so with reservations, and the proportion who strongly disagreed was markedly higher than the proportion who strongly agreed. The faculty confirmed its color-blind perspective even more convincingly on the question whether "any special academic program for Black students should be administered and controlled by Black people." Here only 4 percent agreed strongly and 21 percent with reservations; there was no real variation by type of institution.

The color-blind ethos of the liberal ideology has been shaken by the increasing prominence of race in the social upheavals of the past years. Whereas a significant minority of professors have presumably given up this belief as an anachronism, the majority have not. Commitment to the color-blind ideal lies behind the faculty's distress at the general thrust of third world student politics. But many professors must also sense the truth of an NYU Law Dean's dictum that "the fact of the matter is that if you're color-blind you don't admit minority groups,"[21] and they have therefore reluctantly supported some particularistic programs. As Lawrence Fein points out, this is not really a break with present actualities, for "the structure of the system, which is to say, of our institutions, and the rules according to which they are managed, preserve, in many ways, a reality of particularism and of ascription, elaborately disguised by a mythology of universalism and achievement orientation."[22]*

* In response to these dilemmas, new positions are emerging. One advocates ethnic consciousness for a number of years in the immediate future in order to bring about the conditions in academic and professional life that will make color blindness possible eventually. Whether realistic or not, such a formula seems to be in the spirit of liberalism, which historically in the United States has based its strength on a flexible social doctrine and pragmatic adaptation to new realities rather than on a set of dogmatic principles.

Racial Conflict in Campus Politics and the Classroom

It is obvious that black students—and, on some campuses, Chicanos, Puerto Ricans, and other third world groups—have become a significant force within the political life of American colleges and universities, though their activity and militancy have varied from one place to another. Because the patterns of racial exclusion have been virtually identical throughout higher education, third world students, once their numbers are sufficient for a political base, have a built-in agenda for action against the all-white character of their institutions. This explains why the demands of black students, for example, have been remarkably similar at campuses across the nation.*

At various times and places, some faculty have supported these demands, others have opposed them, and a large number, sometimes the majority, have been indifferent or neutral. The alienation that has developed between many white professors and the black movement on campus is not only a matter of different views of the content or legitimacy of proposals for change. The faculty has a different set of priorities from that of the students, and the liberal professor in particular maintains a belief in the sacredness of procedures—a conception of the "means-ends" problem in political action that diverges from the assumptions of contemporary student movements, both white and third world.

Thus professors may agree that racism should be eliminated from the university, but they see this goal as only one of many reforms that are needed to improve the viability of the institution and its

---

* The number of demands varies with the specific campus crisis, but in almost every case three have been included: first, a rapid increase in the admission of black and other third world students through changing traditional entrance criteria and providing financial aid; second, the hiring of black and third world professors and administrators; and, third, the establishment of a relatively autonomous department or school of Afro-American or ethnic studies. Other frequent demands have been for the disciplining or dismissal of a particular professor or administrative aide charged with racism or insensitivity (Cornell and San Francisco State are examples) and the provision of separate facilities, residence halls, or cultural centers for black students (Northwestern and Cornell). A type of concern that is becoming more central is the university's relation to, or exploitation of, nearby ethnic communities (for example, the case of the Columbia gym) and its financial involvement with corporations doing business in South Africa (Princeton, Cornell, Stanford, among others).

educational mission. The faculty is a heterogeneous body, ranging widely in interests and values. If a hierarchy of its priorities could be drawn up, racial justice would not lead the list. Professional, academic, and intellectual values are much more important, for the majority. The radical faculty has not seen university racism and third world issues as its main concern, either. In recent years its politics has been directed toward antiwar protest and restructuring the university in response to white student interests.*

Third world students have a different set of priorities. Whereas they are not necessarily opposed to traditional academic values— although many professors think they are—the struggle against the racism of the university appears to them to be absolutely essential to their presence and survival in the academic environment. The single-mindedness of minority students on this issue, and the organizational unity that has emerged in certain crisis situations, strikes many professors as narrowminded, anti-intellectual, and totalitarian—not to mention uncouth. From the student standpoint, the faculty's defense of other values appears to be a self-serving clinging to class and racial privileges, a copping out of the central struggle against racial injustice, and, therefore, a confirmation of deep-seated racism. Such a student perception, when articulated, seems like "arrogant nonsense" to many professors.

When priorities are clear-cut and unequivocal, the means of reaching one's goals may become secondary. It is the wholehearted dedication of the black movement to ending racism that makes "by any means necessary" something more than a rhetorical slogan. When priorities are diffuse, diverse, or conflicting, the means or procedures by which decisions are made often become as important as, or even more important than, the content of the political issues. Further, liberal philosophers like John Dewey have argued that, in the chain of public action, every means to an end is also an end or goal itself at some point in the cycle. From such a framework, liberals have come to view

* The low priority of racism on the faculty's political agenda is one of the reasons for the passivity and indifference I have alluded to. During the Harvard strike of April, 1969, the faculty discussion on the black students' proposal for a black studies program revealed that few professors had even read the Rosovsky Report (The Report of the Faculty Committee on African and Afro-American Studies), though they swore by this document, which was the focus for their deliberations.[23]

the procedures or rules of the "political game" as the essence of the democratic system.[24]

Malcolm X's expression "by any means necessary" was therefore a calculated attack on this liberal position and its implicit sanction of the racial *status quo.* Third world people have pointed out that an explicit policy of racial discrimination has not been the primary means by which they have been excluded from various institutions or denied power and autonomy therein. Today, the mechanisms and procedures of admission, hiring, promotion, and decision making, the distribution of income, and the allocation of other resources are much more effective in this regard. On campus, racial confrontations have often erupted because the procedural mechanisms of faculty decision making (secrecy, the slow movement through a series of bureaucratic channels) created a climate of suspicion and a pace of response that could not satisfy the zeal and seriousness of ethnic students. Strikes and confrontational forms of protest attempt to change the means of decision making to the advantage of excluded and relatively powerless groups, and these pressures have usually speeded up the resolution of concrete issues. The faculty, on the other hand, tends to resist negotiation in a situation seen as threatening or involving undue pressure. The widely publicized events at Cornell illustrate these attitudes. There black students seized Straight Hall, and administrators negotiated a settlement of their grievances in exchange for their exodus from the building. In its first meeting the faculty refused to recognize this agreement, many feeling that they were being blackmailed by threats of violence.*

The presence of more than token numbers of third world students has had special effects on the climate of the classroom as well as on the larger politics of the university.** Minority students, especially

---

* The event was overdramatized by the media's emphasis on the blacks' possession of guns; the photo of armed students was flashed around the world. Two days later, after a long student convocation, the faculty agreed to uphold the *entente* with the blacks. Some professors, however, continued to feel that the week of disruption to the orderly procedures of campus life had dealt a death blow to academic freedom and the university itself; several eminent professors resigned.[25]

** These effects are probably most felt in the social sciences and the humanities, and it is sometimes difficult to separate the impact of third world students from effects of other shifts in student behavior and attitude during the past few years.

blacks, have proved to be extremely vocal in classroom discussions. Among the various student groups at Berkeley they are probably the most likely to challenge a professor's lecture, breaking away from the prevailing patterns of passive absorption and indifference to the form and content of the classroom monologue. Third world people are particularly alert to any implications of racism in a professor's interpretation and presentation of social issues. By now there is probably not a sociology department on a major campus in the country whose chairman has not faced a caucus of very upset black students protesting the overt or covert racism of a particular course or professor.[26] Not only professors, but white students also are regularly challenged for their approach to the issues under discussion and for their racial attitudes. In the past five years at Berkeley I have noted a tendency for whites to refrain from a frank and vigorous presentation of their views, generally out of deference to the superior credentials in life experience of third world students; but in some cases they are intimidated by the possibility of being attacked as racists.

The third world presence has catalyzed many lethargic lecture halls. Though the negative implications for free discussion should not be overlooked, the reactions of the faculty are my central interest. I would guess that only a minority have had the security of personality and flexibility of style to respond well to these classroom confrontations. As professors, we tend to be defensive in the face of challenges to our authority, particularly when students question our competence to expound upon a topic within the purview of our presumed expertise. White students, especially the political radicals, also question faculty interpretations of social science problems, but third world students—and particularly the blacks—do so with an aggressive manner and an ethnic flavor which is more abrasive to the professorial mentality.

The most intense expression of this conflict involves those white professors who teach black history, race relations, social problems, poverty, and a host of other courses where racial issues are central. The influx of third world students has radically changed the teaching atmosphere in these fields. When there were few or no third world students, it was possible for the professor to do his academic thing, analyzing racial problems in the abstract, dissecting ethnic groups, their histories, communities, culture, and social movements, as if under a microscope. On the Berkeley campus a number of developments converged in the spring of 1968 to change this situation: the murders of Martin Luther King and Bobby Hutton, the local Panther leader, the rise in black enrollment, and increased acceptance of black power and third world perspectives. The white professor's prevailing monopoly of the analysis of racial conflict and third world experience was seen (and correctly, in my view) as a reflection of academic colonialism.*

The presence of students of color in the classroom and as political actors threatening the disruption of business-as-usual on campus has had a disquieting effect on many professors. In the late 1960s liberals began to realize that these students were different from whites in some important respects despite their own universalistic theories. For the most part, the white professor has not appreciated or respected these differences. But confronted by outspoken third world students, he began to recognize in himself attitudes that were very similar to the "prejudices" he had always associated with less educated, less sophisticated people. In short, (though there are important exceptions) many if not most faculty found that they didn't like third world

* In the spring of 1968 I was teaching an experimental course in race and culture with two other white professors. Though that was the last quarter in which there was still little direct challenge to our authority, the restlessness and tension in the classroom communicated to us the inauthenticity of a race relations course without instructors from racially oppressed groups. The students, black and white—there were still few Chicanos at Berkeley and Asian-American identity remained relatively undeveloped—wanted to hear about the big issues: the black and Mexican communities; the black family, which Moynihan's report had converted into a loaded subject; black culture; and trends within the third world movements. As white instructors we could only "know" about these crucial matters from books, newspapers, and second-hand accounts. The areas in which our expertise seemed legitimate, expostulating theories of race relations, the dynamics of prejudice and racism, were the more abstract and academic issues, which did not grab the students' attention. Pragmatically oriented young people today are also more interested in discussing solutions than intellectual analyses, and our training and situation made us as incompetent to focus on strategies of change as to inject passion and moral indignation into the classroom situation. My own adaptation to this situation has been to use books by third world writers, to deemphasize the lecture format, to encourage students to organize project groups, often ethnically based, and to invite people of color to lecture. But these adjustments have been only partly successful, which underscores the need for both the rapid integration of the teaching faculty and the establishment of ethnic studies departments.

students and were not particularly interested in teaching them. In the abstract, and from a distance, the liberal professor had "identified" with blacks and their causes, but in the flesh he was often offended by their style, their demands, and a conception of education that differed from his own. It appears that this sympathy and identification had often stemmed from paternalistic motives, the perhaps natural desire of an educator to "help" people progress along his own path, to mold the minority student in his image. Those who had participated in programs to bring in third world students expected that they would respond with gratitude and appreciation. But paternalism was no longer accepted nor gratitude dispensed; the racist games of an earlier period were finished.

In many graduate departments that had "brought in" third world students, liberal professors (and even some radicals) were disturbed by their hostility or apparent indifference to them and their courses. They assumed they were being avoided because they were white, and they searched for techniques to bring about better communication. In fact, the tensions were often due to conflicts in style, personality, politics, and professional methodology rather than to skin color per se. Many third world students found it difficult and unrewarding to relate to professors who were "uptight," overintellectual, and excessively professional in their concerns and mannerisms. And, indeed, this type of professor, perhaps the modal ·one in today's academy, often appeared to me to be extremely uncomfortable in interaction with students of color.

A typical response to this situation was to view the students as less able and less well prepared than whites, rather than different in their interests and reasons for attending the university. The third world student was seen as antiintellectual, rather than as being concerned with the fusion of reason and emotion, ideas and social relevance.[27] The great fear of the faculty was that large numbers of minority students would result in the lowering of standards. Obviously, mistakes in admission decisions were made, and there were and are some students who lack either the aptitude or the interest to succeed in a particular field. But this reality inevitably became contaminated through interaction with the classic dynamics of racism. Thus a third world student who was dumb or hopelessly conflicted raised questions about the ability of nonwhites in general and the success of the "special program," while white students who were dumb and messed up were just dumb and messed up, their race or ethnicity never the issue. The professor also faced dilemmas of a "double standard" concerning classroom response, grading, and criticism of papers. Instead of offering a frank evaluation and grading the minority student down when he felt it was deserved, too often he eased up. This tendency was quickly perceived by the students, who resented the patronization involved. Of course racial games were not played by one side only. Many third world students became adept at hustling for grades, working on the professor's guilt, confusion, and general ignorance of the cultural patterns and survival techniques of the racially oppressed.*

Conflicting Conceptions of Racism

The conflict in perspective between white faculty and third world students is related to contrasting conceptions of racial oppression. Though both groups talk about racism, they talk past each other. Contending interests typically define crucial terms in ways that reflect their group position and further its collective needs. Since the Kerner Report introduced the idea to white liberals, racism has become perhaps the most loaded and overloaded word in public discourse. Militants expand its meaning in an attempt to force far-reaching changes upon institutions reluctant to share power with the oppressed. Those who want to contain the pace and style of racial revolution evoke its stigma to attack radical reforms that appear to deviate from accepted procedures. Thus on the campus, proposals for special consideration of racial minorities are often viewed as racism-in-reverse by traditional faculty, just as many liberals experience the most militant trends in the black power and nationalist movements as black racism. The Kerner Report may have contributed to this state of affairs by failing to define and analyze racism seriously. But the realities of American racism are full of complexity and ambiguity, and in situations of group and value conflict, words will become political weapons.

I am placing considerable stress on what might appear to be

---

* It must be pointed out that race and racism are not the only matters involved in these conflicts: many minority professors also have been critical of the third world students and their politics. At Cornell a black economist resigned because he felt that university judiciary procedures had been too lenient in the case of a black student. And some of the strongest attacks on Afro-American studies programs, particularly in their "separatist" tendencies, have come from such liberal blacks as Bayard Rustin, Kenneth Clark, and Roy Wilkins.[28]

simply a semantic problem. This is because I think the racist label, aimed at individual professors and the university as a whole, has contributed significantly to the faculty's disaffection with the student movement. Of course, if the shoe fits, wear it. Much of the hurt must have come because the validity of the charge was understood or intuited at some level of consciousness; the sensitivity would be the greater because the professor prided himself on his equalitarianism and his sympathy with the underdog. But many professors could make no sense of these allegations because they were working with a totally different idea. Particularly galling to the liberal was the militant's tendency to castigate all whites as prima facie racist (rationalized by the idea that embattled people cannot afford the luxury of making distinctions).* An eminent professor of left-liberal persuasion at Cornell compared this phenomenon to the indiscriminate branding of people as Communists during the McCarthy era.[30]

The liberal professor tends to define racism in a much more restricted sense than do people of color and white radicals today. For him, racism connotes conscious acts, where there is an intent to hurt or degrade or disadvantage others because of their color or ethnicity. It implies bigotry and prejudice, hatred and hostility, concrete individual acts, and clear-cut organizational policies of exclusion or segregation on the basis of race. He does not consider the all-white or predominantly white character of an occupation or an institution in itself to be racism.** He does not understand the notion of covert racism, that

* I personally have found that third world militants who use this rhetoric do make distinctions among various whites in their day-to-day relations and political work. One of the problems of the white response to blacks is that we take their rhetoric too seriously, but we do not take them seriously enough as individuals and groups with specific needs and interests. Thus Friedland and Edwards note that Cornell professors were hung-up behind the black student assertion that their demands were nonnegotiable, at the same time that negotiations were taking place.[29]

** Only 38 percent of the professors in the Carnegie sample agreed that "most American colleges and universities are racist whether they mean to be or not." Sixty percent disagreed. More surprising to me was the finding that a majority (52 percent) disagreed with the conclusion of the Kerner Report, that "the main cause of Negro riots in the cities is white racism." Only at the highest prestige universities did a slight majority (52 percent) accept the Kerner findings.

These attitudes underscore the significance of an official position paper of Northwestern University, in which a group of administrators, white people maintain a system of racial oppression by acts of omission, indifference, and failure to challenge the *status quo*. The fact that he leads his daily life in the ambience of an all-white department and neighborhood does not seem racist to him, because he did not choose his colleagues or neighbors for their color. For many liberals the notion of institutional racism is obscurantist propaganda; in another parallel to the McCarthy era they resent its implications of "guilt by association." *

The third world definition of racism tends to be broader and more sociological. It focuses on the society as a whole and on structured relations between people rather than on individual personalities and actions. From this standpoint, the university is racist because people of color are and have been so systematically excluded from full and equal participation and power—as students, professors, administrators, and, particularly, in the historical definition of the character

---

professors, and students boldly noted that campus's institutional racism. Evidently the students in pushing for the following statement, were testing Sartre's dictum, applied by Stokely Carmichael to white America, that "man cannot condemn himself":

> Northwestern University recognizes that throughout its history it has been an institution of the white establishment. This is not to gainsay that many members of its administration, its faculty, and its student body have engaged themselves in activities directed to the righting of racial wrongs. It is also true that for many years a few Blacks have been members of its administration, faculty, and student body. But the fact remains that the University in its overwhelming character has been a white institution. This it has had in common with virtually all institutions of higher learning in the United States. Its members have also had in common with the white community in America, in greater or lesser degree, the racist attitudes that have prevailed historically in the society and which continue to constitute the most important social problem of our times. This University with other institutions must share responsibility for the continuance over many past years of these racist attitudes.[31]

* At certain universities many professors bristle at this term because they see their campuses, Cornell, Berkeley, Stanford, San Francisco State, for example, as well ahead of others in programs relevant to minority students. With the administration already fighting racism, the charge of institutional racism appears as irresponsible rhetorical distortion. From the student standpoint the beginnings of change do not affect the larger picture; the fact that we're more liberal than Columbia or UCLA is irrelevant.

of the institution and its curriculum. Third world students experience racism in the subtle vibrations that emanate from the climate of the classroom and the quadrangle, in the university's dispassionate, intellectual interest in poor people and their problems, and in a myriad of other specifics—that the custodians and dormitory maids are usually black, for example. The students start from the premise that the society and its basic institutions are all based on the dominant position of whites and the subjugation of people of color; in an essentially racist culture all people share racist assumptions and beliefs in varying degrees of intensity and sophistication. Although for many professors third world protest has been an educational challenge, which has deepened their understanding of racism, the majority have probably been antagonized by the blanket condemnation of themselves and their institutions that is implied in the students' usage. Perhaps the faculty feels even more affronted because, as a group of scholars and educators, it believes that it possesses the legitimate monopoly on the correct interpretation of words and ideas, including changes in such interpretations!

Probably the central demand of black students has been the establishment of an Afro-American Studies Department. Since this falls within the faculty's jurisdiction over curriculum, the setting up of black studies has probably aroused more campus controversy than any other racial issue. The debate over black studies illustrated the great disparity between faculty and student definitions of racism and how it should be eliminated. The two sides in the struggle were coming from totally different places as they invoked divergent conceptions of racism to buttress their arguments. For the liberal professor, the strategic idea has been that of *reverse racism.**

The charge of reverse racism is often used to discredit various projects for preferential treatment. In the university context this means special admissions programs for minority students and deliberate efforts to hire third world faculty and other employees. The classical liberal position holds that color and ethnicity should be irrelevant to all such decisions and that the elimination of overt discrimination is as far as any institution should move toward the goal of racial equality.

* Because space limitations do not permit a full discussion here, I treat faculty reaction to Afro-American studies in an appendix to this chapter.

The error in this view is the assumption that patterns of racial subjugation, the exclusion of people of color from an equitable share of
social opportunity, can be eliminated by simply ending discrimination.
Since much of racial exclusion is the present-day reflection or residue
of past racial discrimination and the disadvantages suffered by peoples
of color earlier in their lives, special energies must be expended in an
active effort to reverse inequality.[32] Preferential treatment is not
racism in reverse because its purpose and goal is not to turn our
racial order on its head so that nonwhites will be in the position of
dominance. Why administrators have often been able to see this point
more readily than professors is again puzzling. The cry of reverse
racism is raised not only by white liberals who have been personally
dedicated to civil rights and integration; it is more and more raised by
conservatives, including professors, who have never raised a finger in
the past about white racism. This would seem to confirm the observation made earlier that, in a context of social change, principles
originally associated with liberalism become conservative in character,
just as many ideas that were once radical are now widely accepted by
liberals.

Racism in reverse is a central argument also against black studies
programs and other efforts of third world groups to celebrate and
develop their culture, their ethnic institutions, and their racial pride
and identity. Because a concern with color is in itself supposed to be
racist, according to the universalistic *weltanschauung* of the liberal,
black consciousness, especially in its militant and more abrasive expressions, is perceived as "black racism." Here, I think, white liberals
in general, and many professors in particular, are guilty of a number
of sociological misconceptions. The fundamental point is a confusion
of racism with *ethnocentrism*. As William Graham Sumner pointed
out in his classic *Folkways,* every tribe, ethnic group, and nation tends
to feel that its own values, customs, and ways of life are the most
natural ones, superior to those of its neighbors. Whereas ethnocentrism
can be a component of and a contributor to the systematic racism that
would aggressively deny the value and humanity of "lesser peoples,"
it is not the main cause of racism. The ethnocentric impulse remains
strong among other ethnic groups in America. Liberals do not deny
Jews, Italians, or even Chinese the right to such attitudes, but when
developed by Afro-Americans it is offensive, another example of the
truly racist double standard. The experience of slavery and the system

of racial subordination that followed Emancipation weakened or virtually eliminated the healthy ethnocentrism of Africans and Afro-Americans. Thus from the past to the present the most significant racism that exists among black people in America is not the antiwhite racism that liberals react to, but an antiblack racism derived from the larger society and culture, that is, assumptions and beliefs about their own incapacities. From this perspective, black studies, black cultural movements, and black institution building are antiracist and not racist, for they are efforts to recoup the losses in group integrity and ethnocentric pride that white racist America has historically undermined.

I am not suggesting that there is no racism at all in the third world movements, or among students in particular. The example that has most bothered me is a tendency on the part of some black students to refuse to read books by whites. The interest in black writers and the insight that many students learn best from professors with a similar cultural experience have led in some cases to the feeling that the goal of learning from any source of knowledge that might prove useful is not applicable to black people.* This strikes me as not only racist, but foolish and anti-intellectual. Harold Cruse has put it well, "All race hate is self-defeating in the long run because it distorts the critical faculties."³³ But my example illustrates another fallacy of the liberal's alarmist equation of white and black racism. Because black people are for the most part without effective power, black racism only hurts blacks themselves, though in the short run it can yield psychic comfort. White racism, on the other hand, obviously harms people of color and not primarily whites.

Liberals often fail to recognize this difference because their perspective emphasizes attitudes and intentions, underplaying issues of group power. Attitudes may be similar, but since people of color lack power they cannot impose their will on whites in the same way that white power has been imposed on them for centuries. If we recognize that racism is a system of domination as well as a complex of beliefs and attitudes, and that this objective dimension of racial oppression is

---

* It is also a reaction to the exclusion of the black perspective from the university curriculum, a historic pattern that still remains in some institutions and departments. An informant in Berkeley's School of Education tells me that no white professor has included a book by a black or Chicano author on a required or suggested reading list in the past few years, despite the department's emphasis on urban and minority problems.

the more determining one, the separatist impulse in third world movements cannot be seen as analogous to white racism.

Though most professors have reacted negatively and with de-
fensiveness to such ideas and to the new claims addressed to "their"
jurisdiction and authority, the faculty of many major universities has
not stood pat in its views on race and the role of higher education in
the process of social change. Everywhere there are college teachers
who have become educated about racial oppression in America, understanding and, to a degree, accepting the perspectives of third world
students.[34] Others, and this includes a number of older civil rights era
liberals, have been antagonized by the action, style, rhetoric, and
goals of black student movements; they have reacted with disgust and
hostility much as have the "backlashers" of Middle America. But the
most common response may be another. The modal professor, liberal
in his attitudes, finds himself accepting principles and solutions that
are not mutually consistent. The liberal consensus of the 1950s is
shattered, not only as a coherent social philosophy, but also in terms
of the corporate group that shared the outlook, many in the liberal
center having moved toward the left or toward the right.

Conclusion

Just as the civil rights movement of an earlier period exposed basic
problems of American life that transcended race (poverty, the quality
of education and of the larger culture), the recent student movement
has had an impact on campus life broader than its own goals and the
racial relations on which I have focused my analysis. In emphasizing
the systematic exclusion of people of color, the third world movement
set the stage for the growing reaction against the university's class
elitism and male domination. Though women have been fairly well
represented as college undergraduates, their participation in most
graduate programs and professional schools has been systematically
discouraged. On many campuses today, however, women's liberation
groups are challenging this historical pattern; in some situations third
world and women's movements find themselves in competition for a
limited number of graduate school openings and faculty positions. The
white working class also continues to be systematically disadvantaged
in higher education, and it is possible, though by no means certain, that
significant movements will arise to defend its still unrepresented
interests.

The ethnic presence has given new immediacy also to the relation between university education and contemporary life and society outside its walls. On this issue, often trivialized as the "search for relevance," third world groups were preceded by the general student movement, which was predominantly white. But racial minorities have provided a distinctive approach to the problem in their concern with linking both the educational process and their future careers to those ethnic communities that most colleges and universities had either ignored or exploited.

Furthermore, the racial crisis on campus contributed to the overall weakening of the old liberal consensus and to the rearrangement of political perspectives, which is still going on. As I have stressed in this study, the liberal philosophy on race failed to provide either the general orientation or the specific guidelines to deal with the changing situations of the 1960s. This has been true in the nation as a whole, and on the campus. The racial crisis was only one among many that rendered obsolete old political labels. It is now more and more difficult to characterize specific people as liberal, conservative, radical, or what-have-you. An innovative approach to racial issues may sometimes appear in combination with a hard-line position on traditional academic questions; a professor may be radical on the university's connection with the military and conservative with respect to standards of admission, curriculum, and classroom ceremony.

Finally, a brief consideration of the long-term implications of the changing racial situation within higher education is in order. If current trends continue for the next few years, the proportion of black students on the major campuses will approach the proportion in the general population. Although other third world groups (with the exception of Asian-Americans) are entering at a slower rate, their numbers also will increase. What impact will such a significant presence of people of color have on the university as a whole, on the future course of campus conflict, and on the direction of third world student movements?

Only a fool would try to answer these questions. However, alternative outcomes can be examined. At one extreme, it is possible that there will be no significant transformation in the university's organization and charter of purpose and that third world students will be "co-opted" or absorbed into the present system, which will undergo only minor adaptations. If this turns out to be the case, then future sociologists will interpret the racial conflicts of the late 1960s as a transitional phenomenon, which opened up wedges in the educational monolith through which new groups were able to enter. But an opposite outcome also is possible. Students of color, with a growing number of white allies, may continue to hammer at the racist assumptions buttressing the organization, curriculum, and politics inside the university monolith, to the point that serious cracks appear in its structure. The pieces could then be put together in such a way that cultural pluralism, decentralization, and significant space for group self-determination inform a new concept of higher education.

If neither co-optation nor the institutionalization of a genuine pluralism is likely to occur in the period immediately ahead, how will racial protest develop in a situation offering some possibility of compromise between the two poles? The first wave of racial conflict at the major universities has produced victories for third world students, specifically, black or ethnic studies departments and more favorable admission policies. Slower, more incremental gains in the composition of the faculty are next in the offing, as many professors have come to accept the fact that their institutions and they themselves bear the major responsibility for its all-white character, and as the number of ethnic graduate students grows—for whom, at least at present, the job market has never been more favorable. The question that arises is whether student groups will be relatively satisfied with such reforms and will slow down their political activism, or whether these gains, along with emerging issues, will raise racial conflict to new and more intensified levels.

Thus far the trickling-in of minority (mostly black) faculty seems to have contained militancy. The third world professor or administrator plays a go-between role. To the whites he interprets the students' views and problems; for the students of color he mediates grievances and whenever possible wins concessions from a department or a particular professor. And his availability as a teacher has taken some of the heat off the white faculty. But such middle-man roles are compromising; how long third world faculty will continue to play them is in doubt.[35]

If on some campuses there appears to be a standoff between white faculty and third world students, this is probably only a temporary *modus vivendi*. Also apparent is a retrenchment in the form of an alliance between conservative and liberal professors based on a mutual determination to restore standards and to end past tendencies to make concessions to the demands of students—white as well as colored. But the future of campus race relations probably depends on other uncertainties beyond the political competence of the professoriat. One factor is the larger political context, both national and statewide, and its meaning for higher education. Matters of resources and budget will be important here; a militant student response is to be expected whenever funds are cut back, as Reagan almost carried out with respect to the California State Colleges' Educational Opportunity Program in 1971. At the same time, a repressive national atmosphere tends to take some of the steam out of student activism, as the first three years of Nixon's administration indicate. But events on campus will be most affected by race relations in the nation as a whole and the choices that third world students make about their own social and political direction. On both these counts, the situation is extremely dynamic at present.

NOTES

1. As early as 1963 Murray Friedman diagnosed the situation:

   > Liberal whites are, consequently, caught in the dilemma of believing in equal rights for Negroes and even of working for them, while at the same time attempting to escape from the real and fancied disadvantages of desegregation. . . . The liberal white is increasingly uneasy about the nature and consequences of the Negro revolt. . . . In the final analysis, a liberal, white, middle-class society wants to have change, but without trouble. . . . In other words, to the Negro demand for "now," to which the deep South has replied "never," many liberal whites are increasingly responding "later." But the Negro will accept nothing short of first-class citizenship, now.

   "The White Liberal's Retreat," in Alan Weston, *Freedom Now* (New York: Basic Books, 1964), pp. 320–328. See also Charles Fager, *White Reflections on Black Power* (Grand Rapids, Mich: Eerdmans, 1967); and Charles Levy, *Voluntary Servitude* (New York: Appleton, 1968).

2. See Harry Edwards, *Black Students* (New York: The Free Press, 1970), pp. 64–65. For two accounts dealing with Berkeley, see J. Herman Blake, "Racism at a Great University: The Agony and

the Rage," *Negro Digest, 16,* no. 5 (March 1967), 9–15; and George Napper, "The Black Student Movement: Problems of Unity," Doctoral dissertation, School of Criminology, University of California, Berkeley (1970).

3. These estimates are calculated from data in Christopher Jencks and David Riesman, *The Academic Revolution* (Garden City, N.Y.: Doubleday, 1968), p. 440.

4. The National Survey of the Carnegie Commission on Higher Education (in cooperation with the American Council on Education), directed by Clark Kerr and Logan Wilson, is a study of more than 300 colleges and universities that was conducted in 1969. The findings I quote here and later in the paper are preliminary prepublication data tabulated by the Survey Research Center, University of California, Berkeley. I am grateful to Stephen Steinberg for providing me with these statistics.

5. Cf. Paul Lazarfeld and W. Thielens, *The Academic Mind* (New York: The Free Press, 1958).

6. The liberalism of the university and its professors is stressed by two leading critics of contemporary student movements, Daniel Bell and John Bunzel. See Bell, "Columbia and the New Left" and Bunzel, "Black Studies at San Francisco State." Both appear in *The Public Interest, 13* (Fall 1968). Immanuel Wallerstein and Paul Starr have subtitled vol. 1 of their valuable *The University Crisis Reader,* "The Liberal University Under Attack" (New York: Vintage, 1971).

7. Clark Kerr's analysis of the multiversity, its many publics and constituencies and the mediating role of the university president that follows from them, is also a useful framework for understanding this receptivity of the administrator. C. Kerr, *The Uses of the University* (Cambridge: Harvard University Press, 1963).

8. On the faculty as a privileged group, see Kerr, *op. cit.,* pp. 42–44, 109–110; James Ridgeway, *The Closed Corporation* (New York: Random House, 1968), concentrates on the professor's special opportunities for lucrative consulting and business operations. See also, Richard Lichtman, "The University: Mask for Privilege?" in Wallerstein and Starr, *op. cit.,* vol. 1, pp. 101–120.

9. Provocative discussions of academic values in the face of campus racial conflict appear in Cushing Strout and David I. Grossvogel, eds., *Divided We Stand: Reflections on the Crisis at Cornell*

(Garden City, N.Y.: Doubleday, 1970). See especially the address by George Kahin, "A Personal Narrative of a Rude Awakening" by Cushing Strout and "The University in Transition" by David I. Grossvogel. The latter argues that academic freedom often becomes a shield for privilege and noncommitment.

10. New York Times (July 21, 1968).

11. See Wallerstein and Starr, op. cit., vol. 1, pp. 295ff.

12. New York Times (September 18, 1969), 43. For the changes at Harvard see Lawrence E. Eichel et. al., The Harvard Strike (Boston: Houghton Mifflin, 1970), p. 15; and for Northwestern, see Wallerstein and Starr, op. cit., p. 300.

13. Chronicle for Higher Education, 5 (March 29, 1971).

14. William H. Friedland and Harry Edwards, "Confrontation at Cornell," Trans-Action (June 1969), 32.

15. New York Times (October 14, 1969).

16. Julie Paynter, "Graduate Opportunities for Black Students," unpublished, c/o Julie Paynter, 6753 S. Chappel Ave., Chicago, Illinois 60649.

17. Chronicle of Higher Education, 5 (April 12, 1971).

18. Martin Trow, "Reflections on the Transition from Mass to Universal Higher Education," Daedalus (Winter 1970).

19. Wallerstein and Starr, op. cit., vol. 1, p. 297.

20. In an article which also identifies universalism as central to the liberal philosophy and discusses its implications for race and ethnicity in education, Lawrence Fein makes a parallel point: "The corollary of the liberal ethic that white people ought not to pay attention to the blackness of Negroes was the proposition that Negroes ought not to pay attention to their own blackness." "The Limits of Liberalism," Saturday Review of Books (June 20, 1970), 84.

21. The statement is Peter Winograd's, New York Times (October 9, 1969), in the article "More Blacks Turning to the Study of Law," by Lesley Oelsner.

22. Fein, op. cit., p. 96.

23. Eichel et. al., op. cit., p. 279.

24. An extreme statement of this position is found in Seymour Martin Lipset, Political Man (Garden City, N.Y.: Doubleday, 1960).

25. Strout and Grossvogel, op. cit., and Friedland and Edwards, op. cit.

26. At Cornell it was an economics instructor whose Spring 1968

course on poverty provoked a protest of black students. This proved to be one of the precipitating events that led to the large-scale crisis one year later. See Strout and Grossvogel, *op. cit.*, pp. 5–11.

27. Badi G. Foster, "Toward a Definition of Black Referents" in Vernon J. Dixon and B. Foster, eds., *Beyond Black or White* (Boston: Little, Brown, 1971), esp. pp. 17–19.

28. For example, see Martin Kilson, *et. al., Black Studies: Myths and Realities* (New York: A. Philip Randolph Educational Fund, 1969), which includes contributions by Thomas Sowell, Andrew Brimmer, Norman Hill, Martin Kilson, and C. Vann Woodward as well as Rustin, Clark, and Wilkins.

29. Friedland and Edwards, *op. cit.*, p. 32.

30. George Kahin in Strout and Grossvogel, *op. cit.*, p. 32ff.

31. Wallerstein and Starr, *op. cit.*, vol. 1, p. 306.

32. For a clear formulation of this position see the policy statement of Northwestern black students in Wallerstein and Starr, *op. cit.*, vol. 1, p. 303.

33. Harold Cruse, *The Crisis of the Negro Intellectual* (New York: Morrow, 1967), p. 365.

34. See for example the remarks of the white participants in the Yale symposium, *Black Studies in the University*, ed. Armstead I. Robinson *et. al.* (New Haven: Yale University Press, 1969).

35. On the role of the black administrator, see Roosevelt Johnson, "Black Administrators and Higher Education," *Black Scholar, 1*, no. 1 (November 1969), 66–76.

appendix:
faculty opposition
to black studies

By the end of 1970, according to a *New York Times* estimate, black studies programs had been established at more than 170 colleges and universities, ranging from "several courses to entire departments." According to M. A. Farber, author of the article, critics "seldom attack the academic legitimacy of Black Studies any longer," but the programs still face practical problems on many campuses. Some black educators report that "white schools are thwarting the growth of solid, independent programs by indifference, design or ineptitude." Still it appears that black studies (or in some cases more inclusive ethnic studies programs) are here to stay at most major universities.[1]

The establishment of the new Afro-American field took place despite the opposition of many prestigious professors. The Carnegie survey suggests that only a minority of faculty disagreed with the idea that some new curricular innovation was needed in response to third world students and the growing concentration of concern and scholarship in the area of race and ethnicity.[2] The conflict between the ethnic student initiators and faculty curriculum committees and individual notable professors (who usually came from such related fields as history, sociology, and the humanities) turned instead on the form, the focus, and the status of the program. An examination of this faculty response is useful for further understanding the white professor's perspective on race relations. Though my analysis again is based primarily on my participation in events in Berkeley, accounts of the debates on other campuses suggest that liberal professors elsewhere shared similar ideas and anxieties.

The issues of controversy can be boiled down to the following: (a) Whether the curriculum would be housed in a department or school of its own, or whether it would be an interdisciplinary program cutting across established departments on the campus. This was the question of "autonomy." (b) Whether the traditional faculty (usually white) who are experts in fields of racial research would teach in black studies programs, and the related question of availability of courses and majors for white students. (c) What the credentials of the faculty would be and who would have authority to select them. (d) The demand for student power and participation in the shaping and daily life of the program. (e) The tension between an academic emphasis favored by the faculty and the more political, community-oriented emphasis favored by third world students on most (but not all) campuses.

As these questions became points of contention between faculty and students, they were fed into the cumbersome machinery of campus decision making. From the student perspective, bureaucratic dilly-dallying, the watering down of key demands, and a lack of confidence in the capacity of white faculty to respond to their situation and needs contributed to the outbreak of racial crisis at such places as Berkeley, San Francisco State, Cornell, and Harvard.

1. It is important to understand why a sizable minority of professors could oppose any program at all, even a conventional, degree-granting, interdisciplinary one. A racist society builds up a wall of ignorance that keeps most white Americans unaware of the complex history and culture of blacks and other third world groups. Even many men of knowledge are ignorant of the existence of a hundred years of historiography of the black experience and of the considerable body of poetry, literature, and musical creation by Afro-Americans. Furthermore, many liberal professors have been committed to the belief that blacks have no distinctive history and tradition because they are culturally the same as whites except for the facts of race and poverty. Such people still see black studies as an attempt on the part of a group without a distinctive past to build up an ersatz heritage in order to bolster weak egos and legitimate political nationalism.

Liberal professors particularly have balked in response to the term "the black experience," which is central to contemporary militant rhetoric and is the rationale in-a-nutshell for black studies departments. There is a parallel here to the liberal's early resistance to the adjective "black," although with time he has adapted to this substitution for "Negro" and no longer cringes at the phrase "black people" as he once did. But the notion of an experience based on color seems to him prima facie racist. Yet the same scholar has had no problem with the idea that there has been a Jewish experience in America, or an Irish one. Other groups are granted ethnic cultures and somewhat unique histories, but color should be irrelevant. The third world movement, on the other hand, sees ethnic studies departments as a response to, and a partial antidote for, the university's racist exclusion of their social realities.

2. On many campuses, liberal professors have advocated black studies in the form of an interdisciplinary program, cutting across a variety of departments. Students have generally pushed for a department that would have the same status and autonomy as other departments, and they have also demanded a greater role in the decision making than has been common in the longer-established departments. The faculty who took this position conceded the importance of a number of strands of knowledge related to the black experience, but then argued that these diverse sources do not hang together sufficiently to justify a department. At Berkeley the proponents of a program argued that departments are based on a specific and unique mode of inquiry, the so-called discipline. History, economics, mathematics, philosophy, and sociology are distinct disciplines. Black studies would be a mishmash rather than a discipline and thus should be housed in a multidisciplinary program under the tutelage of legitimate departments. This position is based on an ideal rather than a realistic view of the departmental structure of modern universities, and a naive understanding of the actual conditions under which departments come into existence. A search through most college catalogues would show that there is no inherent logic to the departmental division of labor: there are many that share the same discipline and many others with no distinctive mode of inquiry. There are multidisciplinary departments in such subjects as comparative literature, and as the language and culture departments suggest, there are precedents for organization on the basis of the national experience of ethnic peoples. New academic departments have always originated out of the demands and pressure of interest groups, primarily the faculty but also business

and the military. They do not arise out of some precise Linnaenan classification of the fields of knowledge. What is new in American higher education today is that the demands for curricular innovation are coming from students.*

3. The white faculty has been apprehensive that a department would exclude white scholars from teaching and white students from participation. Blacks and other third world groups have favored a department or school in order to carve out enough self-determination over their education to counteract the racist assumptions and practices of the university effectively. To the white faculty these demands were separatist and therefore *ipso facto* racist.

Although the faculty in at least nine out of ten college departments is likely to be all white, many professors have been seriously disturbed about the possibility of an all-black staff in Afro-American studies. The color-blind ethos and the commitment to integration die hard, and I do not suggest that these principles are without value. But it seems to me that the antiseparatist energies of the white faculty could better be channeled into projects toward integrating their own departments. The concern of many liberal professors for the education of third world students was expressed also in the idea that students of color need to learn from white students and faculty as well as from their own brothers and sisters. This may be true but it is not inconsistent with the proposals for ethnic studies. On most campuses black studies departments did not intend to limit their offerings to black students, and probably none expected that all, or close to a majority, of Afro-American students would major in these new programs. As a matter of fact, the *Times* survey noted that few institutions bar white students from these courses and estimated that perhaps 10 percent of black students may be majoring, or planning to concentrate, in the black studies field.[3] White faculty members who raise the cry of separatism want to decide what is best for third world students. The colonized minorities in America are demanding the right to choose for themselves when and where they will enter mainstream entities or ethnic cultural

* The rebuttal above is not meant to be an argument against the possible appropriateness of an interdisciplinary program on some campuses. However, such forms generally lack the relative prestige and independence of regular departments.

institutions. The function of the university today is to open its doors and resources as widely as possible, permitting third world people to choose their own paths among a variety of possibilities.

Principled objections to racial separation get mixed up with deep-seated white hangups about black autonomy. The slavery experience has affected the white, as much as the black, collective unconscious, and therefore there exist subliminal tendencies among whites to relate to blacks as the possessions and property they once represented. Whites therefore have difficulty accepting the fact that blacks can have their own identities and be independent, self-actualizing agents in the world. At the same time that liberal and radical alike share such paternalistic orientations toward people of color, the thread of guilt in the American racial character makes socially conscious whites especially desirous of the goodwill and respect (if not admiration) of black people. For this reason, separate programs are not only viewed as a disagreement with their own ideas of correct racial strategy; they are also experienced as a personal affront, a deliberate rejection.

4. Many faculty members feared that an independent department would necessarily lower academic standards. Thus the term "academic ghetto" was coined for a department in which predominantly black faculty teach a majority of black students. For some professors the subconscious assumption that blacks are inferior may lie behind this point of view. For others the fear may be a realistic response to the fact that there is a shortage of academically credentialed blacks to fill the teaching positions. Since dozens of universities are searching for minority professors to integrate conventional departments and man new black studies programs, how can each first-rank university compete in this market situation to ensure its traditional excellence?

The argument has merit but seems specious when used to withhold support from the idea of a new department. Since no one wants a "track" within the university where minority people receive an inferior education, a concern with high standards might have been expressed by supporting the department and, at the same time, suggesting those safeguards that any department needs to ensure high performance. At Berkeley I wondered whether the fear-of-standards argument was not a rationalization for other fears and objections. New departments in other fields are begun if the idea

makes sense, if there is a core of interested faculty, and if there is
student demand. They are not expected to become eminent bodies
overnight, either as teaching units or as groups of scholars. In other
contexts it is recognized that it takes time to produce an institution
or program of high quality; yet many faculty members have opposed
black departments because that quality is not available in the
beginning.

5. The other major faculty objection to black studies
departments was the fear that they would become a political base
for militant students and faculty. Since a black department would not
be academic (there is no discipline there), nor of high quality
(not the right faculty or students), it could only become a base for
black power. An eminent liberal economist stated this view bluntly
at a Berkeley Academic Senate meeting when he suggested that
students in this department "will want more and more."

Those who fear black power on campus do not oppose new
departments that attract predominantly white students and faculty
and thus create a broader base of white power. Nor do they cut the
budgets of established fields like sociology, which today attract
white political activists who demand student power. If white power
is a fact of life, then what is wrong with black power—on the
campus as well as in the nation at large? The professors whose views
I am challenging would say that the danger is not black people in
power but the politicization of the university which Afro-American
studies departments further. The black department politicizes the
educational process, and a university is ideally committed to the
separation of intellectual life from group interests and political values.
But this again is an ideology that serves the interests of the *status
quo*. Apparent indifference to political questions in disciplines that
deal with man, society, and culture is in itself a political position.
Certainly political values should not distort our analyses of reality
nor contaminate the search for truth. But the social analyses of
university intellectuals are rarely tested in the laboratories of
community action and social change, and this is why third world
leaders find so much of our social science vacuous and insist on
participation in community affairs as a legitimate component of their
proposed curricula.

From the student perspective on institutional racism, the
university is inherently political because its procedural forms and

educational content express and maintain the privileged position of white people in the society as a whole. The argument that black power on campus would politicize the university is therefore seen as a smokescreen to bolster the myths of objectivity and neutrality, which academic values foster. In actuality, political upheaval on campus has been associated more with the earlier stages of initiating Afro-American studies departments. Once established, it appears that major racial confrontations have tended to subside. Though ethnic studies do increase the political potential of ethnic faculty and students, there is no likelihood at present that the white domination of university culture or politics will be overturned.

NOTES

1. M. A. Farber, "Black Studies Take Hold, But Face Many Problems," *New York Times* (Sunday, December 27, 1970), 1, 42.
2. To the statement "Any institution with a substantial number of Black students should offer a program of Black Studies if they wish it," 26.3 percent strongly agreed, 41.0 percent agreed with reservations, 19.4 percent disagreed with reservations, and 11.8 percent strongly disagreed. The National Survey of the Carnegie Commission on Higher Education, in cooperation with the American Council on Education. Preliminary data supplied by the Survey Research Center, University of California, Berkeley.
3. Farber, "Black Studies Take Hold . . .," *op. cit.*, p. 42.

index

Jews (in the U.S.), 56, 61–66, 68, 78 n., 86, 129, 137, 143, 174 n.
Johnson, Charles S., 194
Jones, James E., 196 n.
Jones, LeRoi, 153 n.
Jordan, Winthrop, 5 n., 45, 118
Jury selection
    racism in, 187–188, 220, 248–251
    the *voir dire* process, 222–232

Katznelson, Ira, 190 n.
Keating, Edward, 246, 254 n.
Keil, Charles, 120, 126–127, 138, 144, 153 n.
Kelley, William Melvin, 143
Kerner Report, 90, 100, 102–103, 192–193, 213–214, 217, 221, 234, 239, 252–253, 275, 276 n.
Kerr, Clark, 285
Kiernan, V. G., 122
King, Martin Luther
    assassination of, 33–35, 265, 273
    in Watts, 206
Kirk, Grayson, 262 n.
Kloosterboer, W., 59 n., 77
Kristol, Irving, 57

Labor
    and colonialism, 29–31, 57–65
    free and unfree, 57–61
Ladner, Joyce A., 160
Levine, Lawrence, 160–161
Lewis, Oscar, 138, 146
Liberalism
    in crisis, 281–282
    institutionalized in the university, 263–264
    as prevailing outlook among professors, 257–258, 263
    and universalism, 266–268, 278–279
        See also White liberals
Liebow, Elliot, 5 n., 159
Lipset, S. M., 46, 50
Los Angeles black community, 185, 197, 206–214